ALL  AND ELBOWS OF SUSCEPTIBILITY AND REFUSAL

READING HISTORY FROM BELOW

BY ANTHONY ILES & TOM ROBERTS

All Knees and Elbows of Susceptibility and Refusal is produced as part of 'knowledge is never neutral', a series of projects exploring knowledge production organised by The Strickland Distribution with Transmission Gallery.

All Knees and Elbows of Susceptibility and Refusal is co-published with Mute Books.

The Strickland Distribution is an artists' group supporting the development of independent research in art related and non-institutional practices: strickdistro.org

Transmission Gallery is a Glasgow based, artist-run, non-commercial art space supporting a large membership of local artists and cultural practitioners: transmissiongallery.org

Mute Books is the new imprint of Mute Publishing specialising in cultural politics, providing a new, expanded space for the kinds of distinctive voices *Mute* magazine has hosted since its inception in 1994: metamute.org

Published 24 November 2012

ISBN: 978-0-9565201-3-5
ISBN: 978-0-9565201-4-2 (Ebook)

Artwork by Rachel Baker
Template design by Mute Books
Layout design by Paul Abbott

Distribution
howard@metamute.org
Tel: +44 (0)20 3287 9005
Mute Books
46 Lexington Street
London
W1F 0LP

The Strickland Distribution · transmission gallery

Mute

CONTENTS

PREFACE

This book began in 2006 as a discussion between two friends. Invited to contribute to an event on histories of self-organisation by Whitechapel Project Space in 2007, we decided to assemble our readings and build a critical (and necessarily partial) picture of the practice of 'history from below'. The pamphlet we produced wove extracts from historians and their sources together with our own commentary. This approach, based on fragments and quotations, was intended to make these sources available to other readers. Invited by The Strickland Distribution to reprint the pamphlet, we felt it necessary to reconsider and expand upon the original, not least because the world was changing fast around us – a renewed and expanded field of conflicts, revolts and revolutions from the Arab Spring to struggles against austerity in Europe presented itself to us as a meaningful context for a revised study.

The completed study of historians and other figures is not intended to be comprehensive. We've veered towards the subjects, areas and materials which interest us. We hope the book attests to the very strength of practices of reading history critically against the present in the culture around us, from the school children and young people we have had contact with through recent student revolts to the memories and experiences of family and friends. The book remains a document of our ongoing readings, understandings and questioning in dialogue with others.

Our approach is informed by open, anti-authoritarian and non-dogmatic Marxist tendencies. We follow communist historians into the debates they were formative in developing, but don't hesitate to involve other voices with something to say. The study we have produced negotiates arguments over whether an emphasis be placed on structure or experience in the understanding of historical change, but we argue strongly that the question of one should never obliterate the other. Equally, we at times breach, but never completely resolve, the gap between history from below as 'radical history' – that is, the history of more or less organised political movements which challenge and sometimes shape the order of things – and history from below as the history of unheard voices and experiences per se. We have attempted to question the inherent Eurocentric (and, given the historical legacy of oppression both within and without radical movements, the male- and hetero-centric) contours of our study. In geographical terms our focus remains located where we find ourselves, in a cosmopolitan and polyglot East London in the United Kingdom, the site of deep social divisions and complex solidarities.

We have structured this book around key areas of debate which we find relevant to the requirements of our times. In the Introduction we establish the core figures and institutions whose work we take as a starting point for exploring the field. In Members Unlimited we discuss the categories of class, 'the people' and 'the below' and explore the ways history from below has critically exploded or expanded these categories. In Lobster Traps we look at questions pertaining to the discovery and use of historical sources. These questions are particularly pressing and relevant in light of the vast digital archive which the internet holds and will no doubt be deployed in the historical research of the future.

In a chapter on Autodidacts, we take a partisan approach to some notable figures who learnt how to speak back from a position as subaltern or under educated, and explore the ways in which, against the odds, they both mastered the the time and space to pursue and facilitate intellectual practice, and developed distribution networks for the dissemination of dissent. The debates from the previous two chapters, on the veracity of sources and on self-education, meet in the following chapter on Authenticity and Ambiguity, which addresses the relationship between history, literary forms and myth making, and investigates how historical subjects constructed their own identities and experiences in relation to the dominant culture. The theme of education is expanded to address institutions, critiques of them and educational protest in the Business University. A chapter on the Big Society, an odious Conservative party formulation, illustrates how forms of historiography are tied closely to state politics in the UK but also how consideration of the vicissitudes of the uses of history are relevant to any territory and time. Our final chapter on Unhistorical Shit rescues some remaining key debates from the rubbish dump of history and tries to draw together some threads that run through the book without closing things down to other readings or uses.

We have written this book as amateurs in relation to the material assembled, it has written us as much as we have written it. It is offered as a contribution as opposed to a definitive statement – a tool and a provocation to other readers and writers of history from below, and by 'writers' we mean makers and active participants in history.

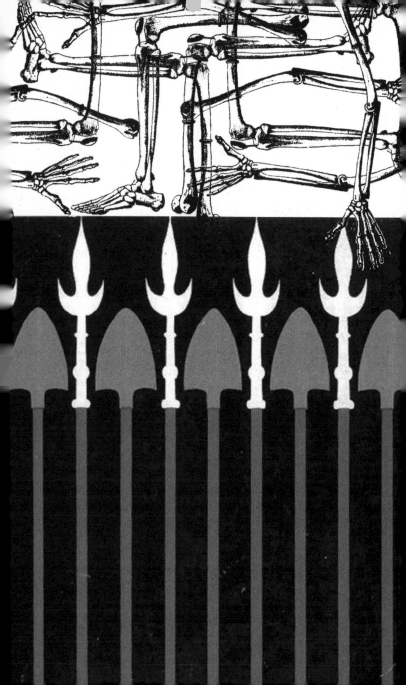

INTRODUCTION

This book is an attempt to sketch what might constitute 'history from below'. In it we have assembled quotations from esteemed historians, their lowly subjects and sometimes even their critics. Here, E.P. Thompson's phrase, from which we have made our clumsy title, will help us express the necessary awkwardness of effecting transformation by writing history.[1] For there are many attractions here but also some obstacles of interest too. Firstly, we will attempt to construct what is 'history from below', introducing some of its key historians, and the origin of different groups and different formulations of radical history they have made, before we explore some tensions inherent in such a project.

Annales

The phrase 'history from below' is the product of a group of French historians known as the Annales School. It is their description of an approach to subjects previously considered historically unimportant, an attempt to surpass history as simply a story of kings, great men and their wars. In many ways the School pursued what August Comte had advocated

---

1   E.P. Thompson, 'An Open Letter to Leszek Kolakowski', *Socialist Register*, 1973, p.91. The full quote reads: 'For one must as an unassimilated socialist in this infinitely assimilative culture, put oneself in a school of awkwardness. One must make one's sensibility all knobbly – all knees and elbows of susceptibility and refusal – if one is not to be pressed through the grid into the universal mish-mash of the received assumptions of the intellectual culture.'

when he called for a 'history without names'.[2]

> The leading ideas behind *Annales* might be summarised briefly
> as follows. In the first place, the substitution of a problem-
> oriented analytic history for a traditional narrative of events.
> In the second place, the history of the whole range of human
> activities in the place of a mainly political history. In the third
> place – in order to achieve the first two aims – a collaboration
> with other disciplines: with geography, sociology, psychology,
> economics, linguistics, social anthropology and so on.[3]

The interdisciplinarity championed by Annales has had
a lasting effect on approaches to history as well as many
of the other disciplines which it touched. However, the
journal, school, or *movement* (which Peter Burke insists is a
better description), has also redefined its approach during
certain phases of its existence. This can be seen through
the variations in its full title. During its appropriately long
history the journal has used five titles: *Annales d'histoire
économique et sociale* (1929-39); *Annales d'histoire sociale* (1939-
42, 1945); *Mélanges d'histoire sociale* (1942-4); *Annales: économies,
sociétiés, civilisations* (1946-1994); and presently: *Annales: Histoire,
Sciences sociales* (1994-).[4] We can conclude, at the very least,
that the meaning of social history and the meaning of social
science in France has changed over the century. Peter Burke
summarises Annales' development:

---

2   Peter Burke, *The French Historical Revolution: The Annales School,
    1929-89*, Malden, MA / Cambridge: Polity Press, 1990, p.9.

3   Ibid., p.2.

4   Also see: Lynn Hunt and Jacques Revel. *Histories: French
    Constructions of the Past*, New York: The New Press, 1994.

This school is often perceived from outside as a monolithic group with a uniform historical practice, quantitative in method, determinist in its assumptions, and hostile, or at best indifferent, to politics and to events. This stereotype [...] ignores divergences between individual members of the group and also developments over time.[5]

The founders of the journal, Lucien Febvre and Marc Bloch, had met at Strasbourg University in 1920, and in 1929 Bloch took the initiative to found a journal 'on the virgin soil of social history'.[6] The group followed leading sociologist Emile Durkheim in his dismissal of events as no more than 'superficial manifestations of a deeper reality', but also cited 19th century historian of the picturesque, Jules Michelet, as a founding father of the school.[7] Effectively, as a movement, Annales encompassed an eclecticism to which it applied methodological rigour.

They could be said to have taken the scope of US historian James Harvey Robinson's then bold assertion: 'History includes every trace and vestige of everything that man has done or thought since first he appeared on the earth'.[8] The Annales historians attempted to develop frameworks within which such totality could be thought, researched and related. Concepts such as 'geo-history' and 'total history' are indicative of this will to totality. Another was the '*longue*

---

5   *The French Historical Revolution,* op. cit., p.2.

6   Ibid., p.22.

7   'Lucien Febvre hailed Michelet as the founding father of the Annales school.' Jacques Rancière, *The Names of History*, Minneapolis: University of Minnesota, 1994, p.42.

8   James Harvey Robinson quoted in Peter Burke, op. cit., p.9.

durée', popularised by the work of Fernand Braudel who became joint director with Febvre in 1949 and effectively took over the school after his death in 1956. Braudel summarised the *longue durée* as '[...] a history whose passage is almost imperceptible [...] a history in which all change is slow, a history of constant repetition, ever recurring cycles'.[9] Braudel became the leading historian in France after Febvre's death until his own in 1985. Despite many other currents and counter-tendencies, it is his approach with which, by and large, the school remains associated. His approach stressed continuities and micro-historical changes rather than events, ruptures or personalities. However, one of the key concepts which Annales developed and for which they are most famous, but which remained extremely weak in Braudel's work, was the concept of *Mentalité* (mentalities). Analogous to the way Braudel studied economic movements and geographical factors over the long term (periods of thousands of years), other Annales historians focussed on the unconscious formation and modulation of ideas, habits and customs over time and their transmission across geographic and socially defined regions.

Whilst some members of Annales were Communist Party members, anti-fascist partisans or Marxists, many were not; Braudel was even profoundly anti-materialist. They are nonetheless by and large associated (especially by conservative critics) with the left. The school became a powerful force in French history, especially after its institutionalisation after the Second World War. It has remained an important point of reference for left social historians across the globe.

---

9   Fernand Braudel, *The Mediterranean*, quoted in Peter Burke, op. cit., p.36.

The archival techniques developed by Annales historians, their problem-oriented approach to history and concept of mentalities left a strong impression on Anglophone proponents of history from below.

The Communist Party Historians Group

Aspects of the Annales approach were taken up by a group of British Marxist historians who developed a set of methodologies and a world view at odds with existing Marxist and historiographical orthodoxies. In 1946 a group consisting of E.P. Thompson, Christopher Hill, Eric Hobsbawm, V.G. Kiernan, George Rudé, Roger Hilton, Maurice Dobbs and Dona Torr, among others, formed the Communist Party Historians Group (CPHG).

Dona Torr was a catalyst for the group, agitating within the Communist Party as early as 1936 for a strong role for historians, establishing a Marxist Historians' Group in 1938, and the Historians' Group (CPHG) in 1946, partly in order to help revise A.L. Morton's influential *A People's History of England*.[10] First published in 1938 by the left book club, it gives a long and accessible overview of English history from a Marxist perspective. The group also worked under the influence of Maurice Dobb's book *Studies in the Development of Capitalism*, and this stressed the importance of certain Marxian concepts for the interpretation of history. Members of the group also took part in founding the academic journal *Past & Present* in 1952 which formed a left-leaning, but open,

---

10 David Parker (Ed.), *Ideology, Absolutism and the English Revolution: Debates of the British Communist Historians 1940-1956*, London: Lawrence & Wishart, 2008.

forum for debate between historians. Up until 1957 the CPHG was organised into a number of different sections focussed on different periods, the 16th-17th century section headed by Christopher Hill being the most productive. This reflected a widespread interest in peasant and pre-industrial rebellions and political movements in communist movements in France, Russia and China throughout the 20th century. In the 1940s and 1950s the reading of the English Civil War as 'The English Revolution' was a foundational discussion which underpinned subsequent attempts to construct and develop radical accounts of British history.

Christopher Hill

Christopher Hill's work already displayed hallmarks of history-writing as intervention into the social dynamics of the present.

> Hill's essay The English Revolution 1640 [...] was written for the soldiers going into battle and the civilians who suffered the Blitz. It is brief, it is lucid, and it does not weigh heavily in a soldier's kit. Its address was to a class excluded from academia or the ruling elite. [...] He explained how revolution was made, and the Communist Party leadership of 1940 did not like what he said. He introduced the idea of the 'bourgeois revolution'. Getting it published was 'a victory for politics as well as theory', wrote Dona Torr. The victory was a lasting one – we see it in the formation of the postwar Communist Party History Group [...].[11]

---

11   Peter Linebaugh, 'An American Tribute to Christopher Hill', *Counterpunch*, May, 2003, http://www.unz.org/Pub/CounterpunchWeb-2003may-00129

In the post-war period Christopher Hill continued to develop his research into radical movements in the period before and after the English Revolution. The introduction to his most influential book, *The World Turned Upside Down*, makes parallels between the atmosphere of dissent and levelling democracy and the debates taking place in the context of post-war reconstruction in Europe. When it came out in the 1970s it quickly became popular with counter cultures such as the squatting and post-punk movements. The book was turned into a play performed at the National Theatre as well as (probably) inspiring numerous bands such as The Levellers, New Model Army, etc.

> This book deals with what from one point of view are subsidiary episodes and ideas in the English Revolution, the attempts of various groups of the common people to impose their own solutions to the problems of their own time, in opposition to the wishes of their betters who had called them into political action.[12]

Hill had delved even further back in time, to the period preceding the English civil war in the 17th century, to uncover the ideas of a revolutionary period that had lessons for his own.

> We do not need to idealise merrie England to realise that much was lost by the disruption of the mediaeval village; but its relative equality and communal spirit had always been accompanied by grinding poverty for the mass of the population,

---

12   Christopher Hill, *The World Turned Upside Down: Radical Ideas During the English Revolution*, London: Penguin, 1991, p.13.

and were doomed by the sixteenth century anyway. Equality and a communal spirit, combined with a reasonable and rising wage, only became attainable after capitalism had completed its historical task of laying the industrial foundation society. Hence to-day we can at last see our way to realising the dreams of the Levellers and Diggers in 1649.[13]

In 1957, Hill left the Communist Party and does not appear to have re-engaged with party politics again. He published a book on Milton, entitled *The Experience of Defeat*, in 1984 and many consider this to be a reflection of his dismay at the failure of organised communism.

Dona Torr

As well as translating key texts by Karl Marx, Dona Torr went on to lend editorial support to the publication of many key works by the new breed of historians she had helped encourage. In a collection of essays published in her honour in 1955, John Saville and E.P. Thompson wrote of her:

> She made us feel history on our pulses. History was not words on a page, not the goings-on of kings and prime ministers, not mere events. History was the sweat, blood, tears, and triumphs of the common people, our people.[14]

Torr frequently put aside her own work to assist that of others, and take part in party activism. Shortly before her

---

13   Christopher Hill, Preface to *The English Revolution 1640*, London: Lawrence & Wishart, 1955.

14   John Saville (Ed.), *Democracy and the Labour Movement: Essays in Honour of Dona Torr*, London: Lawrence & Wishart, 1954.

death A.L. Morton and Christopher Hill assembled a first
volume of her major work on Tom Mann, one of the leaders
of the great dock strike of 1889, and later an Australian Trade
Union organiser, whom she had known personally. Mann
provided a connection between early socialists such as Henry
Hyde and William Morris and the post-WWI communist
movement. Whilst Torr is not associated with the original
research methodologies developed by her protégés, her
approach to Tom Mann set something of a standard in the
attempt to situate recent radical traditions in the UK within
a continuum of class formation and struggle stretching
back to the 17th century. This became a central axiom of the
work which flowed out of her own – that regardless of their
unorthodoxy, untimeliness and obscurity the conflicts of the
past were constitutive of this present. Though attention to
the particularity of the historical development of capitalism
in Britain could sometimes drift into uncritical celebrations
of Englishness, even 'dark spots of nationalism', the outlined
themes of class, democracy and tensions between rhetorical
equality and material inequality were not in themselves
nostalgic.[15]

It is not through some memory of a former state of complete
equality and equal shares that the tradition of democracy
with a material or communal basis subsists, but through the
conjunction of equal rights and unequal shares operating within

15   Dave Renton, 'The History Woman', *Socialist Review*, Issue 224,
     November 1998, http://pubs.socialistreviewindex.org.uk/sr224/renton.
     htm

a class society, in which, inequality increases with wealth.[16]

The question of the relationship of the CPHG's adherence to the Communist Party line is an ongoing subject of debate. Eric Hobsbawm has suggested that the development of the Historians' Group was influenced by the ethos of the Popular Front introduced by the Comintern between 1934 and 1939, wherein broad alliances between communist and socialist, social democratic and liberal parties were advocated against the rise of Fascism in Europe. In 1935 Comintern secretary Giorgi Dimitrov argued that the Fascist use of nationalist historical myth should be met with counter-histories, drawing on the unearthing of radical heritages. As early as 1949 *The Modern Quarterly* (1946-1953), a Marxist journal aligned with the CPGB, dedicated an issue to the 'Puritan Revolution'. If Comintern directives influenced the direction of communist historians, the consequences might be shown to have had subversive and counterproductive results for the Party in the long run. The work of the Historians' Group opened up a legacy of diverse, hidden struggles that contradicted and more or less consciously flew in the face of orthodox Marxist and Stalinist visions of history.

---

16   Dona Torr, *Tom Mann and his Times*, vol. 1, 1956, prepared for publication by Christopher Hill and A.L. Morton. Quoted in Ibid.

Eric Hobsbawm

An early member of the CHG, Eric Hobsbawm was one of the first of this generation of left historians to critically reappraise the Luddites. In an essay for the first issue of the then new journal *Past & Present* written in 1952 he situated Luddism in a much longer historical continuum of machine-breakers and defended their tactics as practical and effective. In the context of post-WWII Labour Party ascendency Hobsbawm controversially disagreed with assumptions that

> the workers must be taught not to run their heads against economic truth, however unpalatable; of Fabians and Liberals, that strong-arm methods in labour action are less effective than peaceful negotiation; of both, that the early labour movement did not know what it was doing, but merely reacted, blindly and gropingly, to the pressure of misery, as animals in the laboratory react to electric currents.[17]

Despite this early radicalism, Hobsbawm was also staunchly loyal to the Communist Party. In 1940 as a student in Cambridge he wrote a pamphlet defending the Soviet invasion of Finland. Later, in 1956, when many others left the Communist Party as Russian tanks rolled into Hungary, Hobsbawm wrote a letter to the *Daily Worker* (9 November 1956), '[A]pproving, with a heavy heart, of what is now

---

17   Eric Hobsbawm, 'The Machine Breakers', 1952, http://libcom.org/
history/machine-breakers-eric-hobsbawm Originally published in
Past & Present, No. 1. February 1952, pp. 57–70.

happening in Hungary'.[18]

Hobsbawm concentrated his work on the 19th century, providing an important link between the emergence in the 20th century of revolutionary communist movements and the focus of others within the CPHG on the 17th and 18th centuries. One of his most significant contributions was the concept of the 'social bandit' developed in two books; *Primitive Rebels* (1959) and *Bandits* (1969). These books argued for an interpretation of banditry as social protest and challenged orthodox interpretations of crime, peasant organisation and capitalist development in a global context stretching from the Brazilian Sertao to the Carpathian mountains, and as such also helped to circulate diverse and pioneering work by left historians from all over the world.

E.P. Thompson & Dorothy Thompson

E.P. Thompson was initially best known for his participation in the Communist Party Writers' Group. Not intending to become a historian, his earliest work, *William Morris: Romantic to Revolutionary*, was a study, co-written with his partner Dorothy Thompson, which began a reappraisal of Morris as critical to the development of Marxist thought in Britain. The Thompsons' research on Morris led them to make close alliances with the Historians' Group. E.P. Thompson also worked as an adult education tutor for the Workers' Educational Association in West Riding from 1946, and drew upon his experiences in working with his students to develop

---

18   Eric Hobsbawm, quoted in James Heartfield, 'Eric Hobsbawm and the
      tragedy of the left', October 2012, http://www.spiked-online.com/site/
      article/12936/

his mode of writing. Dorothy Thompson was a social historian who specialised in studying the Chartist movement. She was also active in the CPHG and later anti-nuclear and women's movements.

The Thompsons both broke from the Communist Party in reaction to the invasion of Hungary in 1956, founding the journal *The New Reasoner*. E.P. Thompson retained a commitment to historical materialism whilst developing a critique of Stalinism. His position was outlined in the article 'Socialist Humanism: An Epistle to the Philistines'.[19] For Thompson, the brutality and reproduction of exploitation under Stalin was founded on 'a mechanical model, operating semi-automatically and independently of conscious human agency'. To counter this tendency involved re-injecting a sense of the agency of real men and women in revolutionary struggles; and rediscovering the making and contesting of moralities 'as difficult as life' in radical movements and the Marxist tradition, including the work of Marx and Engels.

E.P. Thompson's famous study, *The Making of the English Working Class*, published in 1963, was initially intended as a chapter in a textbook on the British labour movement up to 1945. As the book developed, Thompson argued that it became in part a polemical intervention against

abbreviated economistic notations of Marxism, which had become very clearly disclosed [...] inside and outside of the Communist movement from 1956 onward to the creation of the New Left [...]. In this tradition the very simplified notion of

---

19 E.P. Thompson, 'Socialist Humanism: An Epistle to the Philistines', *New Reasoner*, No.1, Summer 1957, pp.105–143, http://www.marxists. org/archive/thompson-ep/1957/sochum.htm

the working class was that of [...] raw material processed into so many yards of class-conscious proletarians.[20]

In his approach Thompson fused an earlier tradition of people's history with the perspectives developed within the CPHG. His specific arguments about the impact of the industrial revolution on the British working population are informed by Barbara and John Hammond, who had written that looked at the impact of the industrial revolution on the working class: *The Village Labourer* (1911), *The Town Labourer* (1911), and *The Skilled Labourer* (1919). Raphael Samuel in particular emphasises this influence:

> In Britain, Marxist historiography was chronologically preceded by, and has always had to co-exist with a more broadly based, if theoretically less demanding 'people's history', radical and democratic rather than socialist in its leading concepts, yet providing very often the groundwork on which Marxist historians have built... [The Hammonds'] *Skilled Labourer* anticipated some of Thompson's major themes (e.g. the centrality accorded to the Luddites) while the vision of the industrial revolution as a cultural disaster, which informs all the Hammonds' work, provides Thompson with his central polemical thrust.[21]

---

20 E.P. Thompson quoted in Henry Abelove, et al, (Eds.), *Visions of History*, Manchester: MARHO: The Radical Historians Organisation & Manchester University Press, 1983, p.7.

21 Raphael Samuel, 'British Marxist Historians 1880–1980', *New Left Review*, I/120, March–April 1980.

The book is a study of the development of class consciousness which radically revises labour history. Thompson examines the complex process by which working people made themselves – coming to constitute themselves as a political body – as much as they were made by the imposition of industrial capitalism. By focussing on the *experience* of material conditions and foregrounding the conflict between agency and determination, Thompson reveals how earlier traditions informed what was to become the workers' movement. Thompson's statement of intent about the book and his method has gone down in history as one of the formative statements of history from below.

> I am seeking to rescue the poor stockinger, the Luddite cropper, the 'obsolete' hand-loom weaver, the 'utopian' artisan, and even the deluded follower of Joanna Southcott, from the enormous condescension of posterity. Their crafts and traditions may have been dying. Their hostility to the new industrialism may have been backward-looking. Their communitarian ideals may have been fantasies. Their insurrectionary conspiracies may have been foolhardy. But they lived through these times of acute social disturbance, and we did not. Their aspirations were valid in terms of their own experience; and, if they were casualties of history, they remain, condemned in their own lives, as casualties.[22]

---

22 E.P. Thompson, *The Making of the English Working Class*, London: Victor Gollancz, 1963, pp.12–13. The quotation has lent itself as a title to a recent film: Luke Fowler, *The Poor Stockinger, The Luddite Cropper and the Deluded Followers of Joanna Southcott*, 2012.

Despite the far-reaching influence of Thompson's work on international histories from below, the book has come under criticism, firstly for leaving out the development of consciousness and revolt on behalf of large sections of the industrial proletariat, including those in the cotton and coal industries, and secondly for its narrow focus on the English nation, which ignores the centrality of global slavery and expropriation to both the development of capitalism and resistance to it. As Thompson's work has recently been appropriated by thinkers associated with the Conservative and Labour parties in the UK, the national focus of his work becomes increasingly problematic, as we will discuss in chapter 7 on the Big Society. As Paul Gilroy presciently noted in 1993:

> England ceaselessly gives birth to itself, seemingly from Britannia's head. [...] For all their enthusiasm for the work of C.L.R. James, the influential British Communist Historians' Group is culpable here. Their predilections for the image of the freeborn Englishman and the dream of socialism in one country that framed their work are both found wanting when it comes to nationalism. [...] [In the work of Thompson] the nation – understood as a stable receptacle for counter-hegemonic class struggle – is the primary focus. These problems within English cultural studies form at the junction point with practical politics and instantiate wider difficulties with nationalism and with the discursive slippage or connotative resonance between 'race', ethnicity, and nation.[23]

---

23   Paul Gilroy, *The Black Atlantic: Modernity and Double Consciousness*, Cambridge, MA: Harvard University Press, 1993, p.15.

Ruskin College

Ruskin College was founded in Oxford in 1899. It was prefigured by 'summer meetings' held at various universities to open access up to working people. This was part of the 'University Extension Movement' – the major educational movement of the 19th century. The college was open 52 weeks of the year and students could visit and choose any length of study. Placements at the college were sponsored by trade unions who would dispatch members for set periods of time. In addition, Ruskin ran correspondence courses, extension classes in other localities, and later developed local Ruskin Halls in Manchester, Birmingham, Liverpool, Stockport and other regional English cities. Initially the founders of Ruskin had used their own funds to establish the school. They had hoped that the co-operative movement would then support the schools' development, but instead it was the trade unions, Oxford Council and the Labour Party which took up some but not all of the financial burden. That there was an enormous demand for adult education in the early 20th century became quickly apparent when by 1902 there were 96 classes in existence and 1,800 correspondence students; by 1904 there were 5,000 correspondence students associated with Ruskin. Working class education rapidly expanded in response to this demand.

From the beginning of Ruskin College, examinations and qualifications were a controversial topic. We will come to some moments of controversy at Ruskin and rival working class educational initiatives, which developed specifically in response, in chapter 6. An early Ruskin syllabus listed the following subjects: English Constitutional Political History,

English Industrial History, The Industrial Revolution, The History of Our Times, The Labour Movement, Trades Unionism, The Co-op Movement, Local Government, Political Economy, The Tariff Problem, Ethics, Sociology, Principles of Politics, English Literature, Psychology. From its beginnings Ruskin put the study of history and specifically the study of the history of the labour movement by union members at its centre.

History Workshop

The History Workshop, initiated at Ruskin College by Raphael Samuel (a student of Christopher Hill's at Balliol College, Oxford), was partly conceived as an 'attack on the examination system at Ruskin' which Samuel felt made the college 'servile' to the 'academic apparatus'. The Workshop was named after Joan Littlewood's Theatre Workshop to emphasise its improvisatory, informal and collective nature. It was an attempt to democratise the practice of history writing and research. From 1966 Raphael Samuel developed a series of seminars, and a journal launched in 1976, with the aim of developing historical studies that included detailed attention to the lives of working people, with Ruskin students and 'amateur' historians from outside the college playing an active role in the production of the Workshops. They published 13 Workshop pamphlets between 1970 and 1974. Looking back later, Samuel described the theoretical basis for the group:

Marxist categories certainly provided us with our basic starting point, above all in the centrality which we gave to class struggle, while more generally one might say that Marxism, like a commitment to the labour movement generally, was one of the common bonds between us [...] [W]hat we were attempting to do, like others, was to re-establish contact between Marxist thought and the reality it purported to address.[24]

According to Samuel, History Workshops could be set up anywhere by anybody without appealing to central control. The History Workshops developed into a popular movement with branches in various parts of the UK. It also spawned parallel initiatives and workshops in Latin America, Germany and South Africa. The History Workshop attracted criticism for under-emphasising quantitative and objective analysis, and there was a later drift toward a mode of discourse that was seen to render class as a largely cultural phenomenon together with a slight 'antiquarian' sensibility. But the History Workshops also worked to promote the understanding of working class women's lives and involvement in history, addressing a bias toward men that is evident in some of the earlier 'histories from below'. The journal of the History Workshop was initially titled *History Workshop: A Journal of Socialist History*. Reflecting the growing contribution of women, this strapline was later extended to *A Journal of Socialist and Feminist History*. One of the key figures still working in the legacy of The History Workshop is Carolyn Steedman. In an obituary for Raphael Samuel, Steedman poses questions

---

24   Raphael Samuel quoted in Roderick Floud, 'Quantitative History and People's History: Two Methods in Conflict?', *Social Science History*, Vol.8, No.2, p.154.

about the Workshop's role in incubating feminist research.

> Histories of feminism in Britain conventionally cite History Workshop as one of the origins of an indigenous women's movement. A notorious argument at the 1968 Workshop, about the failure of the male Left to take the personal and the domestic seriously – as objects of historical inquiry, or as anything at all – is frequently evoked. Did History Workshop give birth to women's history, in its modern mode? Samuel thought it did; it certainly obeyed its injunctions of historical practice, pursuing women as workers into the realms of reproduction, with the result that we now know more about what working-class women actually did during the Long Revolution [Raymond Williams' term], on a day-to-day basis, than we know about working-class men's activities. [...] Samuel understood this form of women's history as a politics, arising from 'a radical discontent with historical explanations which remained wholly external to the object they purported to account for'. It was part of a wider desire of the 1970s, to show 'class consciousness [...] mediated and formed in the crucible of the workplace and the home'.[25]

Steedman describes her work as addressing subjects who she says are 'embarrassing' to 20th century social history: in particular, policemen, soldiers and domestic servants. If the development of 'history from below' has been a matter of introducing areas of history previously neglected, then Steedman questions, often in a very personal way, what it is that informs or guides the inclusions (historical choices) and exclusions of the field. In *Master and Servant* (2007) *and Labours*

---

25   Carolyn Steedman, 'Raphael Samuel, 1934–1996', *Radical Philosophy*, No.82, March 1997.

Lost (2009), she injects the lives of working class women – particularly domestic servants – into the time frame and locations of Thompson's *Making of the English Working Class*.

Anna Davin

Anna Davin was also closely involved in the History Workshop movement during the 1970s. She was a founding member of the editorial collective of the Journal, and was to continue as an active editor for over thirty years. In 1970 she moved to London and started a History PhD at Birkbeck College. In London she joined the Stratford Women's Liberation Group (and helped produce their issue of the London Women's Liberation Network's magazine *Shrew*), and also a feminist study group in Pimlico (the Feminist History Group), and for a time helped in the Women's Liberation office. She was active in a pioneering community history group (People's Autobiography of Hackney); in the Feminist History Group; and also in The Public Library, a short-lived attempt to establish a library of political ephemera. Her best-known publication is an article called 'Imperialism and Motherhood', (*History Workshop Journal*, no 5, 1976). Her book, *Growing Up Poor: Home, School and Street in London 1870-1914* (1996), innovated in writing history from the perspective of the experience of children. Anna Davin's papers on Ruskin College and The History Workshop are held by the Women's Library in London. Anna herself prepared the Raphael Samuel archive at the Bishopsgate Institute which contains a great deal of material on Ruskin and The History Workshop.

Jacques Rancière

A useful way into the discussion of the way the landscape of French historiography changed in the 1960s and 1970s is through the figure of Jacques Rancière. Rancière was a pupil of Louis Althusser at the elite *École normale supérieure*, part of the seminar that assembled *Reading Capital*. His loyalty to Althusser was such that his contribution to that book has been cited as an example of the limits to which his master's philosophy can be taken.[26]

Rancière's initial split with Althusser was prompted by the loyalty Althusser showed to the French Communist Party (PCF) during the events of 1968. Althusser stood behind the line taken by the party that the revolt represented a form of infantile leftism, effectively defending the party and his own role as a party intellectual. Returning to Althusser's theory later, Rancière worked to widen the breach that May 1968 had thrown open.[27] For Rancière, his former teacher's philosophy was thus an effective defence of the status quo, keeping workers in their place as workers and maintaining the hegemony of the party, the state and intellectuals. Henceforth, Rancière follows, in the most minute detail, the mediations which surround subaltern subjects, proletarians or workers. The problem of theory, of Marxist science and the condescension of the intellectual to their subjects, is raised to a general principle traceable back from the perspective of the

---

26 Donald Reid, Introduction to *Proletarian Nights*, London: Verso, 2012, p.xiv.

27 *Althusser's Lesson* was first published in French in 1974. Jacques Rancière, *Althusser's Lesson*, London: Continuum, 2011, p.xvi.

present through the entire history of the left.[28]

The break Rancière was part of in 1968 mirrors the break of UK historians with the Communist Party of Great Britain after the invasion of Hungary by Russian troops in 1956, yet this delay is perhaps significant. During this period much of the European left distanced itself from Stalinist policy, but the primacy of the PCF in France softened this break, arguably helping to defer, and effectively trigger, what in 1968 became an open revolt against the party.

Les Révoltes Logiques

In 1975 Rancière joined a group of philosophers and historians, including many ex-Gauche Prolétarienne (Maoist) militants, to research a television series on the *Meaning of Revolt in the Twentieth Century*. The series never transpired because the state-owned channel Antennae 2 withdrew backing on the advice of Prime Minister Jacques Chirac. But the group developed its research in a journal, *Les Révoltes Logiques (LRL)*, based at the philosophy department of the University of Paris VIII. Inspired by a line from Arthur Rimbaud's poem 'Democracy' and addressed to both an academic and general readership, *LRL* was intended as a 'purposefully inconclusive problematisation of the history of the workers' and women's movements'.[29] Rather than retrieving a continuity of revolt, of invariant class antagonism, the group was more focussed

---

28   Anglophone commentators frequently invoke Rancière as a critic of Marxist economic determinism, yet he is less a critic of Marx than a critic of Althusser who leaves Althusser's interpretation of Marx largely intact.

29   Oliver Davis, *Jacques Rancière*, London: Polity, 2010, p.40.

on the discursive content of working class articulation and the manifold means by which it has been stifled.

Before the formation of the LRL group, Rancière had begun work with Alain Faure on sustained archival research into working class writings from the period 1830-1851. A book collecting the writings (including brochures, letters, poems, articles and posters) of workers of the 19th century across two key revolutionary periods, 1830-34 and 1848-51, was published in 1976.[30] The book, *La Parole Ouvriere 1830-1851*, was divided into five sections with commentary by both authors.[31] Much of the material assembled for *La Parole Ouvriere* provided the foundation for Rancière's writings for the LRL journal and he revisited an expanded selection of material by worker poets previewed there in his major study *Proletarian Nights*.

In a kind of manifesto, printed on the inside back cover of the first issue of the journal, the LRL group vowed to

> listen again to [*réentendre*] the findings of social history and to re-establish thought from below [*la pensée d'en bas*] and the issues which were debated therein.[32]

The collective waged a struggle which churned up the landscape of left history, challenging the tradition of left militancy from which they had come. [33]

---

30 Alain Faure & Jacques Rancière, *La Parole Ouvriere* 1830–1851, Paris: Union générale d'éditions, 1976.

31 See: Adrian Rifkin and Roger Thomas (eds.), *Voices of the People*, New York: Routledge, 1988.

32 *Les Révoltes Logiques* 1 (Winter 1975), quoted in Oliver Davis, op. cit.

33 Jacques Rancière, *Staging the People: The Proletarian and His Double, (Staging the People*, Vol.I), London: Verso, 2011, p.9 and p.11.

> *Les Révoltes Logiques* [questioned] the practices of identification common to the discourse of both activist vanguards and academic historians [...] It was not a history of voices from below against one of discourse from above, a history of individuals against that of collectivity, or of spontaneous movements against that of organisations and institutions. It was a history that questioned the very functioning of these pairs of opposites, and also those that opposed realities to representations.[34]

LRL sought to complicate the framework of post-WWII left history by philosophically developing the trend of turning away from party representation and towards the complex of identification, beliefs and solidarities which made up the (pre-industrial) working class. This general trend, begun after 1956, was compounded by the events of 1968. The strategic response of many left historians in the UK, France and elsewhere, even if they remained complicit with pro-Stalinist parties, had been to steer away from 20th century history; away from battles, revolutionary events, and towards writing and thinking through the minor, and pre-capitalist histories of the proto-working class or early workers' movement. In France, this work had been monopolised by historians working around the journal *Annales*, who had developed microscopic analyses of statistics, interactions of the interdependence of material, environmental and ideological frameworks structuring action, culture and economic change over the long term. Rancière developed strong criticisms of the Annales group, situating them in a left tradition established by pioneers such as Jules Michelet who, as Rancière saw it, founded social history on conditions

---

34 Ibid., p.13.

which constructed and perpetuated the left historian's mediating role between people and their own history.[35] For LRL, Annales historians indulged a particular contemporary spirit of nostalgia, and, through their ultra-localist view, stressed continuity at the expense of revolutionary rupture.[36]

Left Social History in England and France

In some ways this drew LRL and Rancière closer to the studies developed by peers from the CPHG working on history from below (who themselves had been heavily influenced by *Annales*). The groundbreaking post-WWII studies of C.L.R. James, E.P. Thompson and Christopher Hill had flowed into and been modified by the '60s and '70s culture of the new left which no longer bracketed off questions of race, sex and class from revolutionary politics. Rancière and the LRL group share some affinities with the historiography of history from below, especially in the emphasis on agency over structure. Both groups affirm some autonomy, in everyday life and self-perception, in the formation of popular consciousness; both perceive and animate the space for people to think differently with and against the forces determining them.

Rancière's individual work takes a self-consciously workerist perspective, establishing thematic and episodic histories around events and presenting working class subjectivity as active. However, vis-à-vis Thompson and

---

35 This is explored in Jacques Rancière, '"Le Social": The Lost Tradition in French Labour History', in Raphael Samuel (Ed.), *People's History and Socialist Theory*, London: Routledge, 1981; and later in further detail in Jacques Rancière, *The Names of History*, Minneapolis: University of Minnesota, 1994.

36 See Oliver Davis, op. cit., p.42.

history from below in general, LRL maintain a critical economic dimension whilst there is an even more finely tuned awareness of both the authority of the historian and of the forms of domination that are enacted within dominated groups. Equally, LRL's constant sniping at the self-serving nostalgia or revisionism of left intellectuals and historians was an attempt to follow and critically derail the development of left thought as it headed into the relativist impasses of postmodernism.

Commonalities with the UK movement extended to participation in a debate on people's history and socialist theory organised by the History Workshop, which sought, like LRL, to span and connect discussions between professional historians, workers and feminist movements. However, Rancière also caused friction within the History Workshop. The editorial board of its journal is said to have refused to publish some translations of Rancière's articles in 1979 because they 'insulted the working class'. Adrian Rifkin, then a member of History Workshop's editorial collective, speculates that Rancière's exploration of hybridity was incompatible with what he saw as History Workshop's cast-iron conception of class consciousness.

C.L.R. James

The Communist Party Historians Group and History Workshop's post-war collective study of pre-industrial history was preceded by a landmark work of history, *The Black Jacobins* (1938) by C.L.R. James, which had a lasting influence on their project. James established himself in Trinidad as an author, producing the novel *Minty Alley* (1936) and a series of short stories along with *The Life of Captain Cipriani: An Account of British Government in the West Indies (1932)*, a biography of Arthur Andrew Cipriani, the President of the Trinidad Workingmen's Association. Working as a teacher, James taught Eric Williams, later Prime Minster of Trinidad and Tobago, with whom James developed sharp political disagreements. Travelling from Trinidad to the small town of Nelson in Lancashire in 1932, James worked as a cricket correspondent for The *Manchester Guardian* and moved to London in 1933. James began to interpret Marxist thought, joining the international Trotskyist movement. James later split from Trotskyism, forming the Johnson-Forest Tendency, a radical splinter group, with Raya Dunayevskaya and Grace Lee Boggs. Johnson-Forest fully denounced the idea of the 'vanguard party'. James' position as party refusenik, critic of 'state capitalism', and his experience theorising American, Caribbean and African working class self-activity and organisation led him to become a strong influence on autonomist Marxism in Italy and elsewhere.[37]

---

37   See Pier Paolo Frassinelli, 'Cyril Lionel Robert James', http://www. generation-online.org/p/pclrjames.htm and 'A Libertarian Tendency Map', http://amodernmanifesto.tumblr.com/post/26731433122/a-libertarian-marxist-tendency-map-this

James also became involved in editing the journal of the International African Friends of Abyssinia, with Amy Ashwood Garvey and George Padmore among others. His involvement in the development of Pan-Africanism coincided with the writing of *The Black Jacobins*. The book was adapted as a play performed in London's West End starring Paul Robeson as the Haitian Revolutionary leader, Toussaint L'Ouverture. Crucial to James' work is the notion of history as contestation. *The Black Jacobins* was a challenge to the false picture of slavery and slaves which has been passed down to us as history. In the slave revolt in Haiti, James saw the continuity of the same struggle against exploitation that was taking shape in his own time in the African and Caribbean liberation movements of which he was a part. Haiti set an example that the colonised and marginalised peoples of the world could, and would again, play a defining role in its history.

> Effectively for the first time, James gave slaves an agency: *The Black Jacobins* portrayed slaves as agents in their own story rather than being grateful recipients of the largesse of others.[38]

> If you read *The Black Jacobins* carefully you will see that time and again it is Africa to which I am referring, and the political purpose of the book has got little to do with the Caribbean [...] In 1936, Du Bois wrote *The Black Reconstruction* in which he showed the role that Blacks had played in the creation of modern America. In 1938 I wrote *The Black Jacobins* in which I showed the

---

38   From the introduction by James Walvin to C.L.R. James, *The Black Jacobins: Toussaint L'Ouverture and the San Domingo Revolution*, London: Penguin,, 2001, p.viii.

role the Blacks had played in the creation of modern Europe.[39]

Selma James

Selma James is a women's rights and anti-racist campaigner and author born in New York and, since the 1960s, resident in the UK. She worked with C.L.R. James, initially in the Johnson-Forest tendency which she joined at the age of 15, and, after marrying, from 1958 to 1962 they worked together in Trinidad in the movement for Caribbean federation and independence. In 1972, Selma James founded the International Wages for Housework Campaign. She coined the word 'unwaged' to describe the caring work women do, and it has since entered the English language to describe all who work without wages on the land, in the home, and in the community. With Mariarosa Dalla Costa she co-authored the classic pamphlet *The Power of Women and the Subversion of the Community (1972)* which launched the 'domestic labour debate.' She has addressed the power relations within the working class movement, and how to organize across sectors despite divisions of sex, race, and class, South and North.[40]

Peter Linebaugh

Peter Linebaugh was a student of E.P. Thompson at the Centre for the Study of Social History at Warwick University. He is a member of Midnight Notes, a U.S. based collective who have published political magazines and books influenced by

---

39   *Visions of History*, op. cit., p.275.
40   'Selma James', http://www.pmpress.org/content/article.
     php?story=SelmaJames and http://en.wikipedia.org/wiki/Selma_James

autonomist Marxism since the late 1980s. Whilst a student of Thompson's he co-authored a landmark study of social crime in 18th century England, *Albion's Fatal Tree* (1977), with Thompson, Douglas Hay, Cal Winslow and John G. Rule. He went on to develop his essay for that book, 'The Tyburn Riot Against the Surgeons', into the book *The London Hanged*, which took the life, work, crime and deaths of those hanged at Tyburn in the first half of the 18th century as its object of study. Linebaugh's project sought to understand the relationship between crime and the working class in a period of social struggle against new laws governing property and wages.

> Our starting point is neither law nor 'critical law' but the hanged men and women whose views and actions continually challenged both the law and their own class. If we categorize them too quickly as social criminals taking from the rich, or criminal-criminals stealing from the poor, in the process of making these judgments we cloud our attentiveness to theirs.[41]

In the 18th century the beginnings of the criminal justice system, 'law' and the institutions which today we consider almost eternal were somewhat more malleable and fluid. The invention of new criminal offences pertaining to property produced a new criminal class. As much as the law and criminal justice system was imposed from above, the limits of the 'law' were tested by material acts and prior beliefs that emanated from below. The law was shaped not just by the 'great men' who presided over it.

---

41 Peter Linebaugh, *The London Hanged: Crime And Civil Society In The Eighteenth Century*, London: Penguin, 1991, p.23.

As a Marxist project, history from below sought to reconstruct a working class before the term existed in a period in which waged work was by no means a given and was sometimes actively challenged. This jarred with orthodox Marxist schema, yet objects, goods and material were made, circulated and consumed nonetheless. Following the passage of these 'things' leads Linebaugh to some imaginative materialist propositions.

> The archives of the criminal jurisdictions of London and the printed Proceedings of the Old Bailey give us a history of misappropriated things. From them we may derive a history of taking. Rarely do they provide information permitting us to understand how things were made or the exact combinations of materials, tools and expenditure of labouring creativity. For that information we need to begin with the biographies of the men and women who were hanged – from these we may obtain a history of making.[42]

Linebaugh's own biography, as someone from the US who crossed the Atlantic to study with E.P. Thompson and others in the UK, goes some way to explaining his particular approach. His work is as stimulated by the UK communist historians as it is by engagement with activism against the US incarceration industry, and with black power and civil rights movements.

---

42   Ibid. p.27.

Marcus Rediker and the Revolutionary Atlantic

Working together with Marcus Rediker, Linebaugh produced *The Many-Headed Hydra*, a study of the revolutionary Atlantic with a close relation to the work established by Paul Gilroy in *The Black Atlantic*. The book developed Marcus Rediker's work on slavery and piracy, and Linebaugh's attempts in *The London Hanged* to establish accounts of class solidarities which stretched across the world as mercantile capitalism globalised.

> At its most dynamic the eighteenth-century proletariat was often ahead of any fixed consciousness. The changes of geography, language, climate, and relations of family and production were so volatile and sudden that consciousness had to be characterized by a celerity of thought that may be difficult to comprehend to those whose experience has been steadier.[43]

In many ways the book developed and internationalised Thompson's project of uncovering hidden histories of struggle and contestation against the imposition of capitalism. Whilst reverent towards Thompson's work, Rediker and Linebaugh enacted a practical critique undermining the anglophone and national limitations of the focus of *The Making of the English Working Class* and displaced it with a mobile, global, polyglot, ethnically and sexually diverse proletariat. In his book Thompson had hoped that 'causes which were lost in England might, in Asia or Africa, yet be won'. Yet, if Thompson had

---

43   Peter Linebaugh and Marcus Rediker, *The Many Headed Hydra: Sailors, Slaves, Commoners and the Hidden History of the Revolutionary Atlantic*, Boston: Beacon Press, 2000.

been internationalist in aspiration, Rediker and Linebaugh's study forcefully laid the groundwork for a material study of the globalisation of labour history stretching both back and forwards in time.

History, the Present and Beyond

In many ways, reaching into the unexamined sources of pre-capitalism allowed these thinkers not only to study the formation of capitalism, the very moments at which the wage, the law, property and the commodity are 'discovered', but also its reverse; the challenges that met industrial capitalism along the road to its development, the acts and imagination that might have contributed, or might yet contribute, to its undoing. Siding with the marginalised and the censored, history from below has to confront the very terms in which people's daily lives and activity in the dominant society were and are framed.

> It is no longer necessary to apologize too profusely for taking the common people of the past on their own terms and trying to understand them.[44]

Since Hill's statement, we could say that this 'necessity' has receded ever further into the past. Television dramas and documentaries frequently draw on the everyday experience of 'normal' people to reconstruct the past. Since the 1970s, history from below has expanded and proliferated across disciplinary boundaries and throughout the mediascape. This does not necessarily mean it has been recuperated

---

44   *The World Turned Upside Down*, op. cit., p.17.

simply, nor that somehow the problems of the marginality of certain histories has been adequately redressed. In the rest of this book we will explore arguably undigested tensions within the operations of history from below in the present. Its legacy still remains charged in present times. Journalist and broadcaster Paul Mason's best-selling book *Live Working or Die Fighting: How the Working Class Went Global* (2007) draws on a popular form of labour history to make parallels with struggles in the globalised present. In particular, his account draws on moments of international solidarity to emphasise several waves of globalisation and the potential for working class internationalism to develop in the spaces and networks opened up by capital. The intense phase of globalisation over the last two decades has also spurred fierce localisms in response. This has both negative effects and positive ones, but in the field of social history much interesting material, and many groups, associations and practices have developed within the new tensions of a dynamic period of globalisation.

In the last decade radical history groups in the UK have proliferated from anarchist, anti-authoritarian communist, feminist and activist scenes. In our bibliography you'll find references to and resources of such groups, but a brief list of some of the most active we are alert to would include: London Psychogeographical Association, Transpontine, South London Radical History Group, Past Tense Press, Penniless Press, Bristol Radical History Group, Nottingham Radical History, North London Radical History Network, Workers City, The WUSC (Wetherspoons Underground Sykogeosofers Club). Many of these groups assume a critical stance towards professional historians and in their local focus have often crossed over with anti-gentrification struggles wherein knowledge of the recent past has been developed for practical reasons (e.g. contesting planning laws) as well as to lend a legitimacy and authority to their campaigns.

Political movements frequently make use of images of the past to lend authority and continuity to their address to present problems. In this respect we might question whether anti-capitalist and emancipatory politics have been transposed from the present into the past. Challenging the tendency to turn lived history into heritage, we might also consider the turn to history as deriving its energy from an intense period of transformation which appears bent on obliterating not just the past, but for many, the future too. The powerful neoliberal consensus that 'there is no alternative' to sweeping privatisation, welfare reform, and imposition of work has stimulated many to explore the radical alternatives posed in the past as pointing ways out of this dead end. With a widespread loss of legitimacy of both mainstream political parties and extra-parliamentary organisations, there is an objective need for new formations and movements to do their own work of informing their participants of the historical ground of the present in which they operate.

At the same time there is a need to challenge the instrumentalisation of radical history by increasingly desperate professional politicians and their advisers on the right and the so-called left (John Cruddas, Maurice Glasman, Philip Blond) as a means of justifying austerity and 'cohering community' while in fact directing social fracture. As we will discuss in our chapter on the Big Society, thinkers affiliated with UK political parties have been reappraising the 'paternalism' of pre-capitalist society and reconstructing what they hope to be a viable English-British nationalism whilst disguising the violence that such a nationalism requires to function. A dubious celebration of 'working class autonomy', once foregrounded by historians from below, has been circulated by right wing thinkers to characterise austerity as an act of tough love that might reactivate a sanitised and depoliticised independence for the working class.

These are some of the factors at stake in revising our study of history from below. We will begin, in our next chapter, by considering in whom and of what 'the below' consists.

Spinners and Weavers, are ye injured? Least of all persons have ye reason to complain. For four times your number are employed since the invention of machinery :--- and why? because your little children of machinery can earn their own livelihood, and it is easy to rear a

MEMBERS UNLIMITED

The working class did not rise like the sun at an appointed time. It was present at its own making.[1]

The rich are named but not numbered, while the poor are numbered but not named.[2]

The question of who or what constitutes 'the people' and 'the working class' is a problematic object in any historical account because of the political investments which are always made in these categories. The very notion of a 'people' is usually circumscribed by national boundaries. A class implies a unity of interests and conditions, but also antagonism between (and within) classes. Here we explore the definition and redefinition of the working class and the complexity of class interests as developed in 'history from below'. Of particular interest will be attempts to expand or redraw the limits of the working class and the questions these attempts raise.

What the expansion of the category of class reveals is the exclusion of a larger body of people from wider realms of public life than are commonly considered. In the longer view of history and of class, it is possible to trace an evolution of sovereignty which tells us much about the foundation of democracy upon exclusion, a part of the political body kept outside. During the English Revolution of 1640 two ideas of 'the people' emerged, with each side – parliamentarians

---

1   E.P. Thompson, *The Making of the English Working Class*, London: Penguin, 1982, p.9.

2   Anonymous Pamphlet, 1790s.

and royalists – keen to invoke them for the sake of their legitimacy. Within this split were further divisions. On the parliamentarian side there were conflicts between an emerging bourgeoisie and radical democrats. The reduction of democratic interest to those who held property, i.e. an interest in the land, versus a levelling democracy consisting in the manifold interests of those who lived and worked on the land was settled on the side of the former. These conflicting conceptions have fundamentally shaped modern political philosophy and statecraft in Europe, at least.

When we mention the people, we do not mean the confused promiscuous body of the people.[3]

It was the experience of the period of civil war and challenges from all directions to state, church and law that shaped Thomas Hobbes' mechanistic theory of political sovereignty, which insisted on the necessity of centralised authority to safeguard a liberal state. In Hobbes' and some of his peers' conceptions (and in the famous illustration which accompanies his book, *Leviathan*), a mechanical understanding of the body is conflated with a smoothly running political regime.

In mechanical philosophy, the body is described by analogy with the machine, often with emphasis on its *inertia*. The body is conceived as brute matter, wholly divorced from any rational qualities: it does not know, does not want, does not

---

3   Marchamont Needham, mid 17th century political commentator. Quoted in Christopher Hill, *The World Turned Upside Down: Radical Ideas During the English Revolution*, London: Penguin, 1991, p.60.

The working class rises, fully formed, from Glastonbury Tor at the appointed time – the opening ceremony of the 2012 London Olympics.

16th century engraving of an agricultural labourer

feel. [...] the body is a conglomerate of mechanical motions that, lacking autonomous power operates on the basis of an external causation, in a play of attractions and aversions where everything is regulated as in an automaton.[4]

The human body and not the steam engine, and not even the clock, was the first machine produced by capitalism.[5]

---

4   Silvia Federici, *Caliban and The Witch: Women, The Body And Primitive Accumulation*, New York: Autonomedia, 2004.

5   *Caliban and the Witch*, op. cit., p.146.

Christopher Hill shows how during this period two revolutions correspond to, but also exceed, these two powers grappling over a body to direct.

> There were, we may oversimplify, two revolutions in mid-seventeenth century England. The one which succeeded established the sacred rights of property (abolition of feudal tenures, no arbitrary taxation), gave political power to the propertied (sovereignty of Parliament and common law, abolition of prerogative courts), and removed all impediments to the triumph of the ideology of the men of property – the protestant ethic. There was however, another revolution which never happened, though from time to time it threatened. This might have established communal property, a far wider democracy in political and legal institutions, might have destabilised the state church and rejected the protestant ethic.[6]

William Walwyn noted of the Cavaliers and Roundheads 'their quarrel is all whose slaves the poor will be.'[7]

Against the Stalinist/Leninist orthodoxies with which the Communist Party of Great Britain was officially aligned can be countered the longer traditions of dissent, radicalism and revolution that historians from below had begun to unearth in the 1940s and gone on to read in the light of contemporary struggles. This had challenged Marxism's foundation in the modern project in a number of ways. Not only did the myths of linear history become somewhat fractured, but

---

6   Ibid., p.15.
7   Quoted in Peter Linebaugh, 'Days of Villainy: a reply to two critics', *International Socialism Journal*, Issue 63, http://pubs. socialistreviewindex.org.uk/isj63/linebaugh.htm

also the centrality of the industrial proletariat to historical development is put into question. From Christopher Hill and Edward Bernstein's medieval communists to Eric Hobsbawm's 'social bandits', Peter Linebaugh's 'picaresque proletarian' and Silvia Federici's 'witches', tensions, ruptures and singularities are brought to bear upon the definition of the working class.

In the attention to detail that these historians carried out, from the discovery of hidden forms of work and hidden conflicts outside the workplace, we arrive with a picture of the proletarian embedded in struggles for control over both production, and reproduction – all those practices, including care-giving, that sustain life within capitalism, and in effect reproduce labour power.

Peter Linebaugh provides an image of the articulation of these different bodies in the vast augmentation of wealth that intensified throughout the 18th century:

> The factory proletariat propelled the machines of industry; the slave plantation of the West Indies and the plundered indigenous peoples provided the commerce; the young, the unemployed, and the criminalized peopled the towns; the separate public and domestic spheres of women's endeavour reproduced the population on an enlarged scale. The working class was thus composed of waged artisans, criminalized unemployed, unwaged domestic workers as mothers and wives, slaves, and the indigenous and colonized.[8]

---

8   Peter Linebaugh, *'Introduction to the works of Thomas Paine, Rights of Man and The Commonwealth'*, http://libcom.org/history/peter-linebaughs-new-introduction-works-thomas-paine

Those who contributed to and/or opposed that vast accumulation of wealth were quite far from the heroic male white worker celebrated by socialist and communist parties in Europe. Politicising reproduction was a specific challenge to forms of western Marxism which had tended to focus on production as the privileged site of struggle, and reproduction as natural or passive. To pose antagonism within the reproduction of class society not only upset the naturalised understanding of who the proletariat were, but also what its stake in the abolition or continuation of capitalism, class, gender and race relations really meant.

Women, Witches, Workers

For Silvia Federici, women's history is not detached from that of men nor the social system of production which traditionally has been associated exclusively with men's labour. *Caliban and the Witch* (2004) is her study of the enclosure of the female body carried out through the demonisation of women as 'witches' in the 17th century. The book is also a polemic about the construction of race and gender as part of parallel forms of expropriation taking place in Europe, Africa and the Americas over the same historical period, and as Federici argues, this process of primitive accumulation took place not just in the past but continues in the present too.

In *Caliban and the Witch*, Federici like many of the historians from below, revisits the historical origins of capitalism – a 'counter-revolution that destroyed the possibilities that emerged from the anti-feudal struggle'.[9] This is not a lament for a lost Eden, but a call for both an understanding

---

9   *Caliban and the Witch*, op. cit., p.21.

of the violence, exploitation and division at the heart of the capitalist project, and for us to imagine other possibilities at the present juncture. Much of her research was carried out as Federici was working as a teacher in Nigeria in 1984, where, under the auspices of a 'War Against Indiscipline' imposed by the Nigerian government and World Bank, Federici saw 'unfolding under my eyes processes very similar to those that I had studied' in *Caliban and the Witch*.

> Whenever the capitalist system is threatened by a major economic crisis, the capitalist class has to launch a process of 'primitive accumulation': that is, a large-scale process of colonisation and enslavement, such as the one we are witnessing at present.[10]

In her study of primitive accumulation, Federici foregrounds the relationship of women and the enslaved peoples of the colonies to the reproduction of labour-power. In Europe, Federici argues that the process by which capitalism developed (and responded to its own crises, through state intervention) began to limit many women to the home and to domestic work, in order to maintain the labour-power of male workers through clothing, feeding, caring, cleaning, cooking. In this respect Federici's research was partly influenced by the work of Selma James. James co-authored the classic *The Power of Women and the Subversion of the Community* with Maria Dalla Costa which launched the international

---

10   Ibid., p.104.

Wages for Housework Campaign in 1972.[11] James and Costa, Federici argues, understood women's unpaid housework as,

> the effect of a social system of production that does not recognize the production and reproduction of the worker as a social-economic activity and a source of capital accumulation, but mystifies it instead as a natural resource or a personal service, while profiting from the wageless condition of the labor involved.[12]

The population decline of the 16th and 17th centuries in both Europe and European colonies, which was mostly the result of colonial plunder and dispossession, coupled with economic crisis, led the state to attack women's control over their own bodies by regulating sexuality, imposing discipline and criminalising early forms of birth control. At the same time women were increasingly seen as non-workers, and women's labour came to be 'defined as a natural resource, laying outside the sphere of market relations':

> In pre-capitalist Europe women's subordination to men had been tempered by the fact that they had access to the commons and other communal assets, while in the new capitalist regime *women themselves became the commons*.[13]

---

11 Mariarosa Dalla Costa and Selma James, *The power of women and the subversion of the community*, 1972, http://libcom.org/library/power-women-subversion-community-della-costa-selma-james

12 *Caliban and the Witch*, op., cit, p.7.

13 Ibid., p.97.

It was not just the state and capital that produced this environment. Some male workers (for example craftsmen) were complicit, with the authorities, with keeping women out of the workplace and restricted to low paid cottage industry or domestic work. In this light, Federici questions and redraws the concept of wage-slavery: European working class women's situation, Federici asserts, was closer to a form of slavery than that of many male workers. Moreover, this led to a counter-productive 'self-alienation and dis-accumulation' of male worker's power and that of workers generally.

Federici notes that struggles over the wage and reproduction between European workers and employers were dependent upon the wealth generated by the brutality of slave labour in the Americas and the Caribbean. Other historians have also tracked the dispossession inherent in the founding of modern capitalism to stress the centrality of subjects other than the British working class. Peter Fryer:

> Thus, at the dawn of the factory system in Britain, the trade in black slaves directly nourished several important industries and boomed precisely those four provincial towns that, in the 1801 census, ranked immediately after London: Manchester, Liverpool, Birmingham and Bristol [...] There is controversy about the extent to which the threefold profits of the triangular trade as a whole financed Britain's industrial revolution.[14]

---

14   Peter Fryer, *Staying Power: The History of Black People in Britain*, London: Pluto Press, 1984, p.16.

As well as providing a crucial financial input, Federici shares with C.L.R. James the conviction that aspects of the labour process fundamental to capitalism originated in European colonies rather than in Europe itself. The plantation system that began to be imposed wholesale in the colonies in the 1650s prefigured not only the factory, but also the global assembly line along which exploited workers in Africa, Latin America and Asia produce commodities for the production and reproduction of labour power in Europe and America.

> waged-work, rather than providing an alternative to slavery, was made to depend upon slavery for its own existence, as a means (like unpaid female labour) for the expansion of the unpaid part of the waged working-day.[15]

On the whole, European workers did not profit from slavery and importation of goods. They were subjected to disciplinary techniques first 'experimented with' on enslaved people in the plantations, and vice versa. It wasn't until the end of slavery that European wages rose and workers' organisations gained legitimacy. In the colonies any form of combination between the white maritime proletariat and slaves was guarded against through the production of racial division – for example laws to prevent interracial fraternisation and mixed childbirth.

In *Caliban and the Witch*, Federici argues that the witch hunts of the middle ages curtailed the possibilities for resistance to capitalism in both Europe and its colonies, paving the way for the expansion of capitalism by limiting and dividing the working class, peasantry and enslaved people.

---

15   *Caliban and the Witch*, op. cit., p.104.

primitive accumulation has been above all an accumulation of inequalities, hierarchies, divisions, which have alienated workers from each other and even from themselves.[16]

The witch hunts facilitated the dispossession of the peasantry and the imposition of industrial work discipline. These forms of superstition and barbaric punishments were contiguous with the division of male and female workers, reduction of women to mothers or wives, and the propagation of racist and separatist ideologies. Federici contends that the witch hunts were not a simple 'movement from below' but a state-sponsored phenomenon; a tool mobilised to achieve conditions fertile for early capitalism.

Federici contextualises the accusations and confessions directed at women in terms of the political economy of the times. The accusations levelled against the 'witches' reveals a fear of class confrontation. Many of the accused were on public assistance, begged door-to-door or stole milk, food or wine. For Federici the records of the witch trials reveal the class struggle 'played out at the village level'.[17] For Sheila Rowbotham, the 'mania' over accusations of witchcraft reveal a struggle over women's attempts to speak out and for themselves. While '[the peasant's wife] was like cattle, a means of production' whose labour at the same time gave her 'a degree of bargaining power', older women were excluded from production and sometimes took on an outsider's role in relation to the community.

When misfortune came people looked for someone to blame.

---

16   Ibid., p.115.
17   Ibid., p.171.

Old women who argued back were obvious targets. Reginald Scott in his *Discoverie* said the witches' chief fault was that 'they are scolds'. They could also be felt to be trying to gain powers or control which did not suit their station. Thus 'wise' and 'cunning' women became suspect.[18]

'Witches' were purportedly promised money in times of hardship by the Devil, money which subsequently turned to ashes – 'a detail perhaps related to the experience of superinflation at the time'.[19] Ironically, Jean Bodin, a French rationalist and political theorist who wrote the first account of inflation, was a keen participant in witch trials, and was later accused of diabolical magic himself. Effectively, Federici suggests magic was invoked in order to dispel magic.

> In the history of capitalism, 'going back' was a means of stepping forward [...] the devil functioned as a true servant of God [...]. He so well consolidated God's command over human affairs that with the advent of Newtonian physics, God would be able to retire [...].[20]

Thus, by the late 17th and early 18th century witch hunts were ridiculed. They had served their purpose in the imposition of industrial capitalism: the displacement of the church and the establishment of *rational* bourgeoisies across Europe. The recordings of common crimes (theft, damage to property) replaced more superstitious accusations. As one French parliamentarian put it: 'One has ceased therefore to accuse

---

18 Sheila Rowbotham, *Hidden from History: 300 Years of Women's Oppression and the Fight Against It*, London: Pluto Press, 1975, p.5.

19 *Caliban and the Witch*, op. cit., p.171.

20 Ibid., p.203.

them of the uncertain in order to accuse them of the certain'.[21] In Federici's account, women had led the way in battles against enclosure; so-called 'witches' may have been privy to secret gatherings co-ordinating peasant revolts. The witch hunts, through the vagueness of the accusations made against 'witches', were conducive to an atmosphere which allowed for the widespread suppression of dissent.

The witch hunts were an attack on female sexuality, particularly for older women, but also on homosexuality, collective sexuality, and relationships between people of different classes. Forms of social gathering, feasts and festivals, along with 'deviant' sexual practices such as masturbation, were banned as 'non-productive', threatening to the family and therefore dangerous to the capitalist project As Federici points out, across Africa such practices are still often subject to state and communal repression.[22] While in wealthy capitalist states, the demonisation of single mothers and sanctions on non-reproductive sex still sharpen during periods of economic crisis. Recently Melinda Cooper and Angela Mitropoulos have connected this fear of non-reproductive sex and its association with usury to the blame culture which has developed in the wake of the 2008 sub-prime loans crisis.

> Recalling capitalism's bloody inauguration in the enclosures and witch hunts, and its most vicious moments since, sermons against the sin of usury have always implied that crises might be transcended in the determination of a boundary between that which is excessive and that which is proper. [...] Unlike

---

21   Ibid., p.205.
22   Ibid., p.194.

the debt that can be repaid, which in its repayment makes the future a calculable version of the present, usurious debt assumes the existence of an incalculable, unknowable – and, quite possibly inflationary – risk. In its malevolently construed history, usury has signified both unnatural generation and an obstacle to proper generation, not so much non-normative as abnormal. [...] the sin of usury was not only part of that medieval confluence that included the sins of sodomy and prostitution, sermons against gambling, the witch burnings, pogroms and anti-heresy trials.[23]

In the Middle Ages the witch hunts provoked deep fear and alienation between men and women. Perhaps they inculcated self-regulation based on the fear of the trials and horrific 'punishments'. Bodin: 'We must spread terror among some by persecuting many'. In this way, says Federici, the witch hunts were an attack on all women: 'it was not only the "deviant" woman, but the woman as such, that was put on trial'.[24]

Rowbotham and Federici's work establishes not only women's claim to be included in *history*, but specifically locate the position of women in social relations of production, the development of capitalism and resistance to it.

The Enclosure of the Globe

Federici's account rests on research carried out in South America on the relationship between the Conquest, the industrial revolution, and birth of world capitalism. Eduardo

---

23   Melinda Cooper and Angela Mitropoulos, 'In Praise of Usura', http://www.metamute.org/editorial/articles/praise-usura.

24   *Caliban and the Witch*, op. cit., p.185.

Galeano's bestselling history of Latin American conquest and the neo-imperialism which followed it, *The Open Veins of Latin America* (1973), argues that the riches 'discovered' in the New World, and the black and indigenous labour that dug them out of the land, underpinned the dawn of the era of capitalist production in Europe.

> The Latin American colonies were discovered, conquered and colonized within the process of the expansion of commercial capitalism. [...] Neither Spain nor Portugal received the benefits of the sweeping advance of capitalist mercantilism, although it was their colonies that substantially supplied the gold and silver feeding this expansion. [...] It was in other parts of Europe that modern capitalism could be incubated, taking decisive advantage of the expropriation of primitive [sic] American peoples. The rape of accumulated treasure was followed by the systematic exploitation of the forced labour of Indians and abducted Africans in the mines.[25]

In Galeano's words 'Spaniards owned the cow, but others drank the milk'. The Spanish may have overseen the initial process of conquest and primitive accumulation, but it was those European centres most advanced in banking and manufacture which reaped the rewards.

> The metals taken from the new colonial dominions not only stimulated Europe's economic development; one may say that they made it possible.

---

25   Eduardo Galeano, *The Open Veins of Latin America: five centuries of the pillage of a continent*, (Trans. Cedric Belfrage), London: Serpent's Tail, 2009, p.29.

The [Spanish] Crown was mortgaged. It owed nearly all of the silver shipments, before they arrived, to German, Genoese, Flemish, and Spanish bankers.[26]

The narrative established by Galeano has become central to the left revival in Latin American politics of recent years. Both Lula and Chavez have referred to Galeano's research, and direct control of the revenues from mineral extraction in Venezuela and Brazil has been central to each of these figures' political power in the region. Chavez even went so far as to publicly hand Barack Obama a copy of Galeano's book. Nonetheless, Galeano's narrative is not anathema to classically national socialist agendas. A rhetoric of anti-imperialism, energy independence and nationalisation is paired with populism, homophobia and anti-semitism under Hugo Chavez's leadership.

What is emphasised in Federici, Fryer, C.L.R. James and others' related arguments is the way this understanding of colonial 'peripheries' as central to historical process undermines national histories and a key left narrative: that of the European working class as the motor of industrial development. This puts the so-called 'dignity of labour', historically celebrated by elements of the workers' movement, in question, but also pulls apart the certainties that had conscripted the spheres of operations for trade unions and communist or socialist parties within national boundaries.

E.P. Thompson's father, a Methodist clergyman and teacher in Bengal, had related the enclosures of the English countryside to those taking place simultaneously in Europe and its colonies:

---

26   Ibid., both quotes p.23.

The same era that saw the English peasant expropriated from his common lands saw the Bengal peasant made a parasite in his own country.[27]

Peter Linebaugh has taken this connection further, suggesting that not only were the expropriations in England and the colonies simultaneous and connected by the Atlantic trade, but also that there were solidarities between the expropriated proletariat on both sides of the Atlantic. The forms these solidarities took were complex and not always reciprocal. Linebaugh finds evidence of what he takes to be the expression of global solidarity in the action of commoners thrown off their land in England.

> The leader of the Blacks and 15 of his Sooty Tribe appear'd, some in Coats made of Deer-Skins, others with Fur Caps, &c. all well armed and mounted: There were likewise at least 300 People assembled to see the Black Chief and his Sham Negroes [...].

I would put forward the fact that the poachers defended commoning, not just by disguising themselves but by disguising themselves as *Negroes*, and they did so at Farnham, near the heart of what became the quintessence of England as Jane Austen so gently wrote about it, or Gilbert White, the ornithologist, so carefully observed it, or William Cobbett, the

---

27   Edward J. Thompson, 'The Life of Charles. Lord Metcalfe', 1937 quoted in E.P. Thompson, *Customs in Common*, London: Merlin Press, 1991, p.170.

radical journalist, so persistently fulminated about it.[28]

C.L.R. James found in Haiti evidence of alliances between black slaves in revolt and stranded European seamen. Moreover, he set this against a background of proto-industrial conditions.

> The slaves worked on the land, and, like the revolutionary peasants everywhere, they aimed at the extermination of their oppressors. But working and living together in gangs of hundreds on the huge sugar-factories which covered the North Plain, they were closer to a modern proletariat than any group of workers in existence at the time, and the rising was, therefore, a thoroughly planned and organised mass movement[29]

The 'discovery' of a proletariat before the Industrial Revolution overturned the neat distinction between 'primitive' and civilised societies and the racism inherent in the idea of the former occupying static and the latter dynamic time. In revolutionary Haiti, C.L.R. James found both co-operation between many hands of labour and work refusal: a black revolutionary subject organised as collective labour in a proto-factory situation (the plantation) in combination with a force that stood outside of capitalist production and actively refused it (the maroons). This is in no way to say that the conditions experienced by slaves and the European proletariat were the same. James accepted the

---

28 Anonymous, *The History of the Blacks of Waltham in Hampshire*, (1723), quoted in Peter Linebaugh, 'Charters of Liberty in White Face and Black Face: Race, Slavery and the Commons', *Mute* Vol.2 Issue 2, 2006. p.76.

29 C.L.R. James, *The Black Jacobins: Toussaint L'Ouverture and The San Domingo Revolution*, London: Penguin, 2001, p.69.

Marxian distinction between proletarian work as formally 'free' labour and slaves as human commodities to be bought and sold, while detailing the systematic treatment of slaves as far more horrific than anything the European proletariat experienced. It is a polemic that has split communists throughout the 20th century and remains contentious today. Rather than abandoning the working class as some post-autonomist thinkers might pretend to today, James heads directly into this combination – attempting to understand the complexities of who the slaves were, and the forces that made them into a movement.

What was the intellectual level of these slaves? The planters, hating them, called them by every opprobrious name. 'The negroes,' says a memoir published in 1789, 'are unjust, cruel, barbarous, half-human, treacherous, deceitful, thieves, drunkards, proud, lazy, unclean, shameless, jealous to fury, and cowards.' It was by sentiments such as these that they strove to justify the abominable cruelties they practiced. And they took great pains that the negro should remain the brute beast they wanted him to be. 'The safety of the whites demands that we keep the negroes in the most profound ignorance. I have reached the stage of believing firmly that one must treat the negroes as one treats beasts.' Such is the opinion of the Governor of Martinique in a letter addressed to the Minister and such was the opinion of all colonists. Except for the Jews, who spared no energy in making Israelites of all their slaves, the majority of the colonists religiously kept all instruction, religious or otherwise, away from the slaves. [...]

Naturally there were all types of men among them, ranging from native chieftains, as was the father of Toussaint L'Ouverture, to men who had been slaves in their own country [...]. The leaders of a revolution are usually those who have been able to profit by the cultural advantages of the system they are attacking, and the San Domingo revolution was no exception to this rule.[30]

Luddites

The Luddites are a key social movement whose position on the cusp of pre-industrial and industrial capitalism remains contentious for historians of the workers' movement and Marxist historiography. Made up of artisans who sought to collectively protest against and resist the introduction of mechanised looms into the textile industry, their key tactic, for which they are still famous today, was the destruction of machinery.

The Luddites took their name from a youth called Ned Ludd who was alleged to have wrecked several machines in an industrial dispute. As the anonymous, mythic leader of a powerful rebellion, much celebrated in graffiti and song, Ned Ludd quickly became General or King Ludd.[31] As Peter Linebaugh explains, the Luddites were most active in three areas: West Riding of Yorkshire (where croppers were threatened by the gig-mill or shearing machine), Nottinghamshire and the Midlands (where those who weave stockings – stockingers – were being made redundant by the framework-knitting machine) and Lancashire (where cotton

---

30   Ibid., p.13.
31   One of the most well-known songs, 'General Ludd's Triumph', is reproduced at the end of this chapter. That the Luddites continue to be the object of popular celebration and song is evident in the following video made for the televised children's history 'Horrible Histories' http://youtu.be/IgBiGrpWNQU

weavers were losing their jobs due to the introduction of the steam-driven loom).[32] Where and when the movement began – in Scotland in 1810, or in Nottingham in 1811 – is a matter of some dispute. However, its 200th anniversary was widely celebrated in 2011 and 2012.[33]

Though only mentioned in passing, the Luddites are central to the polemics within a key chapter of *Capital* Vol.I in which Karl Marx discusses the introduction of machinery and large-scale industry in England.

> the Luddite movement, gave the anti-Jacobin government, composed of such people as Sidmouth and Castlereagh, a pretext for the most violent and reactionary measures. It took both time and experience before the workers learnt to distinguish between machinery and its employment by capital, and therefore to transfer their attacks from the material instruments of production to the form of society which utilizes those instruments.[34]

Marx points out in a footnote that this form of revolt continued even up until 1865. Rather than machine-breaking being an adolescent stage which workers would leave behind, we can point to its continuation throughout

32 Peter Linebaugh, *Ned Ludd & Queen Mab: Machine-Breaking, Romanticism, and the Several Commons of 1811–12*, Oakland: PM Press, 2012, p.10.

33 Luddites Bicentenary, http://ludditebicentenary.blogspot.co.uk/ and the conference held 6 May 2011 at Birkbeck University of London, The Luddites Without Condescension, http://backdoorbroadcasting. net/2011/05/the-luddites-without-condescension/

34 Karl Marx, *Capital* Vol.I, London: Penguin, 1990, pp.554–555.

the 20th century and into the present.[35] We might continue Marx's list well past the assumed attenuation of this practice by briefly listing some successful deployments of similar measures for collective bargaining recently used by workers. In a spate of bossknappings, equipment hijacking and factory occupations in France which followed the 2008 crisis, in the UK at three Visteon plants in 2009, and all over parts of China, Bangladesh and Egypt throughout the beginning of the 21st century this tactic has seen a widespread resurgence.[36]

On this point Marx does materialism poor service. It is evident that not only did the Luddites attack machines, but also their owners (in Yorkshire but not in Nottinghamshire), moreover, machines were attacked selectively, their wreckers

---

35   The IWW (International Workers of the World), a grass-roots US union, never ceased to advocate sabotage as the following pamphlet testifies Elizabeth Gurley Flynn, *Sabotage: the conscious withdrawal of the workers' industrial efficiency,* (1917), http://archive.org/ details/SabotageTheConsciousWithdrawalOfTheWorkersIndustrialEfficie ncy

36   For a few sources on the recent continuation of similar tactics see: on the Visteon occupations; Alan Woodward, 'Ford Visteon Enfield Workers Occupation', 2009: http://libcom.org/history/ford-visteon- enfield-workers-occupation-alan-woodward and Anon, 'Report and reflections on the UK Ford-Visteon dispute 2009 - a post-Fordist struggle', http://libcom.org/history/report-reflections-uk-ford- visteon-dispute-2009-post-fordist-struggle; on bossknapping in France: Jeanne Neton & Peter Åström, 'How One Can Still Put Forward Demands When No Demands Can Be Satisfied', http://communisation. net/How-one-can-still-put-forward?lang=fr; on destructive strikes in Bangladesh, Anonymous, 'Strike, Riot and Fire amongst the Garment Workers: a working class revolt in Bangladesh', London: 56a Infoshop, 2006, http://zinelibrary.info/strike-riot-and-fire-among-garment- workers-working-class-revolt-bangladesh-0; Hossam el-Hamalawy's collection of links on bossknappings in Egypt: http://www.diigo.com/ user/elhamalawy/bossnapping

discerning carefully between machines which manufactured 'under-price or "cutup" work'.[37] So, while we might side with Marx in his exasperation over choosing one version of capitalism over another, the practice of machine-breaking was not unselective. It distinguished between tools and their uses, and its practice in the case of the Luddites directly affected the price and autonomy of the breakers' labour and that of her class favourably (if only temporarily).

This is the lesson of the Luddites and part of the reason they continue to be of interest today. Presently few radicals would dispute the centrality of the social application of technology in capitalism, nor its importance to a future without capitalism. However, perhaps because in his treatment of this period Marx tries to draw out general rules about the capitalist use of machinery, he instrumentalises a social movement which has other things to teach us.

It's possible that the similarity between recent tactics deployed in class struggle and the actions of the Luddites and their precursors have structural echoes – workers have recourse to such tactics as part of 'desperate struggles', often responding to lockouts from factories, mass layoffs, non-payment of wages or re-location of the means of production elsewhere. These forms of struggle have historically bookended a relatively short period of stable accumulation of capital with correlative successive gains in the living standards and working conditions for labour. In a situation when capital is in retreat or flight, the workers' (soon to be non-workers) response may take the form of destructive revenge because they no longer have anything to gain from standard forms of negotiation. Instead, extracting short term

---

37   *The Making of the English Working Class,* op. cit., p.534.

material gains directly through extra-legal measures (riot, kidnap, taking the means of production hostage, looting) are seen and felt by workers to be their only options. In this respect the teleology attributed by many to Marx – of a transition to socialism through the gradual development of capitalist production – has become uncoupled from the reality of both workers' struggles and the conditions in which they struggle. What's posed in these forms of struggle is not gains within the productive circuit of capital, but social reproduction as a circuit which no longer necessarily passes through the capital-labour relation.

So, whilst Marx's historical reading of the Luddites is limiting, there are important points about the structural formation of the working class and its relationship to welfare, philanthropy and the wage to be drawn from it. After consigning the Luddites' tactics to history's dustbin by conflating the challenge it made to authority with the repression that it unleashed, Marx goes on to sketch a broader dynamic.

> World history offers no spectacle more frightful than the gradual extinction of the English hand-loom weavers; this tragedy dragged on for decades, finally coming to an end in 1838. Many of the weavers died of starvation, many vegetated with their families for a long period on 21/2d. A day.[38]

In a footnote on the same page Marx gives details of why exactly this was the case: 'The competition between hand-weaving and power-weaving in England was prolonged before the introduction of the Poor Law of 1834 by the fact

---

38   Capital Vol.I., op. cit., p.558.

that their wages, which had fallen considerably below the minimum could be supplemented with parish relief.' Karl Polanyi develops this point, arguing that the Speenhamland system of poor relief introduced in 1795 effectively blocked the development of a national labour market.

> The justices of Berkshire, meeting at the Pelican Inn, in Speenhamland, near Newbury, on May 6, 1795, in a time of great distress, decided that subsidies in aid of wages should be granted in accordance to a scale dependent upon the price of bread, so that a minimum income should be assured to the poor *irrespective of their earnings.*[39]

Whilst intended to provide some security to the poor and militate against the wild fluctuations in availability of work and regularity of wages under early capitalism, the effects were in some ways completely opposite. As Marx observes, wages could fall to almost nothing because workers' survival was assured under this system whether paid well or badly. This in turn removed any incentive for workers to apply pressure for wages to rise. As Polanyi points out, the Speenhamland system might well have provided a material base for both unemployed and employed workers to organise. However, the anti-combination laws and the restrictions on movement for workers tied to parish relief effectively

---

39   Karl Polanyi, *The Great Transformation*, Boston: Beacon Press, 2001, p.82.

prevented this.[40]

Instead 'Speenhamland precipitated a social catastrophe.'[41] Not only did wages stagnate, but so did workers. Moreover, the productivity of labour began to rapidly fall since the difference, to workers, between no work and work became more and more arbitrary.

> Speenhamland was designed to prevent the proletarianization of the common people, or at least to slow it down. The outcome was merely the pauperization of the masses, who almost lost their human shape in the process. The Poor Law Reform of 1834 did away with this obstruction of the labor market: the 'right to live' was abolished.[42]

Thus, Polanyi dates the emergence of industrial capitalism and the working class precisely to 1834.

> Not until 1834 was a competitive labor market established in England; hence industrial capitalism as a social system cannot be said to have existed before that date. Yet almost simultaneously the self-protection of society set in: factory laws and social legislation, and a political and industrial working-

---

40 'If laborers had been free to combine for the furtherance of their interests, the allowance system might, of course, have had a contrary effect on standard wages: for trade union action would have been greatly helped by the relief of the unemployed implied in so liberal an administration of the Poor Law [...] Speenhamland might have had the effect of raising wages instead of depressing them as it actually did.' Ibid., p.85.

41 Ibid., p.102.

42 Ibid., p.86.

class movement sprang into being.[43]

The violence of the Poor Law Reform shocked the poor and the middle class, but henceforth, Polanyi argues, the last vestiges of Stuart paternalism were wiped away. Workers were now 'free' to move around the country seeking work, they were also 'free' to seek competitive wages and employers no longer had any excuse for not paying wages fit to reproduce workers.

However, workers were also free to live or die by the labour market (the wage or lack of it) and whilst this situation ushered in modern political movements (e.g. Chartism) and legislation, the ruling class brought in the workhouse and other more or less punitive philanthropic institutions to mediate between the poor and the brutality of the market mechanism, and workers still had no legitimate recourse to self-organisation, since trade unions were outlawed until 1871.

For Polanyi this crucial shift in the form of social reproduction ushered in conceptual transitions too.

It was in the decades following Speenhamland and the Poor Law Reform that the mind of man turned toward his own community with a new anguish of concern: the revolution which the justices of Berkshire had vainly attempted to stem and which the Poor Law Reform eventually freed shifted the vision of men toward their own collective being as if they had overlooked its presence before. A world was uncovered the very existence of which had not been suspected, that of the laws governing a complex society. Although the emergence of society in this new and distinctive sense happened in the economic

---

43   Ibid., p.87.

field, its reference was universal.[44]

Polanyi points out that, by displacing the question of reproduction from the status of individual charity, the developing independence of labour poses the question of 'collective being' as a social question. However, as much as questions of bourgeois conceptual transformation are interesting, we could equally interest ourselves, as many radical historians have, in the continuities between self-conscious forms of struggle before and after the independence of labour Polanyi poses.

Wages, Welfare or Crime

To give a picture of the different class solidarities and alternative forms of welfare which flourished in the 18th century immediately before the point Polanyi marks as the true birth of the working classes, we have recourse to Peter Linebaugh's account of the Tyburn Riots against the Surgeons.

> In the cooper's yard, the sawyer's pit, the apothecary's shop or brewer's house, master and man, if not doing the same job of work, cooperated to make the same product. In the paternalism characteristic of the period of manufacture, Capital and Labour did not oppose each other in inexorable contradiction. [...] Catastrophe came to the master and his journeyman alike. Often they joined together in the Friendly Society, Benefit Society or 'Box Club' to defend themselves against a precarious existence. [...] Mainly the money ensured members of a 'decent

---

44   Ibid., p.88.

funeral'. The Friendly Society and the struggles against the surgeons were the two forms of working-class cooperation in the face of death.[45]

We will return to the question of welfare in the chapter on the Big Society. We foreground welfare here as an important aspect of the formation of the working class because it pertains to 'reproduction', the other side of the coin of 'production'. As Silvia Federici and numerous other feminists have pointed out, the working class would not be available for work without the unwaged work carried out to clothe, bathe, feed and birth them. Different forms of welfare not only composed the working class and made it available for work, it could be self-organised and reflect shared values as well as struggles for stability and autonomy. Welfare, state-administered or otherwise, is the meeting point of ideological and material reproduction, the aspirations of the ruling class for what it wants the labouring class to be and the measure of what is acceptable as means of reproduction by work. In the 18th century, there was a gulf between the wage and the practical question of how a person was to clothe, house and feed themselves, just as there is a gulf between the presentation of their lives and their own experience. Peter Linebaugh's formulation of a 'picaresque proletariat' is in many ways an attempt to bridge this gap which is also characterised by the gap between being in and being out of work, being defined as law-abiding worker or a disorderly criminal.

---

45   Peter Linebaugh, 'The Tyburn Riot Against the Surgeons', in Douglas Hay, Peter Linebaugh, John G. Rule, E.P. Thompson and Cal Winslow, *Albion's Fatal Tree*, London: Penguin, 1977, p.83.

While the Picaro's stance towards the world is active and resourceful – qualities promoted by the literary forms that arose from the individuality of the protagonist – the proletarian as an individual is often left passive and dumb by the historical records, more like a drone or a brute. However, since the proletarian's experience in life is dominated by cooperative action in the production and reproduction of the world, it is within collective experience that his or her individuality is realized. That the world can be hostile and capricious the proletarian knows, but he or she also knows that this need not always be so, because it is the work of his hands and the labour of her body that have created it in the first place.[46]

The argument is significant. In the past few labour historians had been daring enough as to nominate 18th century workers as 'proletarians'. Linebaugh's contention is that this was simply another way to silence and pacify a set of active individuals who collectively must be considered in class terms. Linebaugh builds on these observations to argue that this situation of indistinction and overlapping needs meant that crime was both a recourse for many in lieu of adequate wages, and a measure of class struggle in the absence of strikes or trade unions.

[One] type of solidarity expressed between the condemned and the Tyburn crowd, that of common experience of work, warns us against making too facile a separation between the criminal and the working class.[47]

---

46   Peter Linebaugh, *The London Hanged,* op. cit., p.152.
47   Peter Linebaugh, *Albion's Fatal Tree,* op. cit., p.82

In many ways the analysis of the 18th century relationship between crime, law and class drew its point of departure from the category of the 'social bandit' developed by Eric Hobsbawm. He had initially developed an argument for the understanding of bandits as 'primitive' or 'archaic' forms of social agitation in a book entitled *Primitive Rebels* published in 1959. What had been understood previously by historians as isolated and episodic phenomena, Hobsbawm characterises as essentially social.

> Individual rebelliousness is itself a socially neutral phenomenon, and consequently mirrors the divisions and struggles within society.[48]

Arguing that contrary to the 'archaic' form such social protests took, they had been profligate in the last half of the 19th and whole of the 20th centuries, Hobsbawm's first book opened up an entire field of social history, and he revisited the subject in the 1960s in an immensely popular book simply entitled *Bandits* (1969). His effort to explain the complex through which 'social crimes' were sanctioned, and social criminals protected and romanticised in popular myth, attempted to both build connections and explain fundamental differences between these rebels and modern social movements. The mythical status and political construction of 'social bandits' is explored in our chapter on Authenticity and Ambiguity.

Meaning of the Artisan

What is clear from Linebaugh's description of the 18th

---

48   Eric Hobsbawm, *Primitive Rebels*, New York: Norton, 1965, p.13.

century period of manufacture is that there were workers and there were employers, but their separation was not so simple. Their ties were complex, since wages were highly variable and customary workers in a trade often shared dependencies. So, whilst labour historians might be tempted to follow the radical cut described by Marx and elaborated upon by Polanyi which would consign to oblivion paternalism, custom and a less than modern division of labour, there are strong arguments for seeing the actuality in somewhat muddier but interconnected terms.

> The destruction of farm implements by those working them on American plantations belongs to the story of Luddism, not just because they too were toolbreakers, but they were part of the Atlantic recomposition of textile labor-power. They grew cotton that was spun and woven in Lancashire. The story of the plantation slaves has been separated from the story of the Luddites. Whether [their] separation was owing to misleading distinctions between wage and slave labour or to artificial national or racial differences is unclear.[49]

That Linebaugh and others' work in the 1960s and 1970s on the 18th century spoke so powerfully to their time and our own is because teleological narratives and stable ideals of a working class were quickly becoming contested history, and remain so today. Linebaugh's initial point of contestation is that historians looking back had bracketed off a part of the working class from recognition as such. In other cases we will

---

49   Peter Linebaugh, *Ned Ludd & Queen Mab: Machine-Breaking, Romanticism, and the Several Commons of 1811-12*, Oakland: PM Press, 2012, p.23.

see how the historical framework for existing movements could also be challenged productively.

In his essay 'The Myth of the Artisan', Jacques Rancière re-examines some common premises at work in French labour history and labour movements.

> The works devoted to the labor and socialist movements in France make use of a widely accepted interpretive principle: the relationship between professional qualification (skill) and militant consciousness (militancy). According to this interpretation, the movement developed as the expression of a working-class culture and was based on the actions and attitudes of the most highly skilled workers. Technical ability and pride in work thus created the basis for early labor militancy and it was the Taylorist revolution that spelled the end of this militancy by imposing massive and bureaucratic forms, which led to the creation of a new working population lacking professional skills, collective traditions, and interest in their work.[50]

Not only did this interpretation produce a historical myth by which craft skill would track militancy, but Rancière argues that this myth served to empower a particular labour aristocracy at the point at which their ownership of the struggle (and presumably certain workplace privileges) was threatened.

> This supposed first axiom of labor militancy is most likely a belated interpretation, born of political necessity in some sections of the labor movement which, in order to fend off

---

50   Jacques Rancière, 'The Myth of the Artisan', *International Labor and Working Class History*, Number 24, Fall 1983, p.1.

new and competing militant forces, was led to harken back to a largely imaginary tradition of 'authentic' worker socialism.[51]

One of the hallmarks of the workers' movement in this moment (the 1840s) was the celebration of work and sense of pride of craft expressed in verse, but Rancière questions this, invoking a logic of 'inverse proportionality whereby the men who are loudest in singing the glory of work are those who have most intensely experienced the degeneration of that ideal.'[52]

Rancière also questions the 'stability' of the identification of workers with their trades:

> The term 'artisan' evokes for us a certain stability, a certain identification of an individual with a function. Yet identities are often misleading. [...] The same individual can be found self-employed in one trade, salaried in another, or hired as a clerk or peddler in a third. With the gaps in their time caused by unemployment or the off-seasons, with their businesses crumbling as soon as they are set up [...].[53]

So, we can see class as a process, being made and remade. Questions of identity often manifest forms of idealism, there are problems with the historian taking them at face value and reproducing them, but, however ideal, they frequently become an operative force of containment regulating divisions in the working class, who can enter it, whose grievances are legitimate and whose are not.

Similar dynamics unfold in the discussions which have

---

51 Ibid., p.1.
52 Ibid., p.6.
53 Ibid., p.5.

ensued within labour and social movements following an attempt by Occupy groups to work with unions to shut down ports on the west coast of the United States.

> On November 2, Occupy Oakland shut down the port with a massive, unprecedented march of some 30,000 demonstrators, occupying the port to protest the bloody police attack on the Occupy encampment in front of Oakland City hall [...] It was also called in solidarity with the Longview longshore battle against EGT.[54]

Retired Longshoreman, Jack Heyman's account of Occupy's November 2011 action takes labour historian Cal Winslow to task for reifying the radical history of longshore workers' union, the ILWU.

> [Winslow] imparts his 'wisdom' from above in his CounterPunch article (7/25/12), 'Victory in Longview, A Year On: And Some Lessons From Occupy'. His 'lesson' is a justification for the ILWU union bureaucracy's betrayal of a hard-fought struggle from the bottom up and a gratuitous diatribe against longshore militants and their allied Occupy radicals who organized some of the most powerful labor solidarity actions in years. Tellingly, Winslow evidently did extensive interviews and used quotes from ILWU President Robert McEllrath, union staff and the police but none from working longshoremen, except Dan Coffman, president of

---

54   Jack Heyman, 'A Class Struggle Critique: The ILWU Longshore Struggle in Longview and Beyond', http://www.transportworkers. org/node/90 Heyman's article responds critically to Cal Winslow, 'The ILWU Longshore Struggle in Longview and Beyond', http:// www.counterpunch.org/2012/08/10/the-ilwu-longshore-struggle-in-longview-and-beyond/

Longview Local 21.[55]

Heyman attributes this to a split between 'business unionists' and 'class struggle trades unionists'. As ports have become more technologised and labour forces smaller, union militants have been marginalised within their unions. Heyman relates this change to the need to work with broader social movements outside of the union membership.

> The Occupy activists were trying to work closely with longshoremen in Longview, Portland and Oakland, less so in Seattle and L.A. Occupy was not cowed by bourgeois laws or cops, though some of the infantile anarchist pranks served no good purpose. Yes, there was some anger toward unions expressed but that was because they didn't differentiate between union bureaucrats and the rank and file. I criticized that in my remarks at the Seattle forum when the bureaucratic heavies moved to break the meeting up. Besides Occupy is not one cohesive ideology. It had conflicting politics and practices. Its inchoate left populism and vague anti-capitalist rhetoric has attracted some young workers who want to fight. Winslow speaks for the bureaucrats who after getting in hot water early in the Fall did what their lawyers told them to do to avoid a fight at all costs.[56]

What Heyman presents is the divisive efforts of a union bureaucracy attempting to manage an insular conversation over the organisation of work between themselves and the company management – to protect the best interests of

---

55   Ibid.
56   Ibid.

workers by preserving their authority to discuss and direct their own work. Yet, challenging capitalism is necessarily beyond the remit of this conversation and would threaten union power in the workplace or confuse it with aims other than protecting the workforce. The question of how to build connections between waged and unwaged struggles will be central to social movements in the present we inhabit.

Many of our historians recognised the processes by which divisions were enacted upon and among the working class in the development of capitalism. Raphael Samuel:

> In a rather different direction progressivism has been undermined by a younger generation of Marxist historians. One may note, among labour historians, a shift in attention from 'heroic' periods of struggle, such as Chartism, to more subterranean forms of resistance; a renewal of Marxist interest in such divisive phenomena as the aristocracy of labour and the lumpen proletariat; an increased awareness of the contradictory phenomena involved in 'the battle of ideas'.[57]

For Jacques Rancière, to study the making of a class is a process not just of finding and articulating commonalities and common antagonisms, but also of identifying critical differences:

> The essence of equality is not so much to unify as to declassify, to undo the supposed naturalness of orders and replace it with

---

57   Raphael Samuel, 'British Marxist Historians 1880–1980', *New Left Review*, .Vol.1, No.120, March–April, 1990, p.95.

controversial figures of division.[58]

The Worker, His Wife, Machines

An example of Rancière's attention to the production of divisions and antagonisms within the working class can be found in his 1975 essay for *Revoltes Logiques*, 'Off to the Exhibition...'. He assesses reports made by trade delegations to the Exposition Universelle of 1867, a spectacle, Rancière insists, which 'the workers perceive [...] as a product of their dispossession'. Through them he examines a meeting point of 'class and domestic power' which is both significant and somewhat self-defeating.

The workers remonstrate against employers' deployment of machines as a tool against their class while attacking their employers' efforts to introduce women into the workplace. Machines are attacked because they deskill the worker rather than free him from work time, therefore removing from the worker his power over his own production – his craft and intelligence – 'in order to produce a bit more, to produce regardless.'[59] Though the introduction of women into the workplace would cause wages to fall it is mainly attacked by male workers in these reports for threatening to remove the worker from his power over his domestic situation.

This is not only a matter of scandal judged by contemporary attitudes to gender equality in the workplace,

---

58   Jacques Rancière, *On the Shores of Politics*, (trans. Liz Heron), London and New York 1995, pp.32-3.

59   Shoemakers' report cited in 'Off to the Exhibition: The Worker, His Wife and the Machines', in *Staging the People*, Vol.I, London: Verso, 2011, p.68.

but could already at the time be understood as an outmoded attitude: only a few years later the Women's Union for the Defence of Paris and Aid to the Wounded recognised attempts to discriminate against female workers as the defence of privilege and sought to abolish all competition between male and female workers.[60]

Rancière's presentation of these reports is at first sympathetic. Here, (albeit elite) workers pass judgement on their own conditions, in terms which correspond closely to Karl Marx's analysis on the introduction of machines, so challenging the emerging power of employers to reorganise work, catalyse competition and force downward pressure on the wage across all industries.[61] The reports grasp the machine not as a 'cold-blooded monster to be destroyed' but rather, as Rancière's presentation goes to lengths to show, imagine a moral and social 'collective appropriation of the machines'.[62] Nonetheless, Rancière also gives due attention to a contradiction: here the retort to one particular division of labour production marks a second division in the social reproduction of the working class itself.

While Rancière identifies this moment as a transition from 'corporative thinking' or 'Bonapartiste "socialism"' to a 'new revolutionary working class ideal', a contradiction in the class is not resolved, but rather carried over. In Rancière's somewhat reductive formulation, the foundation of this split is 'the power of the working man over his wife'. If the way forward is for the working class movement to retract from

---

60 See, Adrian Rifkin and Roger Thomas (Eds.), *Voices of the People*, New York: Routledge, 1988, p.14.

61 Karl Marx, *Capital* Vol.I Chapter 15.

62 *Staging the People*, Vol.I, op. cit., p.73.

the compact with bosses and move to open struggle over the means of production, towards either a revolutionary state or workers' control, this trajectory of productivism leaves these two powers – at work and at home – separated and unexamined parts of a never-to-be-whole.

The 1975 essay marks a crucial development in Rancière's thinking. Initially sympathetic to the threats to working class autonomy, he latterly recognised this as a problematic example by which proletarian resistance and power can be formed at the expense of other denigrated subjects I.e. women.[63] Henceforth, it will become impossible for the workers to affirm themselves as workers without reproducing inequality – for their gains will also be their losses – the workers' movement becomes only the movement of those who identify and wield power over other parties as men. The anti-work ethos which Rancière situates elsewhere on more individualistic terms finds, here, a structural rapport.

Similarly Sheila Rowbotham unpicks the complexity of male artisans' resistance to industry in Britain, emphasising traces of gender inequality and frustrated male domination among their often heroicised convictions. For some artisans it was not simply the brutality of factory conditions, low wages or the loss of their way of life, but also the break with men's authority in the home that drove hostility to the factory system:

> Physical violence existed within the family but there it fitted into a customary pattern of relationships. In the factory it became symbolic of a new industrial relationship, the impersonal

---

63 Donald Reid, Introduction to *Proletarian Nights*, London: Verso, 2012, op. cit., pp.xxv–xxvi.

discipline of the cash nexus. In the factory, too, women and children were under the control of overseers and employers, not fathers and husbands. This meant the man's social control in the working class family was threatened [...] even the proud handloom weavers had to face the final humiliation of sending their daughters to the factories, or find their sons were courting factory girls. In one song [...] the father asks his son how he could fancy a factory worker.[64]

Vanguardism

In *The Making of the English Working Class*, Thompson argued forcibly for a study of class as a relationship, that is as a historical relationship:

> If we stop history at a given point, then there are no classes but simply a multitude of individuals with a multitude of experiences. But if we watch these men over an adequate period of social change, we observe patterns in their relationships, their ideas, and their institutions. Class is defined by men as they live their own history, and in the end, this is its only definition.[65]

Marx made the distinction between a 'class in itself' – a way of categorising people as having a common relation to the means of production – and a 'class for itself', that is, the active composition of class by people in terms of their shared interests, conditions and demands. In Thompson's *Making of the English Working Class*, these distinct categories are joined by

---

64   *Hidden from History*, op. cit., p.29.
65   E.P. Thompson, *The Making of the English Working Class*, London: Penguin, 2003, p.11.

the very act of drawing up a 'class on paper' by the historian. In reconstructing the making of the working class, Thompson, and other historians, were insistent on their avoidance of the projection of the party line onto the working class. This was a break from the more 'vanguardist' forms of Marxist analysis, in which it was put forward that the party, the 'tendency', or the state apparatus could stand in and present itself as a cohering force for the motivations of the proletariat.

Vanguardism was a particular form of a common problem within historical reflection: what sociologists call 'homologies', or identifications between the position of the historian and his or her subject that might shave off the differences between their experiences and social position and bring into question the choice of subjects to study. Here, Dorothy Thompson is suspicious of a Labour Historian on his reading of Chartism:

> Not all the histories of the movement make quite such specific demands on the past, but underlying nearly all is the attempt to draw a contemporary moral, and hence, almost inevitably, the historian identifies himself with one or other tendency or sect. The moralising and lesson-drawing have preceded, instead of following, deep research into the facts.[66]

E.P. Thompson confers a retrospective degree of agency on his subjects in their own definition. But this doesn't mean that Thompson et al didn't find points of over-identification with their subjects, nor that they didn't indulge in some wishful thinking about the intentions of what was after all a complex

---

66   Dorothy Thompson, 'The Chartist Challenge', *New Reasoner,* Issue 8, Spring 1959, p.139.

body of people.

However, we should also remember that the accounts of workers which Thompson and others collect in their studies point to self-generated modes of class composition. These vary from accounts in which workers themselves come up with a subjective sense of their relationship to their bosses and between themselves, to attempts at a more objective and widespread analysis of their conditions.

Culturalism and Determination

E.P. Thompson's definition of class becomes most useful when we turn away from the vanguardist projection of desires onto the proletariat, or the dismissal of class struggle as a demonstrable tension in society, and begin instead to look at how people actually experience their social relationships in times when 'class consciousness' is not as publicly visible or self-evident, or when the wider labour movement appears to break down.

In suggesting that the working class was not just the 'product' of the Industrial Revolution, and touching on the continuity of thought and tradition from earlier periods, Thompson expands on the dimensions of class composition. Class is not simply an economic category – 'so many yards of raw material for industry' – but also a 'cultural' category (class actors are reflective upon their own conditions, they attempt to change them, they also argue amongst themselves as to how to change them):

Class happens when some men, as a result of common experiences (inherited or shared), feel and articulate the identity of their interests as between themselves, and as against other men whose interests are different from (and usually opposed to) theirs. The class experience is largely determined by the productive relations into which men are born – or enter involuntarily. Class-consciousness is the way in which these experiences are handled in cultural terms: embodied in traditions, value-systems, ideas, and institutional forms. *If the experience appears as determined, class-consciousness does not.* We can see a logic in the responses of similar occupational groups undergoing similar experiences, but we cannot predicate any law.[67]

What Thompson seems close to saying is that culture, rather than being a 'disinterested' world of practices to be set apart from economic relations, is in fact a terrain of struggles over power amongst the relations within which the working class was directly and productively involved, despite not always having much of a stake in its official production. In this way, we can say that culture is, and was, thereby 'interested'. But this is not the same as saying that culture is ultimately the product of economic determination; instead it is employed in a complex relationship, partly determined by material conditions and partly the attempt to overcome determination.

However different their judgements of value, conservative, radical, and socialist historians suggested the same equation: steam power and the cotton mill = new working class [...] [but] the making of the working class is a fact of political and cultural, as much as of economic, history. It was not the spontaneous

---

67   *The Making of the English Working Class,* op. cit., p.9.

generation of the factory system. Nor should we think of an external force – the 'industrial revolution' – working upon some nondescript undifferentiated raw material of humanity, and turning it out at the other end as a 'fresh race of beings'.

The changing productive relations and working conditions of the Industrial Revolution were imposed, not upon raw material, but upon the free-born Englishman – and the free-born Englishman as Paine had left him or as the Methodists had moulded him. The factory hand or stockinger was also the inheritor of Bunyan, of remembered village rights, of notions of equality before the law, of craft traditions. He was the object of massive religious indoctrination and the creator of political traditions [...] The working class made itself as much as it was made.[68]

But equally this requires us to address how the everyday expression of social relationships is mediated in public culture, and what valuates the mediators of such expression. This means looking also at the institutions that consecrate and reproduce such mediation. As Neil Gray points out in a conversation with Marina Vishmidt, in social movements there is a tension between affirmation and negation:

[T]he notion that in any social movement there needs to be a clear identification of a position of exclusion or injustice, and that this identification is inevitably contradictory or antagonistic in the sense that the excluded group must frame their exclusion in relation to the dominant relation of capitalist hierarchy, patriarchy, race or class. This first moment of affirmation (or self-recognition), then leads to the second moment of negation

---

68   *The Making of the English Working Class,* op. cit., p.213.

whereby the very conditions that frame those hierarchies must be overturned in order to supersede those relations and divisions *per se*.[69]

If, with Marx, we look toward the abolition of class, then we can see that when working people mobilise around the declaration of conditions and convictions held in common, this act of constituting a class can serve a contradictory function. On the one hand it can identify a condition to be overcome – a potential future; and on the other, particularly when mobilised by the state, political parties, trade unions, etc., it can serve to enact limits on such a collective overcoming of determination. If people mobilise less now on the basis of common convictions, then it is possible to understand these as movements which no longer apprehend class society as an arena in which any positive gains can be made.

To properly consider the formation of an expanded working class requires attention to detail where previously there was none. By pursuing this project, one does not find in a class an undifferentiated mass, but rather a variegated and active field of qualities, continuities and differences which in tumultuous times can arrive at shared interests. In Rancière's words this is because, 'there is no single "voice of the people". There are broken, polemical voices, each time dividing the identity they present.'[70]

Here, hopefully we have established briefly the principle of division in three senses: (1) the foundational political

---

69   'The Economy of Abolition/Abolition of the Economy: Neil Gray in Exchange with Marina Vishmidt', *Variant*, issue 42, Winter 2011, http://www.variant.org.uk/42texts/EconomyofAbolition.html

70   Jacques Rancière, *Staging The People: The Proletarian and His Double*, London: Verso, 2011, p.12.

division between the sovereign citizenry whose reason stems from their ownership of property and an 'unreasonable' mob, (2) the distinction between a positive conception of of multiplicity and difference, and the division into hierarchies that can develop between and within classes, and (3) the problem of the historian's acceptance of purported divisions of status, technical ability, or enfranchisement and the need to probe deeper.

A study of what informed and shaped these maligned and ignored actors (in which 'the below' consisted) needs both the reconsideration of old sources read in a new light and the discovery of new ones. In the following chapter we focus on the question of sources which such historical work deployed.

General Ludd's Triumph

Anon., 'General Ludd's Triumph' to the tune of 'Poor Jack', excerpted in E.P. Thompson, *Making of The English Working Class*, p.534 and reproduced in full here, http://campus.murraystate.edu/academic/faculty/kevin.binfield/songs.htm

Chant no more your old rhymes
about bold Robin Hood, His feats
I but little admire / I will sing the
Achievements of General Ludd
Now the Hero of Nottinghamshire
/ Brave Ludd was to measures of
violence unused / Till his sufferings
became so severe / That at last to
defend his own Interest he rous'd
And for the great work did prepare

Now by force unsubdued, and by
threats undismay'd / Death itself
can't his ardour repress / The
presence of Armies can't make him
afraid / Nor impede his career of
success / Whilst the news of his
conquests is spread far and near
How his Enemies take the alarm
His courage, his fortitude, strikes
them with fear / For they dread his
Omnipotent Arm!

The guilty may fear, but no
vengeance he aims / At [the] honest
man's life or Estate / His wrath is
entirely confined to wide frames /
And to those that old prices abate
/ These Engines of mischief were
sentenced to die / By unanimous
vote of the Trade / And Ludd who
can all opposition defy / Was the
grand Executioner made

And when in the work of destruction
employed /He himself to no method
confines /By fire and by water
he gets them destroyed /For the
Elements aid his designs /Whether
guarded by Soldiers along the
Highway / Or closely secured in the
room /He shivers them up both by
night and by day /And nothing can
soften their doom

He may censure great Ludd's
disrespect for the Laws Who ne'er
for a moment reflects / That foul
Imposition alone was the cause
Which produced these unhappy
effects / Let the haughty no longer
the humble oppress / Then shall
Ludd sheath his conquering Sword /
His grievances instantly meet with
redress / Then peace will be quickly
restored

Let the wise and the great lend
their aid and advice / Nor e'er
their assistance withdraw / Till full
fashioned work at the old fashioned
price / Is established by Custom
and Law / Then the Trade when
this arduous contest is o'er / Shall
raise in full splendour its head / And
colting and cutting and squaring
no more / Shall deprive honest
workmen of bread.

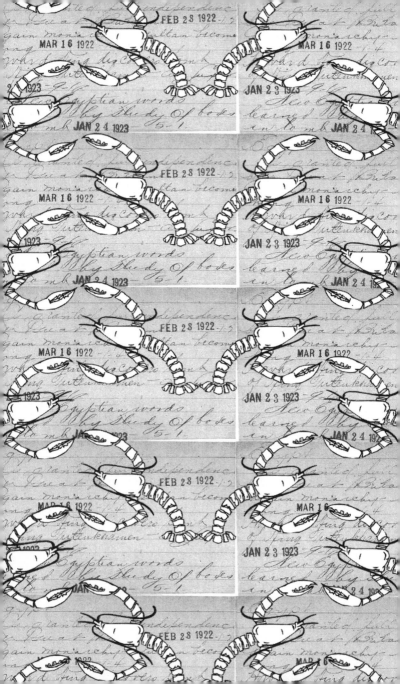

LOBSTER TRAPS

I would Tel you My Name
but My Simplicity Will Not Let Mee.
– Newcastle Collier, 1765[1]

Nothing starts in the Archive, nothing, ever at all, though
things certainly end up there. You find nothing in the
archive but stories told half way through: the middle of
things; discontinuities.[2]

From Despard to Thistlewood and beyond there is a tract of
secret history, buried like the Great Plain of Gwaelod beneath
the sea. We must reconstruct what we can.[3]

Historians from below attempted to displace conservative
histories in which the struggles, experiences and agency of
common people were ignored. This required them to attend
to neglected voices from periods when access to means of
communication were deeply unequal. In response to scant
or heavily mediated sources, the best of these historians
developed creative methodologies to unearth evidence
of how common experience was constituted. There were
few illusions that the reconstructed picture would remain

1   E.P. Thompson, 'The Crime of Anonymity', *The Essential E.P. Thompson*,
    New York: New Press, 2000, p.378.
2   Carolyn Steedman, *Dust*, Manchester: Manchester University Press,
    2001, p.45.
3   E.P. Thompson, *The Making of the English Working Class*, London:
    Camelot Press, 1963, p. 497.

anything other than partial, and incomplete.

In the following chapter we would like to sketch out some of the methods of history from below and ask: how did these Marxist historians, who were often non-conformist Marxists and unorthodox historians, relate to the methodologies of their chosen discipline? What are the problems in constructing subjects from available data? Does the very availability or unavailability of information, the channels it comes to us by, enact limits on our understanding of historical subjects? How does the use of quantitative data reflect or undermine its uses by the state and other agencies as means of social control? How does the development of ideas in a given period, relate to the material conditions in which they are disseminated and recorded?

Speaking Anonymity

To open our discussion on anonymity, sources, and interpretation we begin with a lengthy passage from E.P. Thompson.

> *The London Gazette: Published by Authority* may seem an unlikely source for the student of plebian history. The *Gazette*, which appeared twice-weekly was, of course, the publication of the most august authority [...].
>
> Immediately following, cheek-by-jowl with Princess Lousia-Henrietta Willhemina, there appears a rather different notice, addressed to Sir Richard Betenson of Sevenoaks, Kent.
>
>> Sr: Your Baily or Steward proper is a black guard sort of fellow to the Workmen and if you don't discharge him You may Look

> to Your House being sett on fire if Stones will not Burn You
> damned Sun of a hoare You shall have Your throat cutt from
> Ear to Ear except You Lay £50 under the Second tree of Staple
> Nashes from his house at the frunt of the Great Gates near the
> Rabbit Warrin on Wensdy Morn next...

> This was of course, like the preceding one, an official notice,
> although it was not inserted by the letter's author but by the
> Secretary of State [...]. Hence the *London Gazettes* lie, like so
> many bi-weekly lobster traps, on the sea-bottom of Namier's
> England, catching many curious literary creatures which never,
> in normal circumstances, break the bland surface of the waters
> of eighteenth-century historiography.[4]

Thompson's 'lobster traps' are the sources that allow the
historian to capture traces of their prey. Yet the fragments
of expression within a source like the *London Gazette* arrive
almost without context, emanating from a milieu of which
we have little documentation; and its individual voices,
by their very nature, were covered in anonymity. It is from
these sources that the historian adds the creative work of
imagining the social composition that could produce such
ideas and forms of expression.

Products of 'society' media like the *London Gazette*
attempted to make an example of the discontent of the
subordinate classes, while appealing for help from the
conscientious in catching offenders against property. The
Gazette 'was only involved when an official pardon was
offered for information leading to a conviction; and such

---

4   E.P. Thompson, 'The Crime of Anonymity', *The Essential E.P. Thompson*,
     New York: New Press, 2000, p.378.

authority must be obtained from the secretary of state.'[5] But what drives Thompson to follow the appeal of the Secretary of State is not the offence against property, but instead an interest in the motives and demands of the blackmailer, and more importantly the extent to which they meet collective grievances against the exploitation of labour.

Parallel to the admonishments of the Government, was the awareness on the part of the blackmailers that 'blackmailing [...] thrives on publicity' as much as anonymity. Indexed in the individual blackmail letter such as that of the Newcastle Collier, Thompson finds a play on the unequal conditions of literacy and communication; by sorting the letters by year and checking this against the rough hierarchy of blackmail recipients which runs from 'Gentry and Nobility' to 'Blacklegs', he identifies a cat-and-mouse game between the wider working class and the State. However, Craig Calhoun points out that E.P. Thompson's insight that the evidence might equally indicate the exception as much as the rule.

> If some action of an ordinary worker seemed significant enough to warrant space in *The Times* or another organ of polite society, Thompson rightly and probingly wondered not just how the printed report might be biased by interpretation but to what extent it reflected not generalisable customs but an unusual departure from more typical patterns of action. This was one of the sources of Thompson's longstanding annoyance with attempts to quantify historical evidence [...] above all, with an inadequate sense of the contexts from which the individual

---

5   Ibid., p.378.

cases were torn.[6]

To learn more we must re-place each letter or group of letters within the specificity of its own context. In the end, the form as such can be bound together only by two uniting themes. First, the act of sending such letters, for whatever purpose, constituted a crime; in the eyes of the law all literary styles, elevated or semi-literate, and all grievances, were reduced to a common level [...] Second, these letters are – over many decades – the only literate expression of the 'inarticulate' which has survived [...]. How did a society whose manifest ideology was that of paternalism feel from below?[7]

In the case of clandestine organisations, there are necessarily no records left. The work of recording is after all also a tool of statecraft and social control. Even long after such movements might have extinguished their efforts there still might remain reasons to keep quiet about the identities of their members and the tactics they employed. In the case of the Luddites, Thompson even uses the absence of such records and wariness of working class commentators to lend weight to the probable existence of an 'effective Luddite underground'.[8]

Some historians have gone to extreme lengths to reconstruct hidden lives. In *The Life of an Unknown: The Rediscovered World of a Clog-Maker in Nineteenth Century France*

---

6   Craig Calhoun, 'E.P. Thompson and the Discipline of Historical Context', *Making Histories: Studies in History-Writing and Politics,* Volume 1, Birmingham: CCCS & Taylor and Francis, 1982, p.226.

7   'The Crime of Anonymity', op. cit., p.420.

8   *The Making of the English Working Class*, op. cit., p.497.

(2001), Alain Corbin, a contributor to *Annales*, deliberately chose a single subject at random, with the stipulation that no records existed for him at all beyond a name and occupation in the municipal archives. Corbin happened upon Pinagot, a clog-maker, by running his finger down the registry of 'nondescript locality Origny-le-Butin'. This led the historian to construct a subject from his social milieu, raising questions of generality and exceptionality.

> If we wish to come closer to [Pinagot], we must penetrate the silence and the void that surround him. It was necessary to choose at random one of a myriad of identical social atoms. There was no other way to honour with remembrance a unique individual from an undifferentiated mass. Anyone who [...] left an unusual record of any kind, had to be ruled out [...].[9]

Reconstructing subjects from their milieu requires a lot of suppositions on the part of the historian. The very act of hunting a subject who leaves 'no unusual records' appears to be an implicit critique of exceptionality. As we will discuss later, attention to the particularity of experience can challenge received opinion but it can also sometimes have conservative applications. Despite the school's international connections, from micro-history to the regional surveys conducted by historians associated with *Annales*, it seems the movement has contributed tremendously to the construction

---

9   Alain Corbin, *The Life of an Unknown: The Rediscovered World of a Clog-Maker in Nineteenth Century France,* New York: Columbia University Press 2001, p.ix.

of the national self-image.[10]

Fetishism of locality and tradition became rife during a popularisation of French historiography of the late-1970s and 1980s. Emmanuel Le Roy Ladurie's celebrated book *Montaillou* (1975) was an early example of what came to be called 'microhistory'. The study reconstructed the everyday life of a village in south-west France as a portrait of the microcosm a 'typical' village represented. As such, it fed into a revival and popularisation of social history in France with an attendant heritage industry: fashion, cinema, publishing, and cookery celebrating the rural past. Jacques Rancière sums up the emergence of '*la mode retro*' in this period in France:

> This was a period in which a new enthusiasm for popular culture made itself felt in France, with a profusion of monographs on folkloric customs and biographies of men of the people who were proud of their trade and their traditions. The new tendency marked the cinema as well as academic history, with the success of 'retro' films. [...] Depicted in this way, in place of the strict proletarian of Marxist science we had a noisy and colourful people, reminiscent of what leftist activists glimpsed in their efforts to plumb the depths of the *pays réel*, but also a people that conformed well to its essence, well rooted in its place and time, ready to move from the heroic legend of the poor to the positivity of silent majorities. These people, in fact, was the imaginary correlate of the socialist intelligentsia that was

---

10 For *Annales'* collaborative work on extensive regional studies of France see: Peter Burke, *The French Historical Revolution: The Annales School 1929-89*, Cambridge: Polity, 2007, pp.57-58., and the school's strong ties and dependence upon funding from the French State, ibid., p.106.

about to take power in 1981.[11]

The Archives of Crime

In moments of social upheaval, participants or bystanders in these events often leave few records other than those of the Criminal Justice System, police and court records. Peter Linebaugh discussing the 'Great Negro Plot' in New York, 1741:

> The ideas that propelled so many to such desperate action were not given a full hearing at the trials, because the justices were less interested in what we had to say, than they were in pretending that we were all the stupid agents of the Pope. However, sometimes a few words would slip in, and I can safely leave it to you to read between the lines and to choose for yourself any among the many communitarian traditions alive in our century that they belonged to.[12]

Endearing to us, and to critical literary analysis in general, is that historians like Thompson and Linebaugh treat sources not simply as 'data' but as partisan records of the moral and political convictions borne by class actors. By no means does this suggest such sources are easily categorised. They are open to identifications and the context which the historian constructs. However, this approach implies a leaning toward the material by the historian – a groping for understanding

---

11 Jacques Rancière, *Staging the People: The Proletarian and His Double, (Staging the People,* Vol.I), London: Verso, 2011, p.8.

12 Peter Linebaugh, 'A Letter to Bostons "Radical Americans" from a "loose and disorderly New Yorker"', in *Midnight Notes,* IV No.1.

of the subject in their living context of determinations and limits on speech, form and reception.

> But what of the denizens of 'Satan's Stronghold', the 'harlots and publicans and thieves' whose souls the evangelists wrestled for? If we are concerned with historical change we must attend to the articulate minorities. But these minorities arise from a less articulate majority whose consciousness may be described as being, at this time, 'sub-political' – made up of superstition or passive irreligion, prejudice or patriotism. The inarticulate, by definition, leave few records of their thoughts. We catch glimpses in moments of crisis, like the Gordon Riots, and yet crisis is not a typical condition. It is tempting to follow them into the archives of crime.[13]

The archives of crime also have their own structuring effects, as Peter Linebaugh observed in *The London Hanged*.

> It would not appear that taking tobacco was either lawful or right, for our knowledge of the practice depends on criminal prosecutions for felonious stealing, and the records of such prosecution seems to individualise the actor and to remove him from any community that might sanction such custom.[14]

What traces of life appear in the records of the criminal justice system have usually been assembled to tell a particular narrative – one which would lead to the conviction or exoneration of an individual or individuals – but what other narratives are possible to construct around the very

---

13   *The Making of the English Working Class,* op. cit., p.55.

14   Peter Linebaugh, *The London Hanged*, London: Verso 1991, p.171.

same facts when assembled for another purpose? Some of the most innovative work carried out by the group of historians assembled around Thompson's seminars at the Centre for the Study of Social History at the University of Warwick focused on the question of crime in the 18th century. The book, *Albion's Fatal Tree*, built on Thompson's earlier work which had established a framework for the examination of law as a central aspect of 18th century social history. It was a period in which offences relating to property multiplied and so too did statutes sanctioning death by hanging. In 'The Tyburn Riot Against the Surgeons' Peter Linebaugh assembles a statistical chart of the costs for the Barber-Surgeons Company of acquiring corpses of the hanged at Tyburn. The chart of five-year totals running from 1715 to 1760 puts the development of medical science in grisly material terms, but also proposes an index of the evolving class struggle between the relatives and friends of the condemned who wished to bury their dead, and the surgeons who needed the corpses to extend their teaching practices. In the argument constructed by Linebaugh, the greater the popular opposition to the Surgeons' claiming of bodies, the higher the costs they would need to pay the executioner, coach-driver and other parties (the Barber-Surgeons recorded costs included payment for windows broken by the Tyburn mob).[15] This is a form of economic history of sorts, but, and we think Linebaugh himself would agree, a wilfully perverse one, in the sense that the moral economy of 18th century England required regular hangings and calculative logic to maintain a relatively small elite in power and a large number of working poor in a state

---

15   E.P. Thompson (et al), *Albion's Fatal Tree: Crime and Society in Eighteenth Century England*, London: Random House, 1976, pp.74-77.

of terror.

The archives of crime are not the only legal archives with structuring effects on the voices of the past, though many find their genesis in the management of social reproduction. Riffing on Jules Michelet's vision of the historian as magistrate, Carolyn Steedman examines the records of people of the eighteenth century who were required to account for their life stories to the magistrate in order to be eligible for poor relief.

> The resurrectionist historian creates the past that he purports to restore, in Michelet's case attributing beliefs and desires that he acknowledged were not actually experienced by those he brought back to life [...]. It was in fact a Magistrate, also called History, who did the work of resurrection.[16]

Steedman notes that potential applicants' stories were recorded by the court, producing hundreds of thousands of 'enforced narratives', all structured and shaped by the requirements of the court – entitlements were tied in particular to working in one parish and receiving wages for a year – but with the voice of the questioner an absent presence. Steedman attends to the voice of Charlotte Howe, purchased in America as 'a negro slave', who had been the domestic servant of a Captain and Mrs Howe in Thames Ditton, and who walked free when Captain Howe died. (Steedman cites Douglas Lorimer's suggestion that slave-servants who walked free of their households were 'a major route to the end of slavery in Britain, brought about by the actions of slave-servants themselves'.) When Howe tried to return to

---

16   Carolyn Steedman, *Dust*, Manchester University Press, 2001, p.39.

Thames Ditton to claim poor relief, she was carted back and forth between parishes and ended up in a workhouse in St. Lukes. A legal action declared that as there was no slavery in England, Howe could not be a slave – but neither could she claim settlement. She did not 'answer the description' required by law – the very attempt to do so structured her memoir.

In this respect Steedman throws into sharp relief the origins of the working-class memoir, suggesting that such accounts may have influenced the 19th century idea, evident in melodrama, that the working class were people to whom 'things just *happen*'. Furthermore the effects of legal frameworks on memoir and self-possession are the very basis of the archive.

> The assumption of the modern 'autobiographical turn', that there exists and has existed an *urge* to tell the self, and that it comes from within, is of very little help in hearing these eighteenth-century cases of enforced narration. And for the moment, it is impossible to move beyond these suggestions, that the modern literary articulation of selfhood and character had one of its origins among the poorer sort, when their verbal accounts of themselves, told before a magistrate, were recorded by others. What we can be clearer about is one of the sights of this storytelling, the Magistrate as the necessary and involuntary story-taker, and why it is that the archive contains what it does [...]. Charlotte Howe's story was made for her by legal process... having had the story taken, it was not returned to her, not even in the formulaic autobiography of the settlement certificate, but rather left behind, in the case books and the archive.[17]

---

17   Ibid., p.56.

Quantitative History

Peter Linebaugh's economic history is quite different from the deadly seriousness with which the historians gathered around the *Annales* school invested statistics. Peter Burke evaluates common problems associated with the rise of quantitative history:

> The quantitative approach to history in general, and the quantitative approach to cultural history in particular, can obviously be criticized as reductionist. Generally speaking, what can be measured is not what matters. Quantitative historians can count signatures to marriage registers, books in private libraries, Easter communicants, references to the court of heaven, and so on. The problem remains whether these statistics are reliable indicators of literacy, piety, or whatever the historian wants to investigate. Some historians have argued the case for the reliability of their figures; others assumed it. Some have remembered that they are dealing with real people, others appear to have forgotten it. Any evaluation of the movement must discriminate between the modest and the extreme claims made for the method and also between the manners in which it has been employed, crudely or with finesse.[18]

Michelle Perrot began as a student of Ernest Labrousse, who was one of the more Marxist-orientated of the *Annales* historians. Her first work was a vast project in quantitative and serial history, a study of strikes between 1871 and 1890 - something consciously extended into the 20th century

---

18   *The French Historical Revolution*, op. cit., p.79.

recently by Beverly Silver in her book *Forces of Labour* (2003).[19] In a later preface to Perrot's book the author reflected critically upon the historian's toolbox and the techniques her study applied.

> Only what could be counted seemed to us solid and worthy material: registrations and solicitors' records, tolls and fiscal archives, parish registers and criminal records, voting statistics and figures for religious observance, and so on. The domain of the measurable stretched out as far as the eye could see, and we were discovering the extent to which societies were made up of interlocking patterns of repeated acts. We were in the grip of a statistical madness.[20]

The pull towards quantitative history emanating from France in the 1960s and 1970s was also felt by Marxist historians in the UK. In the foreword to his massive study of the collapse of the medieval church and beginning of the enlightenment, *Religion and the Decline of Magic: Studies in Popular Beliefs in Sixteenth and Seventeenth-Century England* (1971), which covered a period of 200 years, Keith Thomas clearly felt the need to apologise for the paucity of sources and 'proof' for his arguments.

> I particularly regret not having been able to offer more of those exact statistical data upon which the precise analysis of historical change must so often depend. Unfortunately, the

---

19 Beverly J Silver, *Forces of Labor: Workers' Movements and Globalization since 1870*, Cambridge: Cambridge University Press, 2003.

20 Michelle Perrot, 'Workers on Strike: France, 1871–1890' in Lynn Hunt and Jacques Revel (Eds.), *Histories: French Constructions of the Past*, New York: The New Press. 1994, p.415.

sources seldom permit such computation [...] I have only too often had to fall back upon the historian's traditional method of presentation by example and counter-example. Although this technique has some advantages, the computer has made it the intellectual equivalent of the bow and arrow in a nuclear age. But one cannot use the computer unless one has suitable material with which to supply it, and at present there seems to be no genuinely scientific method of measuring changes in the thinking of past generations.[21]

Though the tone of Thomas' statement is apologetic, it's nonetheless lightly satirical too. He points out both the limits of what was becoming the hegemonic method of the time (one can't compute data that doesn't exist) and the inapplicability of such a methodology in approaching what might be thought of as the historian's main task: 'measuring changes in the thinking of past generations.' If ideas were to remain important to the historian, then data, computation and quantitative methods were not necessarily the primary tools. Instead, imagination might still be required. So, while that leaves Thomas with a largely literary analysis, he's particularly burdened by an attempt to pursue the beliefs of the entire population at a time when only as little as 2.5 percent of the male population were well educated (in fact a high tide mark which only began to be exceeded after World War I in the UK) and perhaps half or two thirds could not read and write or at least signed with a mark.[22] However, where he could introduce statistical analysis, he did. A good example

---

21 Keith Thomas, *Religion and the Decline of Magic: Studies in Popular Beliefs in Sixteenth and Seventeenth-Century England*, London: Penguin, 1991, p.x.

22 Ibid., p.5.

of how this might be done is the information on small pox
Thomas gathers (again from the *London Gazette*).

> a study of the newspaper advertisements printed in the *London
> Gazette* between 1667 and 1774 shows that sixteen out of every
> hundred missing persons whose descriptions were given bore
> pockmarks on their faces.[23]

The example is not significant in itself, but it does show
how existing data might be used imaginatively. Moreover,
it demonstrates how historians of the time were learning
from other disciplines (in this case social anthropology) to
introduce information pertaining to diet, illness and other
'environmental' factors which had a bearing on building up a
picture of social conditions and beliefs.

If Thomas recognises that quantitative data might
be unhelpful in reconstructing the thinking of historical
subjects, Silvia Federici reminds us of the duty of the historian
to examine the ideological underpinnings of data-gathering
itself. In *Caliban and the Witch*, census-taking and registers are
identified by Federici as the product of the introduction of
state intervention in workers' reproduction through public
assistance and concomitant forms of social control. We need
to question whether the focus of quantitative history on the
'measurable' might actually reproduce or reflect the power of
state and capital.

> The fact that the 16th and 17th centuries were the heyday of
> Mercantilism, and saw the beginning of demographic recording
> (of births, deaths and marriages), of census-taking, and the

---

23   Ibid., p.8.

formalisation of demography itself as the first 'state-science' is a clear proof of the strategic importance that controlling population movements was acquiring in political circles.[24]

How important is it to measure the reach of ideas in numbers? In a history that seeks to reconstitute protest, revolt and critical thought as a resource for the present, exaggeration is a big temptation as well as, perhaps, one of the tools of the trade. It might be said that quantitative data could help us understand an important aspect of the efficacy of dissenting ideas – their uptake and geographical spread. Equally, we can't account for thought so easily in quantitative terms. Christopher Hill neatly deals with the challenges of quantitative history in the introduction to his book, *The Experience of Defeat* (1984).

I may indeed have exaggerated the numerical significance of radicals – though there is much investigation to be done before this can be stated with assurance. I do not think I exaggerated the historical significance of the ideas, both in themselves, and in the reaction which they provoked.[25]

Prosopography, or Collective Biography

On the other side of the political spectrum (the far-right wing of the Conservative party), there are elements of both history from below and the vast data collation pioneered by *Annales* in the work of Cambridge historian Maurice Cowling. A self-

---

24   Silvia Federici, *Caliban and the Witch: Women, the Body and Primitive Accumulation*, New York: Autonomedia, 2004, p.182.

25   Christopher Hill, *The Experience of Defeat: Milton and Some Contemporaries,* London, Chicago, Melbourne: Bookmarks, 1984, p.4.

styled 'Tory Marxist', Cowling was a controversial figure whose legacy we examine further in chapter 7 on the Big Society. His major works were based on a method known as 'prosopography, or collective biography.' As Colin Kidd notes:

> Cowling's emphasis was on the interplay of individuals within a system, aiming 'to present democratic politicians in a multi-dimensional context where they display on the fragmented nature of God's handiwork the only rational way of acting politically'.[26]

However, in contradistinction to history from below, rather than the study of the convictions and or experiences of those left out of history, Cowling focussed on the ruling class and their preoccupations, distractions and misunderstandings of historical process.

> What seemed important when observed from the outside – the supposed great issues of the day, as well as the structural determinants of politics as studied by historians – was marginal to the largely autonomous machinations of political actors, while the tittle-tattle of the elite (both its passing trivialities and the concessions its members made to the acknowledged temperaments of their peers) turned out to have an inward tactical significance out of all proportion to its wider social irrelevance. To parse politics accurately required an understanding of the way the principal players in the political game – 50 or so figures, including press barons and senior civil servants – variously read and misread the fluid and changing

---

26   Colin Kidd, 'Sabre-Toothed Tory', *London Review of Books*, 31st March 2011, http://www.lrb.co.uk/v33/n07/colin-kidd/sabre-toothed-teacher

'situational necessity' in which they found themselves.[27]

Cowling would take as his set a group of figures from the ruling class and carry out detailed biographical research into their lives, their letters to each other, their motives and their public duties. This exercise, by its very nature, would produce an experiential rather than structural analysis of the situation. Cowling, attuned to hidden agendas, drew great pleasure from the fact that his studies threw up counterintuitive findings; mocking any scientific pretensions in the study of 'political science'. One could also wonder whether it wasn't calculated to undermine more 'heroic' aspects active in the history of ideas, instead affirming political history as the self-interested decisions of the powerful who rule.

Sir Lewis Namier, whose studies of the 18th century ruling class are referenced by E.P. Thompson at the beginning of this chapter, also appeared to resist the idea that power was imposed in a deliberative manner. Instead he analysed the clubbiness and fluctuating social contingencies of elites. Where he is said to differ from Cowling is in his foregrounding of material self-interest:

Namier's obsession with collecting facts such as club membership of various MPs and then attempting to co-relate them to voting patterns led his critics such as Sir Herbert Butterfield to accuse him of 'taking ideas out of history'. Namier was well known for his dislike in ideas and people who believed in them, and made little secret of his belief that the best form of

---

27   Ibid.

government was that of a grubby self-interested elite.[28]

It is worth learning the lesson from Cowling that while attention to the particular, circumstantial and experiential can be emancipatory in demolishing idealist history, it can also just as well carry conservative ideals as liberatory ones. On the other hand, we wouldn't dismiss 'ruling class studies' as a pursuit unworthy of the left historian. Though hopefully some differences of approach, as well as similarities, will be apparent in the following quote by Douglas Hay..

> The course of history is the result of a complex of human actions – and it cannot be reduced to one transcendent purpose. The cunning of a ruling class is a more substantial concept, however, for such a group of men is agreed on ultimate ends. However much they believed in justice (and they did); however sacred they held property (and they worshipped it); however merciful they were to the poor (and many were); the gentlemen of England knew that their duty was, above all, to rule. On that depended everything. They acted accordingly.[29]

Archive Fever

Historians from below have expressed their own experience of attending to the voices of the past as fevered, haunted, even hallucinatory. Carolyn Steedman remarks on the dizziness archives could induce:

---

28   Lewis Bernstein Namier, Wikipedia, http://en.wikipedia.org/wiki/ Lewis_Bernstein_Namier
29   Douglas Hay, 'Property, Authority and the Criminal Law', in *Albion's Fatal Tree*, op. cit., p.53.

I can tell you all about archive fever. Actually, Archive Fever comes on at night, long after the archive has shut for the day. Typically, the fever – more accurately, the precursor fever, the feverlet – starts in the early hours of the morning, in the bed of a cheap hotel, where the historian cannot get to sleep. You cannot get to sleep because you lie so narrowly, in an attempt to avoid contact with anything that isn't shielded by sheets and pillowcase. [...]

What keeps you awake, the sizing and starch in the thin sheets dissolving as you turn again and again within their confines, is actually the archive, and the myriads of its dead, who all day long have pressed their concerns upon you. You think: these people have left me the lot [...] Not a purchase made, not a thing acquired that is not noted and recorded. You think: I could get to hate these people; and, I can never do these people justice; and, finally: I shall never get it done. [...] You know perfectly well that despite the infinite heaps of things they recorded, the notes and traces that these people left behind, it is in fact, practically nothing at all. There is the great, brown, slow-moving strandless river of Everything, and then there is its tiny flotsam that has ended up in the record office you are working in. Your craft is to conjure a social system from a nutmeg grater, and your competence in that was established long ago. [...] Real Archive Fever lasts between sixteen and twenty-four hours, sometimes longer (with an aftermath of weeks rather than days). You think, in the delirium: it was their dust that I breathed in.[30]

Somehow, their subjects' purchases on the historian's mind

---

30   Carolyn Steedman, 'Something She Called a Fever: Michelet, Derrida, and Dust', *American Historical Review*, Vol.106, Issue 4, October, 2001.

must resolve themselves into some kind of narrative, as Marcus Rediker explains.

> I remember hearing while I was in graduate school an admonition about archival and primary sources: 'Go on reading until you hear voices.' It seemed an exhortation to schizophrenia at the time, but memories of my grandfather helped me to grasp the point: humanize the sources, humanize the story. Learn to listen. And, of course, the recovery of voices has been a central purpose of history from below from the very beginning, but storytellers were way ahead of us.[31]

Technology, Sources, and Dissemination

In the brief social and political eruption of the years before the English Civil War, the printed press and the explosion of non-conformist and lay preaching produced a sustained challenge to the dominant society, its philosophy and social practices. Rather than an exception, Christopher Hill establishes this as an unusual moment of legibility for the common beliefs and ideas circulating at the time. Quite rightly, he wondered what else might be otherwise suppressed in more prosaic times.

> In so far as the attempt is successful it may tell us something not only about English history in this period of unique liberty, but also about the more 'normal' periods which preceded and followed it – normal because we are again ignorant of what the

---

31 Marcus Rediker, 'The Poetics of History from Below' in *Perspectives on History,* September 2010, American Historical Association, http://www.historians.org/perspectives/issues/2010/1009/1009art1.cfm

common people were thinking.[32]

The technical innovations of the printing press and the mobility of war, trade and religion permitted rapid distribution of texts and communication of events in 17th century England.

> During the brief years of extensive liberty of the press in England it may have been easier for eccentrics to get into print than ever before or since [...] the printing press was a relatively cheap and portable piece of equipment.[33]

The lead up to the English Civil War was one example of many throughout history in which technological advance coincided with an eruption of social expression. As common people both read and published, the previous distribution of the sensible was ruptured and expanded; existing science, philosophy, and religious orthodoxy were challenged and a part of the rich train of ideas that propelled the men and women of these times to action remained for posterity, as we will go on to explore in chapter 4 on Autodidacts. In the past these eruptions of thought and speech were the stuff of local memory, popular folklore, tales passed on through families; and also physical archives: those of established institutions, self-organised collectives, and labour history bookshops. As Carolyn Steedman puts it in *Dust*:

> Modern students of the discipline are introduced to the idea of

---

32 Christopher Hill, *The World Turned Upside Down: Radical Ideas During the English Revolution*, London: Viking Press 1973, p.18.

33 Ibid., p.17.

an engagement with documentary evidence, collected together in a particular kind of place, as a foundational and paradigmatic activity of historians.[34]

But the position of the physical archive is quickly becoming de-centred as a means of both accessing and housing sources. Paul Mason argues that the unparalleled proliferation of information through the internet, and particularly social media, has effectively ended 'the left's monopoly on critical narratives about capitalism'.

> Today the left is no longer the gatekeeper to subversive knowledge (although it can aspire to be a 'preferred provider'). Those seeking a narrative critical of the world order, and evidence of corporate and state wrongdoing, are free to cut out the middleman.[35]

This would raise the question of the role of the contemporary professional historian in assembling narratives from below. Has the mediating role of the public historian been superseded? A generation may have complained of the 'annihilation of space through time'[36] – and the internet is indisputably a gigantic planetary work-intensification scheme – but few can overlook the intense changes it has wrought in the circulation of struggles in our current anti-austerity moment. It would seem that struggles are written,

---

34 Carolyn Steedman, *Dust*, Manchester: Manchester University Press, 2001, p.x.

35 Paul Mason, *Why It's Kicking Off Everywhere*, London: Verso 2012, p.150.

36 Karl Marx, *Grundrisse: Foundations of the Critique of Political Economy*, London: Penguin, 1993, p.524.

filmed, photographed, blogged, discussed and circulated as they are in their very process of making themselves. By no means is this a death blow to the historian, rather the authority of the historian is available to many. Though while events are historicised quicker and the variety of sources has proliferated, there is still a bias towards professionals conducting such research, since the resources and time needed to sift through so many sources is already beyond the ability of most amateurs.

The August 2011 riots precipitated an avalanche of commentary, two governmental reports, as well as independent reports such as *Reading the Riots*, a collaboration by *The Guardian* newspaper and London School of Economics. *Reading the Riots* had several outputs: generating a report and television documentary as well as numerous other published formats such as interviews and blog entries, and dramatised spin-offs in which testimony by rioters and police were re-enacted by professional actors.

Aspects of the 'reality TV' media approach to contemporary history were anticipated and parodied by filmmakers such as Peter Watkins and Kevin Brownlow. Their films apply formal contemporary film and documentary conventions in 'realistic' re-enactments of historical events such as the Paris commune of 1871, the Diggers' occupation of St. Georges Hill in 1649 and the Battle of Culloden, 1745.[37] These filmmakers owe a debt to history from below, but far from indulging reverence towards their sources the debt is paid

---

37   The films we refer to directly here are Peter Watkins, *La Commune (Paris, 1871)*, France, 2000, Peter Watkins, *Culloden*, UK, 1964 and Kevin Brownlow, *Winstanley*, UK, 1975. Several other films which employ this or related methods are listed in our bibliography.

back with interest in such a way as to draw in and question media forms and the framing of historical and contemporary events. What is perhaps most original and interesting about their shared methodology is its production: an admixture of the experience of radical social movements of the present with those of the past, displacing the perceived authenticity of representation and deploying non-professional actors to inhabit and re-live historic roles.

Such films could also be said to anticipate the popularity of historical re-enactments both as a subcultural leisure activity and in remediated form in contemporary art. A number of contemporary art films, from Jeremy Deller's reenactment of a significant picketing confrontation during the UK Miners Strike in *The Battle of Orgreave* to Anja Kirschner and David Panos' critical reconstruction of the life of legendary thief and escapee Jack Sheppard in *The Last Days of Jack Sheppard*, deal with complex questions of historical reconstruction and lived experience. Deller's film in particular drew a great deal of criticism especially since it's therapeutic approach to historical defeat seemed complicit with New Labour's suppression of class politics.

These sociological enquiries are often reduced to behaviourism as this art nostalgically mourns the ruins of what was social meaning. Deller's 'grand masque' of the Miners' Strike of 1984 substitutes spectacle for critical engagement as he buries the class war in the shroud of a colourful pageant. In this contemporary replay of picturesque aesthetics, subject-matter is discovered/identified in the textured remnants of a fossilised modernity. In these events, history is resurrected as a costume drama.[38]

Despite the obvious connections between re-enactments as a form and the vast means of simulation developed by late capitalism, it's interesting to recognise that the need to reanimate the past through live action and performance is itself surprisingly old. Reviewing an exhibition of contemporary art dealing with the reenactment of historical events, History Will Repeat Itself, Richard Grayson assembles a compelling list.

> The Romans restaged battles in the Colosseum so that the vulgar could celebrate famous victories in which the players were actually killed and, if it was a naval engagement, the arena was filled with water. In 1645 Parliamentary troops re-ran a recent victory on Blackheath although still actively at war with Royalist forces. In 1920, 500 musicians, 6,000 to 8,000 participants and between 45,000 and 100,000 spectators were involved in Nikolai Evreinov's spectacular 'Prolekult' restaging of the 'Storming of the Winter Palace' in Petrograd. [...] This re-enactment was restaged seven years later in Eisenstein's movie *October*, 1927, which has given us images that we hold as iconic of the Revolution itself.[39]

The time lag between social movements and their historicisation or circulation is getting much shorter, and

---

38 Jim Coombes, 'Plink Plink Fizz... Contemporary Art Dissolves the Past', *Variant,* Issue 30, Winter 2007, http://www.variant.org.uk/30texts/hist.html

39 Richard Grayson, 'History Will Repeat Itself: strategies of reenactment in contemporary (media) art and performance', *Art Monthly*, February, 2008, p.28.

this clearly spurs varied forms of self-consciousness and re-circulation. A canny intervention into the burgeoning reenactment culture was made in the early-2000s by the formation of a London Riot Re-enactment Society. The group proposed to re-enact riots from the recent and distant past and took a polemical and good humoured stance on issues of historical accuracy.

> A knowledge of historical costume and weaponry AND some experience of rioting is the ideal combination for a LRRS member, but members can join with knowledge of one, or the other, or neither. After all, many participants in the riots that we are re-enacting had not a clue what they were up to, and we want historical accuracy, do we not?[40]

Local history, traditional social history, and the histories of protest and music have all been injected with the intensification of debate and increased velocity of the circulation of information in recent years. Part of the reason there is no canonical book on, to take an example, the history of rave culture in the UK is because it is being written, collected and shared through the internet. As such, it remains a live culture distributed across many sites, peer to peer networks, on mailing lists and in anecdotes on social media networks. It lives in people's hard drives, on servers and in their record collections. Whilst there are risks involved – there have been a spate of arrests and confiscations of equipment over the last five years, and people charged with organising illegal parties with material gathered on the internet used to prosecute

---

40   'The London Riot Re-enactment Society', http://anathematician. c8.com/lrrs.htm

them – the self-investment in individually and collectively documenting a moment of social change is overwhelming and continues to inspire others who arrive to it later.

There are some caveats to understanding the use of social media, which may confront historians of the future. Firstly we can see from a cursory study of history from below that the voices of the 'common people' do not always come to us pure and direct, but are situated in particular social and economic contexts. Deference and holding one's tongue in one situation might give way to open dissent in another. But the most public forms of social media tend toward a more or less enforced collapse of these different contexts and domains. In the case of Facebook, 'Privacy' tools allowing the user to restrict their posts to particular sets of 'friends' are increasingly being simplified. In the words of Mark Zuckerberg, 'You have one identity. The days of you having a different image for your work friends or co-workers and for the other people you know are probably coming to an end pretty quickly'.[41] In one respect this means the individual is expected to shape themselves into a public persona, one's speech acts always visible to employers, potentially subject to state and even workplace surveillance. Some individuals may be more keen to hold their tongues than others. Secondly, the historian of the future may have to integrate as well as look beyond the gathering and contested forms of evidence and ontology which are partly the product of widespread use of social media: 'Pics or it didn't happen' is becoming, at least

---

41 'Facebook's Zuckerberg: Having two identities for yourself is an example of a lack of integrity', http://michaelzimmer.org/2010/05/14/facebooks-zuckerberg-having-two-identities-for-yourself-is-an-example-of-a-lack-of-integrity/

for some users, 'you don't exist if you're not on Facebook'. While this is evidence of a propensity to distributed demands for veracity – as well as the tendency for news corporations to make use of the unpaid labour of social network users – it also reflects a sense of what makes an active or silent subject, part of which is determined by access to technology in the first place as much as by personal choice. Lastly, despite the distributive nature of social media, the sharing of fragments of information is also increasingly seen as constitutive of the individual; an act of self-curation, in the context of neoliberal capitalism, which raises more questions for the historian of the future.

Not just sources, but circulation is a crucial aspect of rewriting history from the bottom up, and as circulation itself implies, sources circulated trigger new sources from which history is made. Sukhdev Sandhu on the black history boom since the 1960s:

> It was in the wake of increased immigration that academics started taking an interest in the history of blacks in Britain. In the Sixties, Paul Edwards, originally a specialist in Old Icelandic, produced editions of the two most important African-British writers of the 18th century, Ignatius Sancho and Olaudah Equiano. In the Seventies, the Black Power movement's insistence on the need for black people to be aware of their own heritage, and the huge international success of Alex Haley's *Roots*, intensified interest in the subject. Then came the Brixton Riots of 1981. The first International Conference on the History of Blacks in Britain was held in the same year, at the University of London. Studies by Peter Fryer, James Walvin and David Dabydeen appeared in the next few years. Fryer, whose *Staying*

Power is still the most detailed – and most often consulted – account of the subject, gave more than two hundred talks and lectures at adult education centres, schools and public meetings around the country. Local councils began to fund oral history and ethnic workshops; universities set up courses structured around the books of black British writers and uncovering evidence that slavery existed here as well as in the colonies.[42]

Endorsement of oral history and other forms of history workshops are ways to make the historian's role available to many, but also structure the generation of material records. Whilst sponsorship for this kind of historical responsibility appears to have diminished, its legacy in amateur history groups and contemporary fiction-writing is definitely still going strong.

Language

Apart from the clarity of rare moments of revolutionary enunciation, the 'below' is everywhere in history the subject which by definition is not allowed to speak. With recourse to 18th century Canting dictionaries, Peter Linebaugh shows us that when the 'below' speaks it does not necessarily do so in the tones of official legibility or propriety.

The sailor in the Royal Navy used a variety of expressions to signify what he took directly: 'To use the wee riddle', 'to sweat the purser', 'to tosh', 'to sling', 'to cut out', 'to knock off', 'to drop', 'to manarvel', 'to fork' and 'to earn' expressed different forms of

---

42   Sukhdev Sandhu, 'At the Hop', *London Review of Books*, Vol. 19, No. 4, 20th February 1997, pp.23-24.

directly appropriating things in a manner that to the Admiralty was nothing more than stealing. 'To tap the Admiral' meant to insert a goose quill into a wine or brandy barrel and drink at the King's expense. [...] The sailor's 'earnings' thus had a double aspect: customary and legal, picaresque and proletarian. And he might receive a third kind of remuneration in the form of 'prize-money' – if his ship had indeed taken a 'prize' – which meant only what his ship had plundered from the vessels of other seafaring nations. Prize-money was often delayed, and in any case was available only at the Navy Pay Office in London. John Clarke after sixteen years sailing out of Liverpool, had to 'pike to the start' in order to collect his prize-money. Necessity drove him to robbing, and the law drove him up Holborn Hill to his hanging.[43]

Linebaugh has noted that that this study from below requires not only a look at alternative sources and familiar sources in alternative ways but also the very register of unofficial language.

First the ship was not only the means of communication between continents, it was the first place where working people from the continents communicated. Needless to say, the medium of communication could not be the King's English; instead 'vehicular languages' were created – creole, pidgin and 'all-American'. These drew upon parent languages of north-eastern Europe (English, French, Dutch) and western Africa (Yoruba, Fanti).[44]

The vernacular preserves the distinctions that often get lost

---

43   Peter Linebaugh, *The London Hanged*, London: Verso 1991, p.128.
44   Ibid. p.134.

in the learned or 'economic' language of the wage. In the 18th century for concrete and paid labour, the glossary includes cabbage, chips, waxers, sweepings, sockings, wastages, blessing, lays, dead men, onces, primage, furthing, dunnage, portage, wines, vails, tinge, buggings, colting, rumps, birrs, fents, thrums, potching, scrapings, poake, coltage, extra, tret, tare, largess, the con, nobbings, knockdown, boot, tommy, trimmings, poll, gleaning, lops, tops, bontages, keepy back, pin money.[45]

With few precursors, the nautical proletariat had to invent itself as it invented language in the breadth of the Atlantic and on international terms. In the invention of language and forms of life, there is a keen expression of the particular and technical specifications of practices which otherwise remain unrecorded. It is precisely the relation (or tension) between thought, expression, action and material conditions that a history from below struggles to illuminate.

---

45   Peter Linebaugh, 'Days of Villainy: a Reply to Two Critics', *International Socialism Journal*, Summer, 1994, p.63.

AUTODIDACTS

Here we would like to look closer at some of the forms taken by what E.P. Thompson names the 'other kind of knowledge production' in the 1700s-1900s – a period in which literacy grew despite an absence of universal education. This was largely the result of the efforts of the working class to self-educate and self-communicate. Much material drawn upon in the various histories from below was a product of these enterprises. The term 'autodidact' is often used to describe the self-taught person. It's a tricky word because it implies a very individualised and self-contained process of self-education. In much of what follows this was not the case. Working people learned, wrote, and debated both alone and collectively. They initiated and took part in widespread processes of dissemination. In accounting for their activities, we should be careful to give our exploration of autodidact knowledge production a particular degree of awkwardness. For autodidact activity was not simply a self-teaching in the fundamentals of literacy. It was also an appropriation, a borrowing and taking, of the logics and the games of established intellectual discourse – and the invention of new ones. While working class self-education can be appreciated on the terms of the latter, at times it was intended not for the consumption of established interests, but instead for discussion and further use among workmates. Equally, not all workers read, wrote, debated or otherwise produced their culture simply for the purpose of either 'self-improvement' or dissent.

Those who have wished to emphasise the sober constitutional ancestry of the working-class movement have sometimes minimised its more robust and rowdy features. All that we can do is bear the warning in mind. We need more studies of the social attitudes of criminals, of soldiers and sailors, of tavern life; and we should look at the evidence, not with a moralising eye ('Christ's poor' were not always pretty), but with an eye for Brechtian values – the fatalism, the irony in the face of Establishment homilies, the tenacity of self-preservation. And we must also remember the 'underground' of the ballad-singer and the fair-ground which handed on traditions to the 19th century (to the music hall, or Dickens circus folk, or Hardy's pedlars and showmen); for in these ways the 'inarticulate' conserved certain values – a spontaneity, and capacity for enjoyment, and mutual loyalties – despite the inhibiting pressures of magistrates, mill-owners and Methodists.[1]

The diversity of motivations for workers' self-education should not in itself be depoliticised. For, as Jacques Rancière says of the worker-intellectuals of 1820s France:

What was ironically possible was the improvement of the conditions of work and wages, but it was not enough. What they wanted was to become entirely human, with all the possibilities of a human being and not only having what is possible to do for workers.[2]

---

1   E.P. Thompson, *The Making of the English Working Class,* London: Gollancz, 1963, p.59.

2   Interview with Jacques Rancière by Lawrence Liang, Lodi Gardens, Delhi, 5 February 2009, http://kafila.org/2009/02/12/interview-with-jacques-ranciere/

Where historical working-class articulacy risks being absorbed into a flattening textual analysis, we need to remember the material conditions in and against which autodidacts worked, and the monopoly on the official production and distribution of such analyses by the more privileged classes. Where autodidact activity is reduced to a simple and patronising overcoming of obstacles on literacy, we should foreground the innovations in thinking and understanding that self-taught workers developed in line with their experiences of both labour and literature.

> By considering the carpenter Perdiguier, the tailor Troncin. the locksmith Gilland and the engraver Vincard to be representative of the population of skilled artisans, we are not perceiving them for what they really are: a marginal group at the frontier of encounters with the bourgeoisie, characterized by the same migrations and instabilities, the same ambiguities and contradictions that define the working class: but also a particular category of intellectuals, more intellectual, in a sense, than we are, for their intellectuality is a victory over their condition.[3]

Rancière is therefore arguing, at least in the case of 19th century autodidacts, for an understanding of the special condition for those who both worked and produced intellectually. They rarely escaped their condition through intellectual mastery, but their efforts put them in a specific relation to the work they endured and wrote about.

---

3   Jacques Rancière, 'The Myth of the Artisan', *International Labor and Working Class History,* Number 24, Fall 1983, pp.10-11.

Use of Scripture as Dissent

Participation in religious debate and dissent was an early development of autodidact culture. Silvia Federici notes that in the context of the anti-feudal struggle, the popular heresy of the Middle Ages was not simply an attack on the corruption of the church and its doctrines, it was a struggle against the relation of the church to state and landlords. Heretics also developed an international support network disseminating critical knowledge and texts, and providing schools, welfare and safe-houses for dissenters. Moreover, women played a central role in the development of heretical practice.

> Although influenced by Eastern religions brought to Europe by merchants and crusaders, popular heresy was less a deviation from the orthodox doctrine than a protest movement, aspiring to a radical democratization of social life. Heresy was the equivalent of 'liberation theology' for the medieval proletariat. It gave a frame to peoples' demands for spiritual renewal and social justice, challenging both the Church and secular authority by appeal to a higher truth. It denounced social hierarchies, private property and the accumulation of wealth, and it disseminated among the people a new, revolutionary conception of society that, for the first time in the Middle Ages, redefined every aspect of daily life (work, property, sexual reproduction, and the position of women), posing the question of emancipation in truly universal terms... the propagation of the heretical doctrines not only channelled the contempt that people felt for the clergy; it gave them confidence in their views and instigated their resistance to clerical exploitation. Such was the reach of the sects (particularly the Cathars and Waldens,)

and the links they established among themselves with the help of commercial fairs, pilgrimages, and the constant border-crossing of refugees generated by the persecution.[4]

Keith Thomas and Christopher Hill emphasise the role of the Lollards in keeping alive a popular version of John Wyclif's heresies through several centuries. Both historians recover scraps of speech which suggest a widespread current of anti-clericalism and scepticism towards transubstantiation, confession and baptism amongst the lower orders of society which undermined mainstream Christianity and made space for popular beliefs.[5]

Sixteenth-Century conservatives had correctly predicted that the publication of a vernacular Bible would be a subversive and equalitarian act, but not because Scripture was an unambiguously revolutionary text. The danger was that ordinary people would enter into theological debates once reserved for an elite.[6]

Christopher Hill says of the end of press censorship after 1640 that there was a flourishing of authors who were 'illiterate' in the eyes of academics. They knew as little Latin or Greek or Shakespeare. So in the interregnum discussions there was no longer a background of Classical scholarship; the rules of

---

4   Silvia Federici, *Caliban and the Witch: Women, the Body and Primitive Accumulation*, New York: Autonomedia, 2004, pp.33–34.

5   See Christopher Hill, *The World Turned Upside Down*, London: Penguin, 1991, pp.25–26.

6   Jonathan Rose, *The Intellectual Life of the British Working Classes*, New Haven, CT: Yale University Press, 2000, p.15.

logic which structured academic controversy were ignored.[7]

Scripture continued to be invoked, through countless mutations in the hands of autodidacts, constituting a common language of dissent into the 18th century.

> Looking back from the nineteenth century, the victors appeared to be rationalism, political economy, utilitarianism, science, liberalism [...] [but] the authority of the Church, demystified in the seventeenth century, had not yet been replaced by the authority of an academic hierarchy or of public 'experts'.[8]

Talking Back to Books

Participation, then, was not always defined by the exposure of workers to orthodox culture on the terms of its patricians. Instead, in the hands of autodidacts, it became a matter of challenging the terms on which the former operated through a self-initiated questioning of the uses of literature. The fears of the guardians of the canon were not simply that the 'authority' of texts and their selection be challenged, but that their class stranglehold on culture was threatened through such acts of participation. Sheila Rowbotham cites Mary Collier, a washerwoman from Petersfield who wrote a poem in answer to the work of Stephen Duck in 1739. Duck was a farm worker and self-taught poet himself, later discussed in Robert Southey's *An Essay on Uneducated Poets* (1831) and one of a number of poets published in small collections of

---

7   Christopher Hill quoted in *The Intellectual Life of the British Working Classes,* op. cit., p.15.

8   E.P. Thompson, *Witness Against the Beast,* London: The New Press, 1995, p.xv.

verse by working people. In his early work, he drew upon his experience as an agricultural labourer, but as Rowbotham points out:

> Far from being excluded from production, [working class women's] life was one of ceaseless labour [...] Duck had implied that women agricultural workers had 'their wages paid for sitting on the ground'. [Collier] put him right with some precision, pointing out that they sat down to eat after the hay was exposed to the sun [...] the work in the fields was by no means the end of work for women.

> I hope that since we freely toil and sweat
> To earn our Bread, you'll give us time to eat,
> That over, soon we must be up again
> And nimbly turn our Hay upon the plain [...]
> When Ev'ning does approach we homeward hie
> And our domestic Toils incessant ply.[9]

The forms the autodidacts' challenges took were as often a product of irreverent first contact with literature, as they were a growing sense that an initial reverence was (as miner Chester Armstrong put it) 'a spell yet fatal to free initiative and self-reliance in culture'.

It now seems to me obvious that to lean on authority is to acknowledge the philosophy of crutches, which is fatal to culture

---

9   Sheila Rowbotham, *Hidden from History: 300 Years of Women, Oppression and the Fight Against It*, London: Pluto Press, 1975, p.25. Excerpts available at, http://www.marxists.org/subject/women/authors/rowbotham-sheila/hidden-history.htm#s8

and companionship in literature [...] I have good reason to know the spell which canonised writers and others yet cast over the minds of mankind – a spell yet fatal to free initiative and self-reliance in culture [...] I now feel assured that to make an idol of an author or a fetish of a book is tantamount to slavery [...] I still retain, however, my household gods; only that halo round their heads has vanished. I now feel that I can, so to speak, walk arm in arm with them and so converse in familiar terms.[10]

Olaudah Equiano was an African stolen from his village and sold into slavery. He bought his way out of slavery working plantations in America and the West Indies colonies and as a ship hand travelling the Atlantic passage, eventually settling in London as a merchant. *An Interesting Narrative...* was Equiano's account of his life and travels – a narrative shaped by his own experience of slavery and the suffering he saw around him. Equiano's awareness of the conditions around him is presented at each stage in terms of his own self-education and development. Frequently Equiano describes events both as he saw them at the time and as he came to understand them from his new perspective as a 'free subject' – a freedom which included in it the ability to sell his labour power as well as to both read and write.

The following quotation relates Equiano's introduction to literature aboard a merchant ship. Having recognised something useful in books, but not yet perceiving their orthodox use, Equiano invented his own use for them and made the books his own.

---

10   Chester Armstrong, quoted in Jonathan Rose, *The Intellectual Life of the British Working Classes*, op. cit., p.15.

I have often seen my master and Dick employed in reading; and I had a great curiosity to talk to the books, as I thought they did; and so to learn how all things had a beginning: for that purpose I have often taken up a book, and have talked to it, and then put my ears to it, when alone, in hopes it would answer me; and I have been very much concerned when I found it remained silent.[11]

The motif of the 'talking book' can be found in the writings of several black autodidacts of the 18th and 19th centuries. One account Equiano was certainly familiar with and perhaps borrowed from was that of James Albert Ukwasaw Gronniosaw.

I was never so surprised in my life, as when I saw the book talk to my master, for I thought it did, as I observed him to look upon it, and move his lips. I wished it would do so to me. As soon as my master had done reading it, I followed him to the place where he took the book [...] [I was] greatly disappointed when I found it would not speak, this thought presented itself to me, that every body and everything despised me because I was black.[12]

---

11 Olaudah Equiano, *The Interesting Narrative of the Life of Olaudah Equiano, or Gustavas Vassa, The African, Written by Himself*, London: Penguin, 1995, p.68.

12 James Albert Ukwasaw Gronniosaw, *A Narrative of the Most Remarkable Particulars in the Life of James Albert Ukwasaw Gronniosaw, an African Prince, As Related by Himself*, Bath, 1772, http://etext.lib.virginia.edu/etcbin/toccernew2id=GroGron. sgm&images=images/modeng&data=/texts/english/modeng/parsed&ta g=public&part=1&division=div1

Subsequent uses of 'the talking book' were made in the memoirs of John Marrant[13], Ottobah Cugoano[14], Jon Jea[15], and Rebecca Cox Jackson[16]. In *The Signifying Monkey* (1988), Henry Louis Gates argues that these writers produced variations upon the motif as a means of 'signifyin(g)', or referencing and commenting on each other's work and experience. The repetition of the figure also challenged and subverted the expectations the white authorities (and readers) had of slaves and free people of colour. Equiano's description of his discovery of 'talking books' belonging to his master, assumes a knowing air when we consider it part of the author's attempts to provide a persuasive account in the argument for abolition. He provides a powerful metaphor for the movement of the black writer from 'object to subject', as Gates puts it:

> Black people, the evidence suggests, had to represent themselves as 'speaking subjects' before they could even begin to destroy their status as objects, as commodities, within Western culture. In addition to all the myriad reasons for which human beings write books, this particular reason seems to have been

---

13   John Marrant, *A Narrative of the Lord's Wonderful Dealings with John Marrant, a Black*, London, 1785, http://archive.org/details/cihm_20674

14   Ottobah Cugoano, *Narrative of the Enslavement of Ottobah Cugoano, a Native of Africa; Published by Himself in the Year 1787*, London, 1787, http://docsouth.unc.edu/neh/cugoano/menu.html

15   Jon Jea, *The Life, History, and Unparalled Sufferings of John Jea, the African Preacher. Compiled and Written by Himself* (Portsea, 1811), http://docsouth.unc.edu/neh/jeajohn/menu.html

16   Jean McMahon Humez (Ed.), *Gifts of Power: The Writings of Rebecca Jackson, Black Visionary, Shaker Eldress*, Amherst: University of Massachussetts Press, 1987.

paramount for the black slave.[17]

Gates traces the last example of the 'talking book' in this period to the memoirs of Rebecca Cox Jackson (1795-1871), a free African-American dressmaker who became the leader of a Shaker sisterhood in Philadelphia in 1857. Jackson was illiterate until well into her adulthood. She asked her brother, a church leader, to teach her to read the bible and to write letters for her according to her dictation. Not only did he often shirk off this responsibility, he also had a tendency to replace her words with his own. He received a spirited rebuke:

> Thee has put in more than I told Thee [...] I did not tell Thee to word my letter, I told Thee to write it.[18]

Jackson claimed to have learnt to read the bible on her own, when she heard the voice of God ensuring her that it was possible. Gates argues that Jackson reconfigures the talking book to challenge 'male domination of a female's voice and her quest for literacy.'[19] On the role of God in Jackson's attainment of literacy, Gates quotes Alice Walker who asserts, 'Jackson was taught to read and write by the spirit within her.'[20]

The 'talking book' was an important innovation in the development of black and world literature. We believe it is

---

17   Henry Louis Gates, *The Signifying Monkey: A Theory of African-American Literary Criticism*, Oxford: Oxford University Press, 1988, p.129.

18   Rebecca Cox Jackson, quoted in ibid., p.241.

19   Ibid., p.130.

20   Alice Walker, quoted in ibid., p.243.

also an excellent motif for the autodidacts' conviction that books are not something to be distantly revered or their authority deferred to, but rather that this knowledge has to be addressed, participated in and most of all talked back to.

Time and Intellectual Activity

What conditioned the readings, writing and debates of the industrial working class? And how did workers, who were seemingly restricted by working hours and the exhaustion produced by physical labour, manage to take part in such activities? Oral culture, in its various forms, was a means of getting around illiteracy.

> Illiteracy (we should remember) by no means excluded men [or women] from political discourse [...]. The ballad-singers and 'patterers' still had a thriving occupation, with their pavement farces and street-corner parodies, following the popular mood and giving a Radical or anti-papal twist to their satirical monologues or chants, according to the state of the market [...]

> In times of political ferment the illiterate would get their workmates to read aloud from the periodicals; while at Houses of Call the news was read, and at political meetings a prodigious time was spent in reading addresses and passing long strings of resolutions [...].[21]

And it developed to accommodate the growth of literacy, which was by no means universal in the home.

---

21   *The Making of the English Working Class,* op. cit., p.783

In an oral history investigation of social life between 1870 and 1918, half of all working-class interviewees indicated that reading aloud (including bible reading and parents reading to children) was practised in the homes where they were raised [...]. All these influences combined to produce a shared literary culture in which books were practically treated as public property, before public libraries reached most of the country. It was a culture that extended even to Flora Thompson's rural Oxfordshire. 'Modern writers who speak of the booklessness of the poor at that time must mean books as possessions', she wrote; 'there were always books to borrow'.[22]

Being able to read was only the start of it:

The ability to handle abstract and consecutive argument was by no means inborn; it had to be discovered against almost overwhelming difficulties – the lack of leisure, the cost of candles (or of spectacles), as well as educational deprivation.[23]

Central to efforts at learning was the availability of time. The working hours imposed by industry might be seen to have restricted in-depth learning. The imposition of time-discipline over the period of capitalist development was to some extent internalised over a long period by workers, and time itself became the site of struggle.

In *'Time, Work-Discipline, and Industrial Capitalism'* (1967), E.P. Thompson discovers the imposition of time-discipline in the school, which made the teachers as well as the pupils subordinate to the rule of the clock.

---

22 *The Intellectual Life of the English Working Classes,* op. cit., p.76
23 *The Making of the English Working Class,* op. cit., p.784.

Once within the school gates, the child entered the new universe of disciplined time. At the Methodist Sunday Schools in York the teachers were fined for unpunctuality. The first rule to be learned by the scholars was:

> I am to be present at the School. . . a few minutes before half-past nine o'clock . . . .

The onslaught, from so many directions, upon the people's old working habits was not, of course, uncontested. In the first stage, we find simple resistance. But, in the next stage, as the new time discipline is imposed, so the workers begin to fight, not against time, but about it.[24]

In the factories, particularly the textile mills and engineering workshops, employers at first tried to cheat workers of their own knowledge of time.

> in reality there were no regular hours: masters and managers did with us as they liked. The clocks at the factories were often put forward in the morning and back at night, and instead of being instruments for the measurement of time, they were used as cloaks for cheatery and oppression. Though this was known amongst the hands, all were afraid to speak, and a workman then was afraid to carry a watch, as it was no uncommon event to dismiss any one who presumed to know too much about the science of horology.[25]

---

24   E.P. Thompson, *'Time, Work-Discipline, and Industrial Capitalism',* *Past and Present*, 38(1), 1967, p.42..

25   *Ibid.,* p.42.

But the factory was also the scene of attempts to take back time from employers by workers in pursuit of knowledge.

> Despising his job in a Birmingham factory, V.W. Garratt (b.1892) surrounded his workbench with a barricade of boxes, set up a small mirror to provide early warning of the foreman's approach, and studied the Everyman's Library Sartor Restarus when he was being paid to solder gas-fittings.[26]

Here we see an anecdotal trace of what amounted to the taking by workers of the conditions for intellectual activity for themselves. These conditions are, after all, inextricable from its products, and, sometimes, their appreciation.

The Nights of Labour

Jacques Rancière's exhausted artisans stayed up at night, writing, reading, and talking shop. Developed from Rancière's research for his doctoral thesis, *Proletarian Nights* (first published in English in 1989 under the more suggestive title, *Nights of Labour*) is a hefty study of a relatively small group of Paris artisans who were active in writing poetry, prose, polemics, letters and diaries outside of working hours, under the July Monarchy (approximately 1830-1848). In making use of their night hours to pursue an 'other world', Rancière argues that the worker-poets' activities were *'entirely material and entirely intellectual at the same time.'* The artisans not only appropriated languages and discourses, but also time:

---

26   The Intellectual Life of the British Working Classes, op. cit., p.42.

Emancipation for those workers [...] was the attempt to conquer the useless, to conquer the language of the poet [...] the leisure of the loiterer. It is the attempt to take the time that they have not. To go to the places where they are not supposed to have anything to do.[27]

This entails a triple mastery: of time; of the effects of work on the body and mind; and also of the symbolic space of literature itself. Karl Marx suggested in *The Grundrisse* that the '*economy of time, to this all economy ultimately reduces itself.*'[28] For Rancière, time was and is a central object of domination, and thus requires mastering and re-figuring.

In this world, the question is always to subvert the order of time prescribed by domination, to interrupt its continuities and transform the pauses it imposes into regained freedom.[29]

Self-Organised Education

In Britain, institutions were developing to consolidate unofficial learning outside of working hours. Though to what ends was a matter of fierce contestation. The following quotations address the differences between two forms of working class education: the Mechanics' Institutes, which were run on the basis of bourgeois patronage, and the Mutual

---

27 Jaques Rancière, 'Revisiting Nights of Labour', lecture at Sarai 6 February 2009, http://www.youtube.com/watch?v=Lr6ZfzbumVo

28 Karl Marx, *Grundrisse*, http://www.marxists.org/archive/marx/works/1857/grundrisse/ch03.htm

29 Jacques Ranciere, *Proletarian Nights: The Worker's Dream in Nineteenth Century France*, London: Verso, 2012, p.xi.

Improvement Societies, a more diffuse body of groups which ran on a co-operative model and were largely self-organised by workers.

> The mutual improvement society, whether formal or informal, met week by week with the intention of acquiring knowledge, generally under the leadership of one of its own members. Here, and in the Mechanic's institutes, there was some coming-together of the traditions of the chapel and of the Radicals. But the coexistence was uneasy, and not always peaceful. The early history of the Mechanics' Institutes [...] is a story of ideological conflict. The crucial conflicts took place on the questions of control, of financial independence, and on whether or not the Institutes should debate political economy (and if so, whose political economy) [...] Control passed to the middle-class supporters, whose ideology also dominated the political economy of the syllabus. By 1825 the Trades Newspaper regarded the London Institute as a lost cause, which was dependent upon 'the great and wealthy' [...].[30]

With little formal education, William Farish (b. 1818) acquired basic literacy and political knowledge by reading newspapers to Newtown weavers. Farish joined a workingmen's school in Carlisle around 1840:

> Hiring a six-loom weaving shop in the Blue Anchor Lane, we fitted it up ourselves with desks and seats, rude enough, doubtless, but we could not very well complain of our own handiwork, and there was nobody else to please. The Mechanic's Institution, although well managed and liberally

---

30   *The Making of the English Working Class,* op. cit., p.817.

supported, had failed somewhat in its mission, mainly, as was thought, through the reluctance of the weaver in his clogs and fustian jacket to meet in the same room with the better clad, and possibly better mannered, shop assistants and clerks of the city. So these new places were purely democratic, having no master, and not permitting even any in the management but such as lived by weekly wages. Those who could read taught those who could not, and those who could cipher did the same for those less advanced.

Farish himself learned much from an uneducated Irishman who had somehow picked up a broad knowledge of English etymology, and a Cockermouth weaver who was adept in algebra, and yet could scarcely read or write.[31]

The patchwork of shared knowledge described by William Farish, is fascinating in light of a much later and highly contestable (see chapter 5 on Authenticity and Ambiguity) characterisation of the individual autodidact provided by Pierre Bourdieu in his social analysis of 1970s French culture, *Distinction*, which he relates to the official qualifications of state schooling:

[the autodidact] is condemned endlessly to amass disparate, often devalued information which is to legitimate knowledge as his [or her] stamp collection is to an art collection, a miniature culture.[32]

---

31   *The Intellectual Life of the English Working Classes*, op. cit., p.64.

32   Pierre Bourdieu, *Distinction: A Social Critique of the Judgement of Taste*, (Trans. Richard Nice), Cambridge, MA: Harvard University Press, 1984, pp. 328–330.

Here, the 'miniature' cultures of the Mutual Improvement Societies' members, themselves acquired against the odds, are plugged into a shared body of understanding that amounts to a socialisation of knowledge. And it is worth noting that this took place in an environment explicitly set up apart from the patronage of the Mechanics' Institutes.

Tensions in Co-operative Education

The Mechanics Institutes themselves were sometimes forced to accept measures they had previously censored.

As the campaign for the first Reform Bill approached its climax [...]. An agitation was raised by a few of the leading artisans for a mechanics institute. A room was taken over the market-place and opened three evenings a week. Most of the mechanics in the town joined, besides a few innkeepers and shopkeepers [...]. The genteel people would not attend lectures at a mechanic's institute, and they started a literary and scientific institution. It was a bad time for educational work. Bread was dear, trade was bad, and the country was passing through the throes of a political convulsion that was fast ripening into a revolution. The mechanics' institute gradually degenerated into a violent revolutionary club. The door was locked, the passages watched, the most inflammatory and seditious things were read and discussed, and most of the men took an oath and swore that if there was a general rising they would march on the local bank. [...] The following morning found all the shops closed and the militia on the pavement.[33]

---

33   *The Intellectual Life of the English Working Classes*, op. cit., p.63.

The male dominated Mutual Improvement Societies, as well as the Mechanics Institutes were challenged by working-class women, who were generally excluded from the groups until the later 1800s.

> [Alice Foley] complained that when her husband brought home fellow students from the Working Men's College, 'If we asked questions, we heard about Algebra, Shakespeare, or Red Sandstone. What these things were we had no idea; nor did our lords and masters seem to know enough about them to be able to explain them in simple words that we could understand. All that we learned from the conversation of the learned Collegians on Sundays was, that all the teachers of some sort of classes wore double-breasted waistcoats and Albert watchguards of the same pattern. We women felt, naturally, not quite satisfied with this.'[34]

Alice Foley's objections to the self-made 'learned Collegiate' have several implications. The men, jumping ahead of the elementary building blocks of various disciplines, are seen snatching at complex forms of discourse; for Foley, they have developed a more or less arbitrary system of understandings and analysis, in which terms are invested with great meaning – which may or may not meet up with the meanings these terms have developed in professionalized intellectual occupations. Alice sees through this assumption of intellectual prowess – however hard won – through her own exclusion, which presents itself as the condescension of the men.

---

34   Ibid., p.76.

As well as the Mechanics Institutes there were other forms of self-education developing out of the growing workers' movement. Owenism was one example in which women played a central role.

> Like subsequent working-class movements they adopted the Methodist system of class meetings, informal gatherings where a class leader would set off discussion and everyone participate in the debate. Women were not excluded. In Huddersfield for instance in 1838 the Owenite classes included wives and female friends and relatives. Owenite Hans [sic] of Science provided a radical alternative to the Mechanics Institutes patronised by employers and Owenites pioneered co-operative infant and nursery schools where the children were taught not by a system of terror, rewards and punishments, but by making learning pleasurable.[35]

A complex self-organised intellectual culture was integral to Chartism. Although votes for women were not part of hegemonic Chartist demands, women also played a key role in the organisation of this culture, particularly in organising education for participants.

> Chartism, the mass working-class movement of the 1830's and 1840's, with its demands for full political representation and a People's Parliament, was not only accompanied by distinct cultural activities but also did not make, and refused to make,

---

35   Sheila Rowbotham, *Hidden from History: 300 Years of Women, Oppression and the Fight Against It*, London: Pluto Press, 1975. Excerpts available at: http://www.marxists.org/subject/women/ authors/rowbotham-sheila/hidden-history.htm

distinctions between the 'political' and the 'cultural'. A distinct Chartist world was constructed, based on a positive rejection of the existing forms and institutions: radical bookshops, coffee shops, a vigorous press (which easily outsold the 'establishment press') and reading rooms which often promoted public readings of news, of poetry, of serialised novels.[36]

The conditions for autodidact activity were not everywhere as favourable as they were for some sections of the working class. Some degree of education was becoming a criteria for particular forms of labour. Weavers and miners' employers expected them to be educated, and these workers' co-operative educational institutions – libraries, reading societies, etc – fed to an extent these expectations, while the self-organised basis of these centres put them in a productive tension with their employers.

Pamphleteering

E.P. Thompson followed the development of autodidact activity, its innovative readings and discussions, into the practice of pamphleteering in the late 18th century. This was the period of revolution in Haiti, France and America; the combination of internal and international revolt led the Pitt government, terrified of the prospect of revolution in what was then known as the Kingdom of Great Britain, to organise a pronounced suppression of dissent through a combination of measures. The Suspension of Habeas Corpus Act, allowing arrest and indefinite detention without charge, was formally enacted on 16 May 1794 until July 1795. It was revived from

---

36   Anon, *The Republic of Letters*, London: Comedia/Minority Press Group, undated c.1983, p.68.

STEEL LOZENGES

will stop their pain,
And set the Constitution
right again.

My L—ds and G—tl—n,
The foreign powers
Write me word frequently
that they are ours,
Most truly and sincerely,
in compliance

George Cruikshank, Man in the Moon with Fifteen Cuts, c.1820.

April 1798 to March 1801. The army was consolidated into a networked system of barracks, 'so as to prevent contact between the people and the soldiers, who had formerly been billeted in houses and inns'.[37] Industrial areas, according to A.L. Morton, resembled 'a country in the hands of an army of

---

37   A.L. Morton, *A People's History of England*, London: Lawrence & Wishart, 1999, p.299.

occupation'.[38] Added to this, loyalists among the population, such as the 'Church and King' mob, were sponsored by the state to attack dissenters. In this growing climate of repression, we can see how the public distribution of knowledge was subject to working class contestation, as E.P. Thompson notes:

> In this way a reading public which was increasingly working class in character was forced to organize itself [...] The war and post-war years had seen a 'kept' press, on the one hand, and a Radical press on the other. In the Twenties much of the middle-class press freed itself from direct government influence, and made use of some of the advantages that Cobbett and Carlile had gained. *The Times* and Lord Brougham, who disliked the 'pauper press' [...] gave to the term 'Radicalism' a quite different meaning – free trade, cheap government, and utilitarian reform. To some degree [...] they carried the Radical middle-class with them [...].

> So that by 1832 there were two Radical publics: the middle-class, which looked forward to the Anti-Corn Law League, and the working class, whose journalists [...] were already maturing into the Chartist movement [...] the dividing line came to be, increasingly, not alternative 'reform' strategies [...] but alternative notions of political economy. The touchstone can be seen during the field labourer's 'revolt' in 1830, when *The Times* (Cobbett's 'BLOODY OLD TIMES') led the demand for salutary examples to be made of the rioters, while both Cobbett and Carlile were prosecuted once again on charges of inflammatory writing.

> In the contest between 1792 and 1836 the artisans and workers

---

38   Ibid., p.299.

made this tradition peculiarly their own, adding to the claim for free speech and thought their own claim for the untrammelled propagation, in the cheapest possible form, of the products of this thought.[39]

A specific obstacle to the radical press was a series of Stamp Acts, the earliest of which was passed in 1724. According to Ken Worpole, this made the printing of 'fact', reportage or news expensive both to publish and to buy.

Until the 1724 Stamp Act [...] most broadsheet or magazine publications hardly ever distinguished the factual from the fictional. What are wholly distinct categories of writing for us today were then part of a single literary discourse. The Stamp Act unintentionally forced publishers to distinguish the two since the Act put a tax on news and left all other forms of writing intact.[40]

Radical publishers got around this distinction by calling upon the fictional, the satirical and the imaginary to convey news, analysis and polemics. This suggests that their methods were not unfamiliar to their readers, or those who heard their works read out in the alehouses, meeting places and workshops by those who could read. Indeed in the history of working class intellectual culture there were many points of conflict around those who believed that techniques found in fiction would somehow prevent working class readers from seeing the truth of their situation, or indeed that they could not grasp literary allusions.

---

39   *The Making of the English Working Class*, op. cit., p.817.
40   Ken Worpole, *Dockers and Detectives*, London: Verso, 1983, p.14.

Richard Carlile, the intrepid and highly energetic 19th Century publisher and bookseller described himself as 'an implacable enemy of all fiction, allegory, personification and romance'. Despite many periods of imprisonment during 'the war of the unstamped press' in the early part of that century, it does seem likely that given the opportunity Carlile might well have become a quite ruthless censor himself.[41]

What really counted in the pamphleteering culture of the late-18th century was not just the mode of address, or the radicalism of the ideas, but also their dissemination. Later Stamp Acts, passed in the context of increased government repression between the 1770s and 1819, clamped down further on the ability to print and circulate materials. This however led to the development of innovative methods to get around the law, which helped further expand the circulation of 'seditious' materials.

[...] a series of Stamp Acts [...] attempted to take printed materials out of the hands of the working class by making the paper used in books so expensive that the 'cover price' of a book or journal would be far beyond the means of an average individual. There were a variety of responses to this: coffee houses, where one could go, have a drink and read a journal or magazine subscribed to 'by the house' for a fee smaller than the cover price of the journal, reading societies and subscription societies, in which a group of individuals pooled economic resources to purchase a book or journal in common, and frequently read it aloud to one another, and alternate media: radical tracts were published on all sorts of material, including muslin and other cloth, which

---

41   Ibid., p.17.

was not taxed, and some publishers sold other objects (like straw, matches and rocks), and gave away the printed material as a 'bonus' to people buying the other item, thus evading the letter of the law entirely.[42]

Without Contraries is No Progression

Two figures, Thomas Spence and Robert Wedderburn, who have been unjustly sidelined, provide us with innovative and important contributions to pamphleteering and the dissemination of dissent in the late-18th and early-19th century. Wedderburn's biographer, Martin Hoyles, surveys the scene at the agitator's dissenting Unitarian Chapel in Hopkins Street, Soho, in August 1819:

> In one corner stood some bales of hay which had obviously been sat upon, providing a balcony view of the proceedings. The walls were covered in slogans, daubed in bright colours:
>
> EXUBERANCE IS BEAUTY
>
> AN HOUR OF VIRTUOUS LIBERTY IS WORTH A WHOLE ETERNITY OF BONDAGE
>
> WITHOUT CONTRARIES IS NO PROGRESSION
> UNIVERSAL SUFFRAGE AND ANNUAL
> PARLIAMENTS
> KNOWLEDGE IS POWER

---

42   Marc Demarest, *Controlling Dissemination Mechanisms: The Unstamped Press and the 'Net,* http://www.noumenal.com/marc/unstamped.html

> OUR RIGHTS – PEACABLY IF WE MAY,
> FORCIBLY IF WE MUST.
>
> There were a few benches in the room and at one end a table
> standing on a dias. Behind this were hung pictures of Tom
> Paine and Toussaint L'Ouverture and beside them several flags
> – a skull and crossbones, a red, white and green tricolour, and a
> red flag.[43]

We have no way of knowing for sure if the chapel really
looked or sounded like this. Much of the information on
Wedderburn comes to us by way of the evidence of police spies
and informers who heavily infiltrated extra-parliamentary
movements in the 18th and 19th centuries, and is probably
embellished by Hoyle. But Wedderburn was clearly operating
on a different level to many of his contemporaries. The overt
internationalism is striking in the context of working class
agitation, which historians traditionally perceived to be
limited to national and racial boundaries. Wedderburn not
only placed the Haitian revolution at the forefront of world
revolution, he also believed that mass uprisings in the West
Indies would be accompanied by proletarian revolution in
Europe. Important too is the notion of both the necessity of
struggle, and the conflicts that take place *within* struggles.
Lastly there is the projected wholeness of the subject, invoked
by the use of legendary artist William Blake's famous poem,
The Marriage between Heaven and Hell.

Palestinian-Lebanese-American scholar, Saree Makdisi,
in his exploration of Blake's critical position in relation to
what he perceived as the 'narrow conception of freedom'

---

43   Martin Hoyles, *The Axe Laid to the Root: The Story of Robert Wedderburn*, London: Hansib, 2004, p.60.

evidenced in the radicalism of the 1790s, unpicks the dynamic through which writers and activists struggled for hegemony over the form and content of dissent, in the process setting aside some ideas and practices as legitimate and others as illegitimate.

> The presence of a strand of radicalism that sought to rise above the fray and to assert its own legitimacy, partly by making its own claims on 'respectable' political discourse, partly by denying, excluding, and disassociating itself from other forms and subcultures of radicalism (which it regarded as inarticulate, unrespectable, unenlightened, and hence illegitimate), and partly by working to assimilate as many grievances as possible into its own agenda for reform, re-articulating them when necessary – and thereby exercising, in effect, a form of hegemony, albeit one whose dominance was still very much in question at the time and would fade altogether amid the deepening crises of 1796-97, only to return early in the nineteenth century... [Later allowing] historians to conclude that 'radicalism' at the end of the eighteenth century primarily meant a wish to reform a corrupt parliament and to extend the franchise.[44]

Silvia Federici has noted that until the 18th century,

> When the populace appealed to reason, it was to voice anti-authoritarian demands, since self-mastery at the popular level meant the rejection of the established authority, rather than the interiorisation of social rule.[45]

---

44 Saree Makdisi, *William Blake and the Impossible History of the 1790s,* Chicago: University of Chicago Press, 2003, p.301.

45 *Caliban and the Witch,* op. cit., p.152.

Whereas, as Makdisi points out, a new breed of radical saw an opportunity to appeal both to the new conceptions of self and society that accompanied the growth of capitalism, and insert their own demands and criticisms into the making of the modern world. Among radical leaders a tendency to appeal to order so as to shape it, was the product of a complex of factors: partly a reaction to state suppression of dissent; partly to dissociate themselves from conservative criticism, which tended to conflate the different strands of the radical movement. This led to a tendency for activists struggling for hegemony to rein in the extent of their demands, creating in the process a basic dichotomy between respectable and unrespectable activism.

> The leaderships of the various radical societies tried to steer a determined course away from the spectacle of mob violence and levelling so often imputed to them by conservative and reactionary writers, for whom 'republicanism' and 'levelling' were the same thing, both equally reminiscent of the madness of the seventeenth century; and hence they had to steer away from more enthusiastic and plebeian forms of radicalism. Whether real or imagined, actual or potential, this tension between what the organized radical movements repeatedly declared themselves to be – movements for political equality in a properly bourgeois sense, and hence for strictly individual representational right – and what in the eyes of some they threatened to become – movements for economic equality, and hence collective rights, mob rule, sans culotte levelling, and so on – was a highly significant feature of the 1790s radicalism and the conservative response to it.[46]

---

46   *William Blake and the Impossible History of the 1790s,* op. cit., p.27.

In Makdisi's estimation, this reflected the broader development of a narrow, orientalist conception of the subject criticised by Blake.

> The relationship among moral virtue, choice, freedom, and self-regulation that was developed in much of the radical discourse of the 1790s, and in romanticism itself, was profoundly Orientalist in nature – to an extent that has hitherto gone almost entirely unrecognized in scholarship. As much in the work of Wordsworth or Coleridge as in that of Paine or Thelwall, this discourse sought to authorize a modern Western set of values, a modern Western sense of citizenship, above all a modern Western sense of self, as against what it perceived to be an Oriental culture supposedly incompatible with and hostile to all those values.[47]

Thomas Spence and Robert Wedderburn were less disposed to mobilise the contradictions of their age as successfully as better known writers and activists such as Thomas Paine, Olaudah Equiano or Mary Wollstonecraft, whom, as Makdisi points out, appealed to influence and bourgeois democracy, as part of their strategy. We should remember that to 'rise above the fray' for these latter figures was by no means an easy matter in itself. It involved complex acts of self-construction, ambivalence, the smuggling of deep conflicts under acceptable speech, and some measure of difficult transcendence of long held and justified resentments, as we will discuss in chapter 5 on the 'authenticity and ambiguity' of Olaudah Equiano. Sheila Rowbotham unpicks the contradictions in Wollstonecraft's seminal feminist discourse:

---

47   Ibid., p.4.

Ironically, it is only by acquiring a bourgeois state of mind, submitting to the discipline of methodical and regular work, the exact and synchronised time-spirit, the rejection of custom, the delight in innovation, technological and intellectual, that women can cast off their traditional fetters [...] there are many aspects of her radicalism which are quite hostile to the way capitalism was already breaking humanity into method [...] but she is fastened in her own dilemma: how to shatter a whole system of domination with no social basis for a movement of the oppressed. She knew education alone could not end the oppression of women because it could not really be of a different kind until 'society be differently constituted'.[48]

Peter Linebaugh paints Tom Paine as a very ambivalent or torn figure, both a 'planetary revolutionary' and an 'adjunct to the bourgeois revolution':

His own soul was divided; so has been his legacy [...]. While he gave voice to the age, he would bend, if not kneel, to power. Power and Empire have claimed him as one of their own [...]. As a patriot, as a citizen, as a populist, was Paine not an adjunct to the bourgeois revolution? We must take a fresh look. [...] In relation to power, Paine's life and thought was [...] divided. He took part in three attempts at revolution: in America and France it succeeded while in Britain it failed. He was a class-conscious man, sensitive to the differences of power and money. He wrote and spoke for the common people. You see this in his first major writing, which is about the central capitalist relation, the wage; you see it also in his last major writing, which is

---

48   Sheila Rowbotham, *Women, Resistance and Revolution*, London: Penguin Books, 1974, pp.44-45.

about commoning. The Case of the Excise Officers denounced the relations of money and wages, while Agrarian Justice called for social reparations for class injustice. It is between these two major concerns that we place Paine's concepts of revolution and constitution.[49]

Linebaugh goes on to unpick the unheard legacies, struggles and contrary voices that informed Paine's work, and which were also drawn upon by maligned radicals such as Spence and Wedderburn. The latter had their own aspirations toward a different world, and wanted to compete with and influence the 'top layer' of radicalism. Although often fondly regarded by their peers, they were generally sidelined as 'disrespectable levellers' and found a support network and coterie of like-minded thinkers in the alehouses and workshops. To some extent they played up to the encroaching divisions between activists, revelling in their own notoriety.

A history from below has a duty to reanimate and reconstruct these differences and better understand how the terrain of dissent might function; ideas living or dying by their currency and the ability of actors to propagate their value and somehow enact the worlds they seek to create.

The Currency of Dissent

Although friction with the external world causes other entities to lose their idealism, the coin becomes increasingly ideal as a result of practice. The disparity between its nominal content and its real content, brought about by the process

---

49 Peter Linebaugh, 'Introduction to the works of Thomas Paine, Rights of Man and The Commonwealth', http://libcom.org/history/peter-linebaughs-new-introduction-works-thomas-paine

1773 halfpenny counter-marked by Thomas Spence.

of circulation itself, has been taken advantage of both by governments and individual adventurers who debased the coinage in a variety of ways.[50]

Thomas Spence's story certainly takes in idealism, friction with the external world, and some fascinating interventions into the circulation of ideas. Spence was born on Newcastle's quayside in 1750, the son of impoverished Scottish immigrants, a net maker and stocking seller. One of nineteen children, Spence grew up in a dissenter religious family; reading the bible at his parents' stalls on the quayside he was taught to question his readings, igniting his active intelligence and imagination. Spence became a clerk, and later an English teacher in a grammar school, before setting up his own school where he lived.

Spence had been exposed to dissenting currents all his life. The town was full of people dispossessed by the Highland Clearances. French Jacobins visited and gave lectures. In 1771, the sale of 89 acres of Newcastle Town

---

50   Karl Marx, *Preface to A Contribution to the Critique of Political Economy*, http://www.marxists.org/archive/marx/works/1859/critique-pol-economy/preface.htm

Moor to builders was successfully challenged by the town freemen, greatly influencing the development of Spence's ideas for land reform and common ownership, which he developed into a plan he continued to tinker with throughout his life. Through contacts in the church, he was able to make an address to the Newcastle Philosophical Society, Property in Land, in 1775. Believing that 'the right to deprive anything of the means of living supposes a right to deprive it of life'[51], Spence laid out a new social system.

1. The end of aristocracy and landlords;
2. All land should be publicly owned by 'democratic parishes', which should be largely self-governing;
3. Rents of land in parishes to be shared equally amongst parishioners;
4. Universal suffrage (including female suffrage) at both parish level and through a system of deputies elected by parishes to a national senate;
5. A social guarantee extended to provide income for those unable to work;
6. The rights of infants to be free from abuse and poverty.[52]

The parish rents would go toward free healthcare, childcare and libraries. In his advocacy for women and children, Spence was possibly alone among male radicals. Sheila Rowbotham suggests Spence recognised that political reform might not alter family relations and that economic change and a change in family life and the reproduction of labour should

---

51   Thomas Spence quoted in Olive Durant Rudkin, *Thomas Spence and His Connections*, New York: Augustus M. Kelley Publishers, 1966, p.38.

52   'Thomas Spence', http://en.wikipedia.org/wiki/Thomas_Spence

go hand in hand.

> What signifies Reforms of government or Redress of Public
> Grievances, if people cannot have their domestic grievances
> redressed.[53]

Spence was promptly kicked out of the Newcastle
Philosophical Institution. Spence's biographer Olive Rudd
argues that Spence had a counter-productive tendency to
irritate people who might have helped him develop his
arguments and perhaps elevate him to a position of influence.
But we can also see that Spence's actions followed their own
logic. The real reason for Spence's expulsion seems to have
been that he began selling his address as a cheap handbill on
the streets of Newcastle, thereby sidelining the Institution
and entering the fray of popular discourse. This was also the
beginning of Spence's full time commitment to political
agitation, which saw him imprisoned in London's Newgate
Gaol several times for sedition under the Suspension of
Habeas Corpus. Spence moved to London in 1792, having lost
his school and his marriage due to his increasing irascibility
and dedication to his Plan. He opened a stall on Chancery
Lane, and later a shop called The Hive of Liberty on Little
Turnstile, Holborn, distributing political pamphlets and a
hot drink with Turkish roots, drawn from orchid tubers,
called Saloop. The sale of Saloop may have been intended
to get around the Stamp Acts. It has been pointed out that
Spence's parochial fixation on land as the principle object
of power and its appropriation, was both short-sighted and
nostalgic, and unsuited to his audience of urban workers. But

---

53   Thomas Spence quoted in *Hidden from History*, op. cit., p.22.

in a typically reparative reading, Linebaugh argues Spence's readers understood that,

> Agrarian communism was really a communism that included all capital – the mines, the potheads, the canals, the ships, the machines [...] The struggle to preserve the commons was not restricted to the common rights of field, wood and copse, but belonged also to workshop, mine and wharf.[54]

Spence's communism looked forward to the future – Marx and Engels held him in fond regard – and this has made him a marginal but well-regarded figure in some quarters. He was honoured with a plaque on Newcastle Quayside by the City Council in June 2010. His communism was deemed 'impossible' in the context of his times. Despite this, he picked up a movement of followers known as the Spencean Philanthropists who upheld his legacy into the 1820s, breaking off to join groups including the national radical association headed by Henry 'Orator' Hunt, as well as inspiring some ill-fated attempts at armed insurrection.

Spence also contributed to a rich vein of thought on debt and communisation that continues to this day. Linebaugh situates Spence in a long tradition of pan-Atlantic struggle against slavery, enclosure and debt animated by the Biblical trope of 'Jubilee' – cyclical debt forgiveness – and developed, as we shall see, by Spence's peer Robert Wedderburn amongst others. Spence's Jubilee hymn, to the tune of *God Save the King*, derives from his critical reading of Leviticus

---

54   Peter Linebaugh, 'Jubilating; Or, How the Atlantic Working Class Used the Biblical Jubilee Against Capitalism, With Some Success', Midnight Notes 10, 1990 p.89.

as a younger man. Spence thought Moses' designation of a 'Jubilee day' every seven years 'childish', arguing that emancipation should happen once and for all. We might argue that Spence's own view was a bit naïve. But the Jubilee hymn gives us a chance to reconsider this legacy:

Hark how the trumpet's sound
Proclaims the land around
    The Jubilee!
Tells all the poor oppress'd
No more they shall be
Nor landlords more molest
Their property.[55]

The Jubilee continues to be invoked by organisations pressing for debt relief, such as: Jubilee 2000, 'an international coalition [...] that called for cancellation of third world debt by the year 2000'; the anti-debtors movements in Latin America, and resistance of Latin American governments to Structural Adjustment Policies by the World Bank and International Monetary Fund; Occupy's Strike Debt Campaign, which in the U.S. seeks to mobilise an 'invisible army' of those who are already in debt default, by necessity or choice, for instance by collectively buying up debt that is in default in order to abolish it in a 'Rolling Jubilee'.[56] The idea of a debt jubilee has come under criticism as a brake that keeps capital's motor

---

55 'Jubilee – the trumpet shall sound', *History is Made at Night*: http://history-is-made-at-night.blogspot.co.uk/2010/10/jubilee-trumpet-shall-sound.htm

56 Nicholad Smirzoeff, Back to organising, http://www.nicholasmirzoeff.com/02012/category/strike-debt/

running. Linebaugh argues that Atlantic Jubilee need not be taken literally as a demand upon the state and financial capital – nor as an invocation of some biblical law – but is instead an active movement to resist their domination from below.

> A prevailing view is that the Jubilee was an anti-accumulation device, similar to the potlach or the carnival, in that it actually preserved accumulation. In placing restrictions on debt, slavery, and landownership, jubilee strengthened a social system based upon money, credit and exploitation [...] [however, this] reduces justice to the opinion of judges [...] Jubilee language is neither legal insistence nor didactic proposal. 'It is a linguistic act that continues to have dangerous power in all sorts of contexts that are neither legislative nor didactic', Sharon Ringe argues. Its meaning is explicated through the experiences and struggles of the oppressed [...] The year of the Lords favor, all commentators agree, is the jubilee [...] It is clear from this passage that jubilee is not a social-democratic deal of laws to preserve a system of commodity exchange against periodic revolt. [...] The class no longer begs for reforms; it demands justice.[57]

George Caffentzis, a fellow contributor with Linebaugh to the Midnight Notes collective, has called in recent writings, for an international 'debtor's cartel'.

> Debt repayment depends upon isolating and making the debtor feel both morally ashamed and practically vulnerable. Once the debtors are united, however, they can 'turn the tables' on the creditors and liberate themselves. We can see why debtors'

---

57   Ibid., p.84.

solidarity is a path to liberation, because debt is not simply a way for a creditor to get rich, but in the world of contemporary capitalism, it is a way of controlling individuals', societies' and governments behaviour. The whole desire of getting out of debt is not simply to have more disposable income, but to liberate yourself from the control of creditors![58]

Moreover, Spence's techniques for distributing his ideas were startlingly innovative and provoke a shock of recognition in a modern context. In his own way he piggy-backed upon the knowledge and fame of others. Spence distributed Thomas Paine's enormously popular book, *The Rights of Man*, and (possibly deliberately) contributed to the historical controversy over who first wrote a book of that name.

Spence claimed that he was the first writer to use the phrase 'the Rights of Man'. Visiting a miner who had retired to live on Marsden Rock in 1780 to escape from a landlord, he chalked over the hearth:

Ye landlords vile, whose man's place mar
Come levy rents here if you can, Your steward and lawyers
I defy
And live with all the Rights of Man.[59]

His own active participation in producing confusion over this matter not only boosted the sale of his own works but also situates him in a reading-writing relationship to Paines work and ideas.

58 George Caffentzis, 'Summer 2012, A Report from Greece', http://uninomade.org/report-from-greece/

59 Mary Kemp-Ashraf, 'An Annotated Bibliography of the Works of Thomas Spence', http://thomas-spence-society.co.uk/5.html

Young Man: I hear there is another RIGHTS OF MAN by
Spence, that goes farther than Paines.
Old Man: Yet it goes no farther than it ought.
Y.M: I understand it suffers no private Property in Land, but
gives it all to the Parishes.
O.M.: In so doing it does right, the earth was not made for
Individuals.[60]

Spence published a journal called *Pigs Meat or Lessons for the
Swinish Multitude*. The title played on the words of Edmund
Burke who had referred to the lower classes as 'the swinish
multitude' in his pamphlet, *Reflections on the French Revolution*.
What may seem like an ironic appropriation could be thrown
into question by the revelation that Spence sometimes
detested his fellow man as 'despicable willing slaves'.[61]
He certainly drew on a current adopted by contemporary
pamphleteers: other popular titles of the time included
'Hogswash', 'Mast & Acorns: collected by Old Hubert', 'Politics
for the People: salmagundy for swine' (with contributions
from Brother Grunter and Porculus).

Regardless of porcine slurs, the journal reveals the very
process of learning, questioning, collecting and rejecting
that informed the 18th century self-taught radical. *Pigs Meat*
begins, 'A good editor is better than a bad author', and goes
on to piece together fragments from texts Spence had been
collecting from books and newspapers since his childhood,
together with his own polemics in song. In this respect,
Spence's work as an editor and re-publisher of texts explicitly

---

60   Thomas Spence, *The End of Oppression*, (first published 1795), http://
      thomas-spence-society.co.uk/7.htm

61   *Thomas Spence and His Connections*, op. cit., p.47.

performs the bricolage intellectual culture in which better known radicals such as Mary Wollstonecraft and Thomas Paine synthesised their ideas. As with these figures, bricolage tends toward additive, connective and reparative culture, as well as dialectical thought and practice.

Lastly, an aspect of Spence's materialist practice is worth retrieving in this context; a practice which quite literally tried to give his ideas currency and keep them in circulation. Spence minted his own coins and defaced existing ones. In the late 18th century there was a shortage of small coinage, and many workers wages were unevenly split between other forms of payment. Payment in kind, credit, customary rights to the trimmings of the workplace, and taking material goods they could glean formed the subsistence of many. While counterfeiting met harsh punishments, until 1796 the government generally turned a blind eye to the production of unofficial coins and tokens. Spence somehow acquired the equipment to make 27 stamps for counter-marking existing currency with a combination of words and phrases from his *Plan*.

These coins must have been intended to re-enter circulation, but they also picked up a notoriety value which may have made them attractive to some collectors. Alongside his pamphlets, Spence sold (and authored) books on coin-collecting. Spence is also said to have thrown handfuls of coins out of his window to passers-by. Another run of coins used the technique of 'muling', where the design of a coin is different on both sides, and turning the coin links disparate images in the mind. So many of these two-sided coins were produced, with endless variations between messages, that the *Gentleman's Magazine* put them 'almost beyond the powers of calculation'.[62]

Truth, Self-Supported

Robert Wedderburn (1762-1834) was born on the Bluecastle Estate in Jamaica. His mother Rosanna, was initially owned by Lady Douglas as a maid. Robert Wedderburn's father, James Wedderburn, descended from a landed Scottish family who lost their wealth in the Jacobite Rebellion, was the owner of one of the largest sugar plantations. Wedderburn senior bought Rosanna from Lady Douglas through deception via a fellow doctor, when Rosanna made it clear she would refuse to be bought by him. Once installed as Wedderburn's housekeeper, Rosanna in common with other female slaves on the plantation was subjected to repeated physical and sexual abuse. On her third pregnancy, her rebellion against her 'master' eventually persuaded James Wedderburn to sell her back to Lady Douglas on stipulation that her child be born free.

From the age of five, Robert Wedderburn was looked after by his grandmother Talkee Amy, an African-born enslaved woman who sold her master Joseph Payne's 'cheese, checks, chintz, gingerbread, milk etc.'[63] and acted as a smugglers agent in Kingston. Amy was a great influence on Wedderburn, pressing upon him his African heritage and teaching him the Obeah traditions. Obeah is believed to have originated among the Ashanti and Koromantin tribes of Africa, and was circulating among slaves in the Carribean

---

62   John Barrell, 'Radicalism, Visual Culture, and Spectacle in the 1790s', http://www.erudit.org/revue/ron/2007/v/n46/016131ar.html

63   *The Horrors of Slavery*, op. cit., p.48.

from the 17th century. Obeah had a complex role to play in enslaved society - it helped transmit a sense of African heritage, and was the subject of both fear and protection for slaves, while actively providing a form of resistance to colonial powers. When Amy's master's smuggling ship was sunk, she was accused of witchcraft and flogged almost to death - a memory that, together with the treatment of his mother Rosanna, haunted Wedderburn's later writings. Amy also convinced Wedderburn of the need for slaves to create a common future by defending and extending the provision grounds they were allotted for the cultivation of their own crops. As Wedderburn would later declare:

> hold on to the land you now possess as slaves; for without that, freedom is not worth possessing; for if you once give up the possession of your lands, your oppressors will have power to starve you to death, through making laws for their own accommodation; which will force you to commit crimes in order to obtain subsistence; as the landholders in Europe are serving those dispossessed of lands; for it is a fact, that thousands of families are now in a starving state; the prisons are full: humanity impells the executive power to withdraw the sentence of death on criminals, whilst the landholders, in fact, are surrounded with every necessity of life.[64]

For a time enslaved women like Amy came to almost monopolise the islands' internal economies, as Silvia Federici points out:

---

64   *The Horrors of Slavery*, op. cit., p.82.

Their main achievement was the development of a politics of self-reliance, grounded in survival strategies and female networks [...] They created not only a new female African identity, but also the foundations for a new society committed - against the capitalist attempt to impose scarcity and dependence as structural conditions of life - to the reappropriation and concentration in women's hands of the fundamental means of subsistence, starting from the land, the production of food, and the inter-generational transmission of knowledge and cooperation.[65]

Wedderburn joined the navy and travelled to London in 1779, where he moved among a group of immigrants – black, Irish and Jewish – known as the London Blackbirds, who made a living as 'musicians, actors, street entertainers, prize fighters, casual labourers, and thieves'[66] in the area around St Giles in the Fields. In 1785, Wedderburn converted to Methodism at Seven Dials. He eventually broke away from Methodism for its preaching of passive obedience to slaves, despite its founder John Wesley's opposition to slavery.

Which is the greater crime, to preach passive obedience to the Poor Black Slaves [...] or to extort from them at the rate of £18,000 per annum under the pretence of supporting the Gospel?[67]

Working his way through the scriptures, Wedderburn eventually became a licensed dissenting preacher. A strong

---

65   *Caliban and the Witch*, op. cit., p.115.
66   *The Horrors of Slavery*, op. cit., p.7.
67   Robert Wedderburn quoted in Peter Fryer, *Staying Power: The History of Black People in Britain*, London: Pluto Press, 1984, p.224.

example of the complex role of religion in the dissenting currents of his times, for Wedderburn, the scriptures were to become a revolutionary toolbox and a means of conveying political dissent. He first met Thomas Spence in around 1813 at the age of fifty, a year before Spence's death. The Spencean Philanthropists, a group of activists gathered around Spence, were one of the few radical organisations to continue throughout the repression of dissent in the early 19th century. By 1817, just as an Act of Parliament was passed to outlaw the group, Wedderburn had become the de facto head of the Spencean Philanthropists. He began publishing his own journal, *The Axe Laid to the Root, or a Fatal Blow to the Oppressors, Being an Address to the Planters and Negroes of the Island of Jamaica* which added Spencean ideas on the redistribution of land and property to fierce attacks on colonial slavery. *The Axe*, in common with much of Wedderburn's practices of dissent, was dependent on oral and not just literary modes of address. Ian McCalman argues that the journal was intended to be read out loud to a multicultural, semi-literate working class audience in London's alehouses and workshops.

> Its impact must also have been enhanced by Wedderburn's skilful incorporation of other familiar plebian modes such as melodramatic balladry, Bunyanesque dream visions and humorous burlesque.[68]

Central to *The Axe Laid to the Root* is the correspondence between Wedderburn and a character he says is his half-sister, Elizabeth Campbell, heir to the plantation to which

---

68   Ian McCalman (ed.), *The Horrors of Slavery and Other Writings by Robert Wedderburn*, Princeton: Markus Weiner Publishers, 1997, p.18.

his mother Rosanna was eventually sold. Ian McCalman asserts that the letters are most probably fictitious, although Elizabeth Campbell is said to have existed; Peter Linebaugh and Peter Fryer take them to be true. Wedderburn asks Campbell to set her slaves free, reminding her of her Maroon ancestry. Campbell's response suggests that *The Axe Laid to the Root*, along with issues of *Cobbett's Political Register*, are being read by the free mulattos of Kingston, a fascinating detail if true. *The Axe*'s lucid, dramatic dual address to the enslaved people and planters of the West Indies, and the London radicals, artisans and unemployed, afforded an international dimension to dissent that was rare in English working class radicalism. Wedderburn, like Spence, put great value on a multiplicity of registers and meanings, while developing a core argument against slavery and capitalism and for non-hierachical democracies based on the ownership of land in common. He informed his audience about the Maroons' resistance to slavery and the revolution enacted by the enslaved people of Haiti. He also drew upon older currencies of dissent, such as William Cobbett's invocation of 'Old Corruption', a popular discourse analysed below by Alex Benchimol:

[...] a populist discourse struggling to come to terms with the complex totality of the new capitalist hegemony, using older symbols of political corruption to engage with the new abstractions of nineteenth century political economy. It was, by necessity, a cultural hybrid constructed in the plebian public sphere where 'Power used commercial hands but wore an aristocratic face', as Jon Klancher has put it.[69]

As Peter Fryer points out, the close relationship between religious and political dissent, religious rhetoric and political economy in Wedderburn's work eventually made it easier for the state to convict him. In 1820 he was jailed for two years, the initial charge of sedition – for asking his congregation at his Hopkins Street chapel whether it was right for a slave to kill his master – dropped in favour of 'blasphemous libel'. Wedderburn's defence, which apparently drew the admiration of the lord chief justice, made clear his class strategy for using biblical rhetoric.

> What, after all, is my crime? - it consists merely in having spoken in the same plain and homely language which Christ and his disciples uniformly used [...] There seems to be a conspiracy against the poor, to keep them in ignorance and superstition; the rich may have as many copies as they like of [...] sceptical writers [..] Am I to be condemned, when I find two pages in the Bible most palpably contradicting each other, for asserting that one of them must be a LIE?[70]

Wedderburn's relationship to his patron, George Cannon, reveals a problematic in the study of working class publishers. Much of his work while Wedderburn was in Dorchester State Prison was ghostwritten by Cannon, a shady character and

---

69   Alex Benchimol, *Intellectual Politics and Cultural Conflict in the Romantic Period: Scottish Whigs, English Radicals and the Making of the British Public Sphere*, Farnham: Ashgate Publishing Limited, 2010, p.166.

70   Robert Wedderburn quoted in *Staying Power: The History of Blacks in Britain*, op. cit., p.226.

later pornographer, who acted as Wedderburn's lawyer. It is unclear how much Cannon acted as ventriloquist, and how much Wedderburn inserted his own ideas into these publications. Historian Ian McCalman suggests George Cannon used Wedderburn – a much braver speaker – as a mouthpiece for furthering his own agenda. But it might also be possible that Wedderburn outsourced the work of making dissent legible in print to his acquaintance while he was in prison. One of his last works, *The Cast Iron Parsons*, is a remarkable satire on corruption, political economy, mechanisation and mechanical philosophy.

> Happening to pass the old church of St.Paul, Shadwell, in the county of Middlesex, when it was taking down, I asked the Churchwarden [...] whether the intended structure was to be of wood or stone? 'Of neither, he replied, but of CAST-IRON'. 'Would to God the Parson were of cast-iron too', exclaimed an old woman, who over heard our conversation. [...] Finding that the routine of duty required by the Clergy of the *legitimate* Church, was so completely mechanical, and that nothing was so much in vogue as the dispensing of human labour by the means of machinery, it struck me that it might one day be possible to substitute a CAST-IRON PARSON. [The advantages of the proposed plan] are threefold; - I. To religion. II. To society. III. To the state. [...] And is this not a most important consideration at a period when we can hardly keep our heads above water, and are threatened every moment either with bankruptcy or revolution?[71]

---

71   Robert Wedderburn, 'The Cast-Iron Parsons', in Ian McCalman (ed.), *The Horrors of Slavery and Other Writings*, Princeton: Markus Weiner Publishers, 1991, p.144.

Jubilee Hymn, Or, A Song to be Sung at the Commencement of the Millennium, if Not Sooner

Thomas Spence, reproduced in full in Peter Linebaugh, 'Jubilating; Or, How the Atlantic Working Class Used the Biblical Jubilee Against Capitalism, With Some Success', Midnight Notes 10, 1990, p.85. and available here, http://www.midnightnotes.org/pdfnewenc12.pdf

Hark! How the Trumpets Sound
Proclaims the Land around
The Jubilee!
Tells all the Poor oppress'd,
No more they shall be cess'd,
Nor landlords more molest
Their property.

Rents to ourselves we pay,
Dreading no Quarter-day,
Fraught with Distress.
Welcome that day draws near,
For then our rents we share,
Earths rightful Lords are we,
Ordain'd for this.

Now hath the Oppressor ceas'd
And all the World releas'd
From Misery!
The fir-trees all rejoice,
And Cedars lift their voice,
Ceas'd now the Fellar's noise,
Long rais'd by thee!

The Sceptre now is broke,
with which continual stroke,
The Nations smote!
Hell from beneath doth rise,
To meet thy Lofty Eyes,
From the most pompous size
Now brought to nought!

Since then this Jubilee
Sets all at Liberty
Let us be glad.
Behold each one return
To their right, and their own,
No more like Doves to mourn
By landlords sad!

AUTHENTICITY AND AMBIGUITY

Here we will explore some aspects of 'history from below' that demonstrate a conflict over the definition of 'authenticity', both in terms of historical evidence and sources, and of the self-construction and societal construction of historical subjects. We will look at the complex identifications of working class and/or subaltern subjects with and against dominant cultures, and the status of history as literature and/or 'fact'.

Romanticism and Myth

Marcus Rediker, remembering his grandfather, Fred Robertson, a Kentucky coal miner, identifies the passing of knowledge and stories between the static and travelling subject at the foundations of his and Peter Linebaugh's historical project.

> In his brilliant essay 'The Storyteller', Walter Benjamin explained that historically there have been two main types: the peasant storyteller who had a deep knowledge of locality and its lore, and the sailor storyteller who brought exotic tales from afar. My grandfather was, I suppose, a variant of the former; he helped me to understand the people I studied, the very embodiment of the latter.[1]

---

1   Marcus Rediker, 'The Poetics of History from Below', http://www. historians.org/perspectives/issues/2010/1009/1009art1.cfm

In Benjamin's original formulation:

> The actual extension of the realm of storytelling in its
> full historical breadth is inconceivable without the most
> intimate interpenetration of these two archaic types. Such an
> interpenetration was achieved particularly by the Middle Ages
> in their trade structure. The resident master craftsman and
> the traveling journeymen worked together in the same rooms;
> and every master had been a traveling journeyman before he
> settled down in his home town or somewhere else. If peasants
> and seamen were past masters of storytelling, the artisan class
> was its university. In it was combined the lore of faraway places,
> such as a much-traveled man brings home, with the lore of the
> past, as it best reveals itself to natives of a place.[2]

The use of poetic logic and the broad sweep of associations
made by Linebaugh and Rediker in their trans-Atlantic
histories, is an attempt to thread together geographically
remote, but economically and politically networked, points
in space and time. They take disparate events and struggles
and link them on the basis of scant evidence, often because
no sources, or only fragmentary sources, are available. They
aim to fill out context where there is none. This is the creative
work of the historian. With any historical event, the historian
must use his or her imagination to an extent, because with
all the evidence in the world we cannot account for the true
experience of its participants.

---

2   Walter Benjamin, 'The Storyteller: Reflections on the Works of Nikolai
     Leskov', *Walter Benjamin: 1935–1938 Volume 3: Selected Writings*,
     Boston: Harvard University Press, 2006, p.85.

Poetry can get the historian close to the experience and consciousness of working people and can evoke people, places, and events in multidimensional, dynamic ways. Sailor-poet James Field Stanfield crafted memorable, graphic images in his epic poem 'The Guinea Voyage' and in his grimly poetic letters about life aboard a slave ship. He described, for example, the second mate of his vessel, lying sick, near death, on the medicine chest, his long hair clotted with filth as it brushed the deck of the ship. He depicted the nightmarish enslavement, flogging, and eventual death of an African woman named Abyeda. Such images can arrest the reader as surely as a surrealist object, disclosing in poetic fashion important connections, relations, parallels, and unities. Christopher Hill once wrote, 'Good – imaginative – history is akin to retrospective poetry. It is about life as lived – as much of it as we can recapture.'[3]

In *The London Hanged*, Linebaugh argues for the inseparability of the literature of the times and the subjects which animated it; poetry and song were a valid and valuable part of the experience of the people who lived during the period Linebaugh studied.

The picaresque as a prose narrative with its episodic structure, its individualist attention to the protagonist, its structural resolution by accident, fate or fortune, was ill-suited to showing the collective power of the proletarian in the face of its many enemies or through the course of its history. Still it remains a valuable and symptomatic source of evidence. The contradiction between the individualism of picaresque presentation and the collectivism of proletarian experience is nowhere more evident

---

3   'The Poetics of History from Below', op. cit.

than in the life of a sailor, especially one about to be hanged [...].[4]

Anja Kirschner and David Panos' film, *The Last Days of Jack Sheppard* (2009), enters shared territory with Linebaugh's historical work, specifically *The London Hanged*.[5] Linebaugh reviewed the film in *Mute* magazine. In their response, Kirschner and Panos questioned the poetic logic of Linebaugh's work.

Having seen Peter Linebaugh talk in public last year we were struck by the way that his deployment of social history to articulate a contemporary sense of injustice sometimes means drawing continuities and connections which seemed to do some violence to their historical specificity and separateness. As Peter Linebaugh's article above perhaps shows, his associative approach can be inspiring and productive. We ourselves often take a similar approach to historical material in our work – by juxtaposing different epochs and genres in our films and riffing on images and symbols. But what might make for interesting poetic provocations in a fictional/filmic work of art might be more problematic in the writing of history.[6]

---

4   Peter Linebaugh, *The London Hanged: Crime and Civil Society in Eighteenth Century England*, London: Verso, p.122.

5   See The Last Days of Jack Sheppard, http://kirschner-panos.info/index.php?/projects/the-last-days-of-jack-sheppard-2009/

6   Anja Kirschner and David Panos, 'A Response to Peter Linebaugh', January 2010, http://www.metamute.org/community/your-posts/response-to-peter-linebaugh

Here Kirschner and Panos bring into tension the fictional and the factual and the designation of each domain to literature and history respectively. Their criticisms assume a harder division between the two, than may obtain in Linebaugh's work. The critique participates in an ordering of these forms which places (as in classical European education) history above literature in a hierarchy of reason. Linebaugh responded to the filmmakers' criticisms:

> The film makers call my historical treatment romantic [...] History changes as we learn more about our past, and what was once a romantic ideal has a way of becoming empirical facts, but it takes some digging to establish them. That is the historical labor. I am not interested in projecting back but in bringing forward, forward to Sheppard, and forward from Sheppard.
>
> The social bandit is given the picaresque biography or the subject matter can dictate the form of presentation. As we become aware of this, the form becomes as important a subject as the material was to begin with. This is an important stage in research, and the historian learns to describe the evidence and interpretations in an historiographical introduction before returning to the subject, which is the bandit not the picaresque. There is an interplay between evidence and story. The means has replaced the material, form over content, the signifier over the signified, the documents over the story. What has happened in this film is that the traditional relation is inverted and the story becomes the document.[7]

---

7   Peter Linebaugh, 'Jack's Back! In the Movies at last!', http://www. metamute.org/editorial/articles/jacks-back-movies-last

Further criticism from Kirschner and Panos towards Linebaugh concerns his reconstruction of Jack Sheppard as an exemplar of proletarian subjectivity from documents which were quite probably falsified by his publishers. It might be very difficult if not impossible to pick apart Jack's own thought from its mediation through the years. The artists accuse Linebaugh of claiming authenticity where it is inappropriate.

> Our intention was to present a double aspect to many of the themes in the Jack Sheppard story: Jack is held up both as a symbol of working class desire and irrepressibility AND a mythologised figure that is so resonant of his time that upper class mediators try to use his story to think through their own problems. We are also very interested in how such semi-mythical constructions around an event or character can become operative in political struggles, sometimes in a progressive way.[8]

The debate is extremely constructive because myth making is part of the self-creation of social movements.

> Such mythological figures [as Ned Ludd], like the porter in *Macbeth*, open the gates to history from below. English history is replete with them – Robin Hood, Piers Ploughman, Lady Skimmington, Captain Swing for example – and so is Irish history especially in this period (1811-12) when Captain Knockabout or Captain Rock joined Ned Ludd as anonymous, avenging avatars who meted out

---

8   Anja Kirschner and David Panos, 'A Response to Peter Linebaugh', *Mute*, 27 January 2010, http://www.metamute.org/community/your-posts/response-to-peter-linebaugh

justice that was otherwise denied.[9]

For Linebaugh it is important to mobilise historical storytelling in the interests of the reconstruction of the present, but there are no shortcuts to the past without deforming the possibilities and difficulties of the present.

However, self-creation is not the whole story either. Myth can also be understood structurally, shaping the agency of the historical actors the myth clings to. Eric Hobsbawm's discussion of social bandits explains the uniformity of both myth and reality across diverse temporalities and geographies in terms of their social construction.

> It does not greatly matter whether a man began his career for quasi-political reasons like [Salvatore] Giuliano, who had a grudge against the police and government, or whether he simply robs because it is a natural thing for an outlaw to do. He will almost certainly try to conform to the Robin Hood stereotype in some respects; that is he will try to be a 'man who took from the rich to give to the poor and never killed but in self-defense or just revenge'. He is virtually obliged to, for there is more to take from the rich than from the poor, and if he takes from the poor or becomes an 'illegitimate' killer, he forfeits his most powerful asset, public aid and sympathy. If he is free-handed with his gains, it may only be because a man in his position in a society of pre-capitalist values shows his power and status by largesse. And if he does not regard his actions as a social protest, the public will, so that even a purely professional criminal may

---

9   Peter Linebaugh, *Ned Ludd & Queen Mab: Machine-Breaking, Romanticism, and the Several Commons of 1811-12*, Oakland: PM Press, 2012, p.10.

come to pander to its view.[10]

Bandits were subject to necessity which bound them to the people, usually peasants, with whom they shared cultural political and economic conditions. Despite being rebels, they were conditioned by the myths which they were expected to fall into line with. Even if they may have deviated from their own representations, this was the interpretation into which their lives and histories fell. And this wasn't simply myth-making, for they themselves and their mode of operation were made by those around them, upon whom they depended.

Equiano, Sancho, Cugoano and Self-Invention

The literary adventures of three black writers and abolitionists of the 18th century – Gustavas Vassa a.k.a Olaudah Equiano, Ignatius Sancho and Ottobah Cugoano – provide extraordinary documents of globalisation and political struggle in the 18th century. Their works occupy unusual territories in literature, biography and critical historical sources, with each of these aspects being emphasised differently during different periods, allowing the opening up of some particularly difficult questions whereby authenticity becomes animated by discourses of race.

Ottobah Cugoano wrote the first directly abolitionist publication in English by an African: *Thoughts and Sentiments on the Evil and Wicked Traffic of the Commerce of the Human Species*, published in 1787. Ignatius Sancho wrote a large number of

---

10   Eric Hobsbawm, *Primitive Rebels*, New York: Norton, (1959) 1965, pp.19-20.

letters which were collected and published in 1782, two years after his death. Olaudah Equiano's autobiographical novel, *The Interesting Narrative of the Life of Olaudah Equiano, or Gustavas Vassa, The African, Written by Himself,* published in 1789, was the first book-length autobiographical slave narrative. Equiano's precursor, James Albert Ukawsaw Gronniosaw, had published *A Narrative of the Most remarkable Particulars in the Life of James Albert Ukawsaw Gronniosaw, an African Prince, As related by himself* in 1772, giving him the claim to have published the first autobiography by a Black African in Britain and the first slave narrative in the English language. However, Gronniosaw did not directly deal with the question of abolition, and though his narrative was certainly influential on Equiano's and provided ammunition for the abolitionists, it contains elements which would later undermine his standing as a class and race conscious black author in some critics' eyes.

> A reference to his white-skinned sister, his willingness to leave Africa as his family believed in many deities instead of one almighty God, the fact that the closer to a white European he became – through clothing but mostly via language – the happier he was, his description of another black servant at his master's house as a 'devil', have led critics to the conclusion that the narrative is devoid of the anti-slavery backlash ubiquitous in subsequent slave narratives.[11]

Olaudah Equiano's importance stems from his centrality to the British campaign for the abolition of slavery and his widely celebrated literary skill. His narrative became '[...] the

---

11   'Ukawsaw Gronniosaw', http://en.wikipedia.org/wiki/Ukawsaw_ Gronniosaw

most important single literary contribution to the campaign for abolition.'[12] Moreover, Equiano's well documented life and practical involvement in the campaign for abolition has made him a crucial source for historical research into the trans Atlantic slave trade and the political and cultural life of blacks in Britain in the 18th century. Unsurprisingly, this made Equiano's life the scene of contestation over both the authenticity of black identity in general and the authenticity of his account as a historical record in his own lifetime, especially between proponents of abolition and those invested in the slave trade who fiercely defended their interests. More recently, controversy has again exploded, this time between historians, and as we will show, this has a political and historical content relevant to the material we have assembled in this study.

According to his *Interesting Narrative*, Equiano was born an Igbo in Africa, kidnapped there and taken to Barbados in the West Indies. He was sold initially to a planter, then sold on again to Michael Henry Pascal, an officer in the British Navy. He came to London in 1757 with Pascal, who named him Gustavas Vassa. With Pascal, Equiano served seven years in the Royal Navy before being sold again to a merchant captain and returning to the West Indies. There, Equiano/ Vassa eventually purchased his freedom and remained for some time as a free man employed by his former master, a Quaker called Robert King. During this time he made several trading trips to Savannah, Georgia, and Philadelphia, Pennsylvania, and worked from London on commercial vessels sailing to the Mediterranean and the West Indies.

---

12   Peter Fryer, *Staying Power: The History of Black People in Britain Since 1504*, London: Pluto Press, 1984, p.107.

Daniel Orme, after W. Denton, Portrait of Olaudah Equiano from the
frontispiece of The Interesting Narrative (1789).

He joined an expedition to the Arctic in 1773, and took part
as an overseer and driver of black slaves in an expedition to
establish a plantation in Central America in 1775-76. Leaving
this position in disgust, he returned to London.[13] In London,
Equiano/Vassa briefly worked as a hairdresser, was involved in
a controversial scheme to resettle poor blacks in Sierra Leone,

---

13   Vincent Carretta, Introduction to Olaudah Equiano, *The Interesting
     Narrative and Other Writings*, London: Penguin, 2003, pp.ix-x.

became increasingly involved in the movement for abolition of slavery, married English woman Susan Cullen, and published his *Narrative*.[14] From the very beginning Equiano's account was assessed in terms of its authenticity. Upon its publication in 1789 the *Monthly Review* wrote: 'We entertain no doubt of the general authenticity of this intelligent African's interesting story [...]. *The Narrative* wears an honest face: and we have conceived a good opinion of the man'.[15] It's worth drawing attention to three aspects of this comment: firstly that the *Narrative* was 'authentic' and that the reviewer is certain of this (though we will have something to say about the interpretation of this crucial term later): secondly that Equiano is 'intelligent' and lastly that his book is 'honest', with honesty being connected to appearance – 'face'. The significance of such a statement of Equiano's intelligence in its time cannot be underestimated – at the time even Thomas Jefferson believed black people incapable of creative thought. Opposition to abolition drew strength from the fact that people of colour were widely considered racially and culturally inferior and therefore incapable of intelligence. Olaudah was living proof, and his book material evidence, of the illegitimacy of such claims, especially as a justification for slavery, for this black man was both intelligent and free. His capabilities as a writer and as a former employee of the government were both well known and self-evident.

Another significant aspect of Equiano's legitimacy or honesty (and that of his narrative) stems from his having

---

14 For a full discussion of the Sierra Leone project and The Committee for the Relief of the Black Poor see *Staying Power* pp.102–108, pp.196–204 and Vincent Carretta, *The Narrative*, op. cit., pp.xii–xiii.

15 *Staying Power*, op. cit., p.107.

been a witness to the worst atrocities of the slave trade. Many had written accounts of the tortuous middle passage, but his was the first written by an African, and this novelty ensured him the enormous commercial success which met the book. No less than eight editions were published in his lifetime. His detractors immediately focussed on Equiano's origins or pedigree. In 1792 *The Oracle* newspaper slandered Equiano, claiming he was from Santo Cruz, an island in the Lesser Antilles. This claim could not be supported with evidence and was quickly quashed by Equiano's increasingly powerful supporters. A further aspect of the legitimacy of *The Narrative* was built into the chain of solidarities constructed around its production and distribution. Each edition of *The Narrative* was published by subscription. This meant buyers committed to purchasing copies prior to the publication of each edition thus providing Equiano with an income stream and funds towards the costs of printing while he was writing. The list of subscribers was published in each edition, showing Equiano's credibility as well as promoting those proud to be associated with his work. The same mechanism connected Equiano to other Afro-British writers -- Cugoano, Sancho, and Gronniosaw -- and other notables who were part of the growing movement against the slave trade. As we shall see, other aspects of the book also directly link Equiano's narrative to that of others; his inclusion of the motif of a 'talking book', discussed in chapter 4 on Autodidacts, was a direct reference to Gronniosaw's own book.

Goodbye Equiano the African?

Recently, Equiano's status and the credibility of his account of his capture and ensuing adventures has been reappraised. Vincent Carretta, Equiano's biographer and editor of his major work, has pointed out that Equiano appears to have been much younger when he entered Pascal's service than he claims and that he seems to have arrived in England two years earlier than the date given in *The Narrative*. More controversially, Carretta has discovered a baptismal record and naval records that suggest Equiano was in fact born in South Carolina, not in Africa.[16] These newly uncovered facts along with the information about his participation in slavery, as a free man, and his role in the highly questionable venture in Sierra Leone, have been used to cast critical light on his perceived heroism and attitudes towards 'racialised slavery', suggesting that these were more a product of conducive environment than individual conviction.[17] This is not as negative as it sounds, nor as black and white. In the account cited above, Nicholas Guyatt establishes the historical development of racial slavery and the rapidity with which ideas were changing in the late 18th century in the wake of the colonial war in America. Equiano was a crucial catalyst of this change and this is the position Vincent Carretta and others have attempted to develop against the empiricist bias of more reductive critics.

---

16   See Carretta, op. cit., pp.x–xi.

17   See Nicholas Guyatt, 'Our Slaves Are Black', *London Review of Books*, Vol.29, No.19, 4 October 2007, pp.19–22.

Equiano was unable to resist, Carretta implies, the siren lure
of becoming an authentic African voice describing the horrors
of the transatlantic slave trade at a time when the abolitionist
movement most needed such a voice. In market terms (and
Equiano was acutely attuned to marketplace concerns – his
construction of an Igbo identity was not a disinterested
intellectual act but brought him sizeable financial benefits).
Equiano saw a market need for a first-hand account of how
Africans experienced the Middle Passage and proceeded to
supply that voice, creating in the process an Igbo identity
that probably did not exist at the time. If we accept Carretta's
contention that Equiano was actually an American slave who
had never lived in Africa, then Equiano is guilty of perpetrating
two lies. He pretended to be offering an authentic account of
himself as a victim of one of the great crimes in Western history
when he was not a victim – partly in order to advance an
honorable cause, partly to make money. He also invented himself
as an Igbo and attempted to create, through his writings, a pan-
Igbo identity that suggests more connections between peoples
in Africa than actually existed. These are serious charges, which
should lead us, in my opinion, to question whether Vassa is a
reliable witness in other areas and which, by casting doubt upon
his truthfulness, should also lead us to be more suspicious of his
character and less effusive about his 'genius'.[18]

Against this attempt to build a picture of Equiano's account
as opportunistic deception, Carretta himself replied to his
critics: 'I feel a bit like Equiano, who believed that some of

---

18   Trevor Burnard, 'Goodbye, Equiano, the African', *Historically Speaking: The Bulletin of the Historical Society*, Volume VII, Number 3, January 2006.

his critics wrote "with a view to hurt [his] character, and to discredit and prevent the sale of [his] book'". Carretta instead emphasises the essentially collective, creative and self-constituting production of *The Narrative*.

External contradictions are especially intriguing because Equiano's account of his life is generally remarkably verifiable when tested against documentary and historical evidence, so much so that deviations from truth seem more likely to have been the result of artistic premeditation than absentmindedness.[19] Carretta points to the author's 'dual identity': on the level of visual presentation, 'an indisputably African body in European dress'; in his very name -- Olaudah Equiano, or Gustavas Vassa, the African -- and in his prose. Each of these moves, according to Carretta, is part of a sophisticated and wilful process of self-invention. One could argue that the author of *The Interesting Narrative* invented an African identity rather than reclaimed one. If so, Equiano's literary achievements have been underestimated.[20] We could say that Equiano from the start is openly duplicitous – as a former slave he would know more than most about how to hide his feelings, feign loyalties and convictions. Carretta's editorial notes in the Penguin edition of Equiano's *The Narrative*, frequently indicate Equiano's extensive credited and uncredited borrowings from other authors. At times these are so close to the letter as to appear more like exercises in literary allusion (common practice in the 18th century) than deception. Descriptions of sea battles which Equiano most likely could not have witnessed are liberally borrowed from well known sources. In fact, authenticity in Equiano's time

---

19   *The Interesting Narrative*, op. cit., p.xi.
20   Ibid., p.xi.

meant precisely embellishing an account with recognisable tropes; what could possibly seem more plausible than a narrative that conformed to existing literary tropes and a common experience of the world to the contemporary reader? Moreover, what could more forcefully and entertainingly prove Equiano's contested intelligence than the masterly talent with which he stitches together biblical and religious allusions, biography, fiction and historical account? When one attempts to prove or disprove that Equiano and others were truly eyewitness to the events and world they described, it is easy to overlook that the knowledge of the trans-Atlantic diaspora was *their experience*. Through reading, writing, communicating it they lived, transformed and shared it.

In his excellent history of black and Asian writing about London, Sukhdev Sandhu explicitly argues for restoring the role of 'imagination' in black literature.

> For too long black literature has been considered in extra-literary terms. It is treated as a species of journalism, one that furnishes eyewitness accounts of sectors of British society to which mainstream newspapers and broadcasters have little access. Given that interest in black and Asian people tends to be at its highest when they are attacked, rioting, or the subject of official reports documenting prejudice in some tranche of daily life, it is hardly surprising if black writing comes to be viewed as a kind of emergency literature, one that is tough, angry, 'real'. It was ever thus [...].[21]

Sandhu goes on to discuss Ignatious Sancho's friendship

---

21 Sukhdev Sandhu, *London Calling: How Black and Asian Authors Imagined a City*, London: Harper Perennial, 2004, p.xxiii–xxiv.

with proto-modernist author Lawrence Sterne, arguing that their own literary exchange emphasised the value of 'irony, contingency and solidarity'.[22] Quoting John Lennard, Sandhu establishes the circuitous literary innovations Sancho adopted from Sterne as an implicit critique of the values which had been used to disempower him as a subject.

Sancho, like Sterne, chose to use dashes extensively 'to mock assumptions about the elegant measured unity of Enlightened discourse.'[23]

Nuances of literary form can constitute the terrain of struggle wherein stereotypes and forms of domination are contested and subverted. Sandhu invokes Sancho's complex negotiation of literary mastery in order to undermine a discourse of authenticity and heroism which itself has come to be hegemonic in black historiographies of the struggle for abolition.[24] Yet, Sancho himself was not averse to producing 'emergency literature'. His account of the Gordon Riots of 1780 invoked 'the worse than Negro barbarity of the populace' and displays some of the worst reactionary qualities of an 'enlightened' English gentleman of the times.[25] Because Sancho wrote, we know much of his life, his inner motivations and his responses to the society around him. We know much less of two free black Londoners, who participated in the riots and were at the forefront of the 'excarceration' of

---

22 Ibid., p.42.

23 *London Calling*, op. cit., p.42.

24 Sukhdev Sandhu, 'At the Hop', *London Review of Books*, Vol. 19 No. 4 · 20 February 1997.

25 'Ignatius Sancho Describes the Gordon Riots', http://www. brycchancarey.com/sancho/letter2.htm

prisoners from Newgate Prison on the 6th June 1780.[26] And even though they wrote, we also as yet know little of the activist organisation, 'The Sons of Africa', of which Ottobah Cugoano and Olaudah Equiano were members, who met in Whitechapel to co-ordinate the campaign for abolition and better conditions for free blacks.[27] There is no need though to contrast these lesser known activist figures as more or less authentic than their better known literary counterparts: after all, some could turn in a short time from being 'quiet, honest, sober' students into revolutionaries. Rather, the vicissitudes of proletarian subjectivity and the operative or liberating status of fictions need to be acknowledged for us to understand the pressures and liberties of the times in which others lived and left us their records.

Literalism and Realism

A persistent intellectual tradition, running alongside the 'scientific' equation of the masses with savages, women, children, bacilli or animals, was the image of the mass as exclusively preoccupied with fact and more or less mundane realism. As intellectuals saw it, it was the dogged literalism of the masses that unfitted them for the appreciation of art, and banished them from the higher aesthetic reaches.[28]

---

26   Peter Linebaugh, *The London Hanged*, London: Verso, 1991, pp.348–349.

27   *Staying Power*, op. cit., p.108.

28   John Carey, *The Intellectuals and the Masses: Pride and Prejudice Among the Literary Intelligentsia, 1880–1939*, London: Faber, 1992, p.31.

A tendency towards literalism has always been evenly distributed across societies. A useful reference in this regard is *Dockers and Detectives*, a study of British working class reading by Ken Worpole. Worpole set up the Centerprise local publishing project on Kingsland High Street in Hackney in the 1970s, which subsequently became an African Caribbean cultural centre and bookshop, and is currently under threat of closure by Hackney Council. As we saw earlier in our discussion of 18th century pamphleteers, Worpole locates the 1724 Stamp Act as a 'turning point in the history of the press and consequently of the novel', as it enacted an economic distinction between factual and fictional publications.[29] Many working class pamphleteers actively used allegory, poetry, song, metaphor, and allusion in their work. Other agitators, such as Richard Carlile, declared themselves vehemently opposed to such methods,

> Everything of this kind should now go in the fire. He who burns a romance purifies the human mind.[30]

Worpole goes on to explore how a false dichotomy between fact and fiction, experience and the imagination was continually enacted in political rhetoric about what the working classes should or should not be reading. While some readers did take fiction as fact, all the while 'most people have moved easily between the two, as they continue to do today'.[31]

---

29 Ken Worpole, *Dockers and Detectives*, London: Verso, 1983, p.14.
30 Richard Carlile, quoted in Ken Worpole, *Dockers and Detectives*, London: Verso, 1983, p.17.
31 Ibid., p.20.

Evangelicals made their flock feel guilty about reading imaginative literature; Utilitarians believed imaginative literature 'produced no direct and measurable benefits to those who read it' and did not 'contribute to material progress'.[32]

A book published by the Federation of Worker Writers and Community Publishers, *The Republic of Letters*, contains a history of working class writing and writers' organisations from the London Corresponding Society of the 1790s to those of the 1980s.[33] Describing the climate for working class writers in the 1930s, they also observed the tendency on the part of patrons and publishers to emphasise the form of the worker's memoir.

In the 1930's the characteristic publishing process was very much controlled by sympathetic middle-class intellectuals like John Lehmann and George Orwell, who encouraged working-class people, particularly men, to write down their experiences, either in direct autobiography or fictionalised form. The system was one of patronage, well intentioned but liable to founder in the case of personal animosity between patron and writer.

---

32 Ibid., p.18.

33 Anon., *The Republic of Letters*, London: Comedia/Minority Press Group, (undated c.1983). Readers interested to follow up discussions of 20th century working class literature from a working class perspective should see: Howard Slater, '*Working Class Novelists 1930-1950*', London: Working Press, Research Pamphlet, http://www.themodernnovel.com/lists/theirs/other/working.htm, Stefan Szczelkun, 'Working Press 1987 to 1997: An account of the first ten years of an umbrella imprint for working class artists and writers who wished to self-publish', 1997, http://www.stefan-szczelkun.org.uk/taste/ExtrasA2-Working%20Press.html, and publisher and resource Penniless Press, http://www.pennilesspress.co.uk/

Work of great significance was also published in this period by members of the Women's Co-Operative Guild. *Maternity* in 1915 and *Life as We Have Known It*. The Communist Party played no small part in encouraging the publication of working-class autobiographies like Phil Piratin's *Our Flag Stays Red* and Lewis Jones' *Cwmardy* and *We Live*, though the emphasis lay very heavily on novels and autobiographies with very little attention to poetry.[34]

William Morris took issue with the idea of working class readers being exposed to 'the new [modernist] concern with exploring the individual psyche and focussing on the more subjective forms of human alienation'.[35] Worpole explains that in Morris' own 'narrative poems and prose works, individual subjective states are pushed aside in the excessive attention to social activity and the emphasis on the physical constraints of life and labour.'[36] But, 'the notion that the communism of property would automatically usher in an end to mental distress, was not, in retrospect, a particularly useful contribution to socialist theory'.[37] It is certainly true that British and French working class readers assembled for themselves what Jonathan Rose calls a 'mongrel library' out of the materials at hand. For Rose this led to a mode of reading in which books were 'framed' by readers in ways which exceeded the author's (and some commentators') intentions, rejecting and accepting parts of a discourse according to their own experience and reason.

When it comes to reading the accounts of the historical

---

34   *The Republic of Letters*, ibid., p.69.

35   Ibid., p.20.

36   Ibid., p.20.

37   Ibid., p.20.

working class, Jacques Rancière questions the 'fetishist passion for lived experience' which he believes produces,

> A distribution of roles that gives the people speech in order to verify that they are indeed speaking the language of the people [...] so as to better reserve for [intellectuals] the privilege of the creative imagination and the explanatory word. [38]

Obviously not every interest in lived experience or its expression is fetishist or idealist. For historians from below it was a matter of undermining idealist narratives, and also paying attention to how living in relation to different social and economic structures felt. Rancière says the post-Gauchist intellectuals in France came to see the worker as an idealised image of political agency, and suggests that this was a reflection of their uncertainty about their own political roles. This led to a double alienation in which 'the difference in conditions' between workers and intellectuals came to be accepted 'as a difference in natures'.[39]

The workers' narratives studied by the historian in *Proletarian Nights* 'constructed a world of experience'. We have no way of knowing for sure if they were true or false. For Rancière, the worker's voice is not the simple, stable domain of truth or authenticity, but is subject to intermittent fabrications and sophistications, just like anybody else's. Moreover, the voice of the worker for Rancière *mobilises* these qualities to enact a relation to the world which includes more than one voice ever could.

---

38   Jacques Rancière, *Proletarian Nights: The Workers Dream in Eighteenth Century France*, London: Verso, 2012, p.x.

39   Ibid., p.xi.

> These words had to be removed from their status as evidence of
> a social reality to show them as writing and thinking at work on
> the construction of a different social world.[40]

We can recognise in Rancière's account the same active,
situated 'work of social construction' which we could take to
be a form of authenticity.

Hybridity Against Sociology

As we have seen, working class experience in different places
and times has tended toward hybrid voices, ideas, identities,
and consciousness. In the 1980s Rancière made the idea of
hybridity central to his attack on the renowned sociologist of
inequalities, Pierre Bourdieu. It appears Rancière's thinking
in this regard was based on the French Socialist Party taking
Bourdieu's *The Inheritors*, *Reproduction* and *Distinction* 'as its
program' in the early 1980s. But Rancière's distrust of the
sociologist goes back further. It may be partially located
in the role he sees sociology taking in the early part of the
20th century. It was sociologists, he suggests, rather than
historians, who began the history of the working class
movement in France. Their role in this history had its basis
in the logic of the state management of workers on behalf
of capital.

> Sociology was the official science of the new radical republic
> [...] the science of social relations as production curves, of
> unions conceived as a force of negotiation, of discussion with

---

40   Ibid, p.xi.

All Knees and Elbows of Susceptibility and Refusal

the state rather than struggle.[41]

Bourdieu's sociology is partly an attempt to map forms of economic determination unexplored by classical economics, by expanding on the concept of capital to include 'symbolic capitals' such as cultural capital. These forms of capital are not merely symbolic; they act as the transformation of economic power into other forms of power which more or less hide their economic determination. In so doing, they actively present another order of inequalities: in speech, dispositions of the body, know how, sociability, opportunities, etc., which are related to material inequality and effectively transform it into symbolic inequality. People's thought and movement in the world are structured, for Bourdieu, in the first instance by 'habitus' – the internalised beliefs, expectations, identifications, and sense of what is possible in life. The 'habitus' is accumulated over a lifetime, and may change in relation to changed circumstances. For Bourdieu it is most affected in the first instance by our socio economic background and our relation to those around us. The 'habitus' more or less unconsciously structures our choices and actions, sometimes in contradictory ways.

In this respect, Bourdieu provides a rigorous analysis of the role of culture and education in the reproduction of inequalities. But he is oddly reticent about acts of transgression toward these structures by working class people. The autodidact or self-taught worker in particular is modelled in Bourdieu's *Distinction* as a tragic figure:

41   Jacques Rancière, "Le Social': The Lost Tradition in French Labour History', in *People's History and Socialist Theory*, London: History Workshop Series / Routledge, 1981, p.269.

s/he is both unable to operate according to the demands of the academic system and is given little validation or recognition by Bourdieu himself. In respect to the autodidact we are left in Bourdieu's work with a critique of educational inequalities that, despite its stated aim to provide a key to understanding their logic of domination, oddly seems to reflect and not radically overcome or supplant that logic. For Rancière, Bourdieu's concept of 'habitus' is too static, entailing a 'homogeneity' of thought, feeling and identifications. This homogeneity becomes a presupposition in the political appeal to the working class, and also symbolically conforms working people to both economic and intellectual determination.

> The hybrid intellectuals of the *Nights of Labour* would be inconceivable on [Bourdieu's] model since [...] no-one ever strays from his or her own habitus.[42]

It should be pointed out that Bourdieu's definition of the habitus, like his own habitus, changed over time, to embrace 'a generative spontaneity which asserts itself in an improvised confrontation'. Bourdieu himself would have been the first to emphasise that the subjects of his analyses were not in any way static. But for Rancière, Bourdieu's critical investigation of the habitus enacts and reproduces the very exclusions and impossibilities he seeks to disclose. He symbolically keeps everybody in their place and sorts out 'what is suitable for each'. The division of roles and habitus fit for each is traced back to Plato, whose *Republic* allots each person just one task.

As we have seen in our discussion of 'autodidacts' and

---

42   Andrew Parker, Introduction to *The Philosopher and his Poor*, North Carolina: Duke University Press, 2004, p.xvii.

elsewhere, and identifications between agents of different classes were not a matter of pure antagonism, but a complex interplay which went hand-in-hand with 'dominated' subjects appropriating, mastering, taking aside, and also *shaping* and changing the logic of 'dominant' cultures. In this sense Rancière taps into a vein of critical thought that takes in Raymond Williams' argument that 'boundaries are there to be crossed', and bell hooks' writing on critical education.[43]

'Bussed to white schools' in the 1960s, bell hooks recalls, 'we soon learned that obedience, and not zealous will to learn, was what was expected of us'. Too much eagerness to learn she regarded as something that could easily be seen as a threat to white authority.[44]

Saint-Simonian Pariahs

Curiosity holds a danger, both for the ruling class at certain times in history, and, sometimes, for the Marxist critic, because it might exceed or circumvent their expectations or desires for the subject. Rancière's worker intellectuals are a very particular and limited sample. But they also, in their very particular ways, present a challenge to both bourgeois power in the 19th century, and to the place which labour history (and perhaps orthodox Marxism) shapes for the worker. In *Proletarian Nights* he explores the relationships between the Saint-Simonians, a group of utopian socialists, and those workers whom they recruited.

---

43   Raymond Williams quoted in 1970 on the BBC documentary *Border Country*, from the series *One Pair of Eyes*.

44   'bell hooks on education', http://www.infed.org/thinkers/hooks.htm

what new forms of false construction affect that paradox when the discourse of workers infatuated with the night of the intellectuals meets the discourse of intellectuals infatuated with the glorious working days of the masses?[45]

The Saint-Simonians were disciples of Claude Henri de Rouvroy, Comte de Saint-Simon, an early French socialist from an aristocratic lineage. After Saint-Simon's death in 1825 the movement came under the leadership of Barthélemy Prosper Enfantin and Amand Bazard. In November 1831, Bazard split from the sect as Enfantin, naming himself 'Le Père', developed it into a religious formation based around a doctrine that sought the abolition of inheritances, emphasized the moral virtue of work while seeking to end competition between workers, and argued for female emancipation while challenging the traditional family unit. Following Saint-Simon's conception of a New Christianity, Enfantin believed the messiah would arrive in the shape of La Mère. Eventually Enfantin and his remaining followers went on an ill-fated expedition to Egypt to to find La Mère and create a Suez Canal.

The main body of Saint-Simonians, according to Rancière, emerged from a section of the bourgeoisie, and had refused their 'destiny' as part of 'a split in the process reproducing the ruling class'. The Saint-Simonians at first seemed to offer some artisans a sense of freedom from the 'egoism' they perceived in their workmates because the socialists lent themselves to the task of 'improving the material and moral condition of the labouring class'. 'I could not imagine that such unselfish people existed', said one working class Saint-

---

45   *Proletarian Nights,* op. cit., p.x.

Simonian, Guerineau, in a profession of faith.[46] The Saint-Simonians also attracted converts through their assertion of the group as an open family, bonded by affirmations of 'filial love'. Worker recruits were not drawn from unionised labour, but generally employed in relatively precarious artisanal trades. However, the Saint-Simonians required and depended upon an authentic image of the working class, while the worker intellectuals they came into contact with were precisely trying to *escape* this image. In this way, some of those workers disposed to join the Saint-Simonians, like the joiner Gabriel Gauny, became more or less ambivalent about their ideology. They found instead an expanded sense of intellectual possibilities, which led them to begin to occupy the symbolic spaces of the intellectuals. In the process, it was not simply their *image*, but also their *condition* that the artisans were trying to escape. As Rancière has argued, they wanted to accomplish a break from determination. This was not an easy process. Gauny describes himself as tongue-tied and alienated by the discourse of the Saint-Simonian leadership.

While seeking to avoid projecting contemporary concerns, Rancière hints at echoes between the Saint-Simonians and the *établi* of the 1970s, only in reverse. *Établi* or 'establishment' was a tactic by which activists, often students or intellectuals, were clandestinely placed in factories to promote worker agitation with the support of militant left groups. Rancière discusses the phenomenon in the article, 'Factory Nostalgia' in *The Intellectual and His People: Staging the People Volume 2*, in which, among other books, he reviews Robert Linhart's novel, *L'établi*.

It is clear how Rancière can see the worker intellectuals

---

46   both preceding quotes from *Proletarian Nights*, op. cit., p.159.

Philippe Joseph Machereau, Saint-Simonian Temple and City, 1832.
Architectural plan by the Saint-Simonian commune founded in the
Parisian neighborhood of Ménilmontant

as a radical break with the classic Marxist requirement of working class subjects. A requirement which runs the danger of reproducing and constraining the worker by making work, and images and conceptions of labour, the principle revolutionary destiny of the working class. Rancière points to a contradiction between the mobilisation of the working class as a political body, and the declared aim of Marxism to struggle toward the self-abolition of the working class and of class generally.

The hybridity of Rancière's worker intellectuals is tied to a sense of appropriation: of time, and also of a fragment of the habitus of the 18th century French bourgeoisie. Rancière draws upon a text by Gauny about a fictional floor layer who temporarily makes himself at home whilst working alone and unwatched in unfinished bourgeois houses.

> Believing himself at home [...] he loves the arrangement of a room, so long as he has not yet finished laying the floor. If the window opens out onto a garden or commands a view of a picturesque horizon, he stops his arms and glides in imagination toward the spacious view to enjoy it better than the possessors of the neighbouring residences.[47]

Rancière has often called upon this example in discussions of politics and aesthetics, stating that 'what is at stake in emancipation [is] getting out of the ordinary ways of sensory experience. This thought has been important for my idea of politics, not being about the relations of power but being about the framing of the sensory world itself.'[48] The problem is that the framing of the sensory world is surely enacted and reinforced not just by subjects but by the forces that more or less determine their lives. Making oneself at home where one supposedly 'does not belong' might be a precondition for radical change. However, the connection between sensory distribution and material inequalities and conditions is very ambiguous in the above passage and in Rancière's later work. While the insights and dreams found in Gauny's writings were part of a shared culture, the sense of a development

---

47 *Proletarian Nights*, op. cit., p.81.

48 Jacques Rancière 'Art is Going Elsewhere and Politics has to Catch it', *Krisis*, 2008, Issue 1, http://www.egs.edu/faculty/jacques-Rancière/articles/art-is-going-elsewhere-and-politics-has-to-catch-it/ 2010, p.40.

toward a less individualised casting off of the habitus of the worker or dominated subject remains unresolved. Rancière suggests that the 'night-time socialisation of vanities' contributed towards opening up a much broader space of possibilities for the working class, a 'general movement of people getting out of their condition', and 'prepared for' the July revolution of 1830 as well as providing comfort during the hunger and repressions that followed. They may well have had a motivating effect, but the development of such a 'general movement' is sadly not adequately explored in *Proletarian Nights*.

The contradictory relationships between working class Saint-Simonians and the group's leadership, were also played out in terms of gender relations. While, as Sheila Rowbotham points out, some women drew self-confidence and an expanded sense of intellectual accomplishment and independence from their dealings with Saint-Simonian practice, they also took issue with the expectations the group had of them. Enfantin's doctrine sought to break with traditional conceptions of the family and of monogamous relationships while retaining the sanctity of the holy 'couple'. He expected women to 'confess' their infidelities in order to develop a new sexual morality; he then made these known to the rest of the group. Claire Bazard wrote that:

> Among us, we are obliged to reveal all the secrets of the heart [...] we lose, little by little, our spontaneity; we withdraw into ourselves [...] This farce that we can love everyone in the same

way results in loving no one.[49]

Claire Démar went much further than Enfantin. She wrote *Appeal to the People on the Emancipation of Women* (1833) which staked the emancipation of the working class on women's emancipation, and challenged the concepts of maternity and paternity and the roles assigned them. She also attacked the intrusive Saint-Simonian practice of confession, arguing that women can 'keep the secrets of the heart to themselves' and share them as they see fit. Démar caused controversy among working class Saint-Simonians, some of whom felt her political ideas went too far in the rejection of moral regulation and the social and economic complexities of child care and bonded relationships. Due to this, and her status as a recent convert to the sect, she experienced isolation within the group. In August 1832, she and her lover committed suicide. Adrienne Baissac reported on the chauvinistic and ignorant attitudes of a male dominated Saint-Simonian meeting held shortly after Claire Démar's death, at which one man declared:

> The time has not yet come [...] when the women must be free; they must still suffer. And if two hundred, three hundred suicides are necessary, we must let them commit this so they may serve as an example to other women. Only when they will have felt all of their sorrows will they arise with all of their force to break their chains.[50]

---

49   Claire Bazard quoted in Claire Goldberg Moses, *French Feminism in the Nineteenth Century*, New York: State University of New York Press, 1984, p.76.

50   Adrienne Baissac quoted in *French Feminism in the Nineteenth Century*, op. cit., pp. 78–79.

Baissac's response was unequivocal:

> Do you hear this, Mesdames? Two hundred, three hundred suicides, and the way he said this number he could have said two thousand, three thousand. Doesn't this thought make you sick? It repulses me and I firmly believe [...] that we must immediately find some ways to make these sorrows cease and not to put women into situations of self-destruction.[51]

Some women broke with the group to develop distinct working class feminist practices of their own which did not require the abstractions of the Saint-Simonian doctrine, or the authority of 'Le Père'. While contradicting Rancière's emphasis on the radical break made by workers from their own work, they made significant contributions to the workers movement and to gender struggles. For example, Flora Tristan, a lithography workshop colourist and former Saint-Simonian, produced a book, *L'Union Ouvriere*, in 1843. She expounded an early idea for an independent Worker's International, and travelled France agitating for male workers to support equal wages for women. Tristan experienced hostility from workers, unions and bosses, because of her ideas and also because she was a single mother. Undaunted, she appropriated for herself the status of 'pariah'.

Questions of historical 'truth' circulate in a field of tensions, authorising and directing what is possible, what is plausible, and what is denigrated. For historians, their subjects can open up some of the complex and contradictory identifications between actors and cultures which challenge the established field, pose wider political questions and in

---

51   Ibid, p.79.

turn reflect the struggles of hitherto marginalised subjects in their efforts to break with external determinations and determine their own lives and agency.

THE BUSINESS UNIVERSITY

As much as we would like to detach the project of history from below from its academic base, the problem of who writes history, and under what conditions that writing is published and read, demands more than a straightforward withdrawal from the systems of instituted thought.

It is important to recognise that the study of history from below was subject to struggles from a relative 'above' – that is to say, it was a matter of institutional relations in the worlds of education and academia, as well as in the political sphere. E.P. Thompson may have taught history for the Workers' Educational Association (WEA) and A.L. Morton taught at the progressive school Summerhill, but both were themselves educated at Cambridge University.

In the last few years the UK has seen an unprecedented wave of student protest against tuition fees, the scrapping of the Educational Maintenance Allowance (EMA), and the commercialisation of higher education in general – unprecedented, that is, within post-war welfarist relations. At points, this has also combined with protests by university staff, including teaching staff and cleaners. UK protests have coincided with a global wave of protest movements in education which is ongoing at the time of writing (particularly in Chile and Quebec).

In this chapter we'll revisit some of the connections between radical history and educational struggles, before discussing more recent waves of education struggles.

Beyond their attempts to change the way history was seen and written, the historians from below had some limited agency in the transformation of the world of higher education. There was a diversity of approaches to these struggles – from E.P. Thompson's battle with the 'Business University' at Warwick, which anticipated the struggle against the commercialisation of Higher Education, to the History Workshop movement's efforts towards a democratisation of the study of history itself.

Therefore, the different practices of these historians can be seen as forms of institutional critique in practice. How they got on, where they lost out, and where they misrecognised their own roles in the power relations of knowledge production, is as worthy of debate as the historical knowledge of people's struggles they circulated. It is also key to uncovering the potential in these practices.

Unrest at Ruskin

Shortly after the founding of Ruskin College in 1899, several issues, which have continued to be points of agitation within workers' education, came to a head. The key issues were examinations, patronage and funding of the college 'the influence of other Oxford colleges' and student control. But conflict over these concerns was initiated via a question of personal loyalty. In 1909 a strike broke out at Ruskin in support of Dennis Hirds, who was Principal at the college. The strike closed the college for two weeks, with the students passing the following resolution:

1. That all lectures in the Institution be boycotted, with the exception of Mr Hirds'.
2. That all house duties be carried on as usual.
3. That the Committee be instructed to form classes among the students in accordance with the present curriculum.
4. That should any student, or number of students, be victimised by any Member of the Faculty, or by the Executive Council, all the students, now in residence at Ruskin College, will leave in a body.
5. That Mr Dennis Hirds' resignation be withdrawn, and the resignations of Messrs. Buxton and Wilson be tendered instead.
6. That no student shall allow himself to be interviewed by any Member of the Faculty or the Executive Council. All matters between the students and the staff [to] be carried on by correspondence.
7. That the Working Committee be instructed to draw up a circular re present situation, and send copies to Trade unions, Labour and Socialist organisations, the Press and past students.[1]

The exact reasons behind the strike are a little obscure. Hirds seems to have been beloved by the students, but was accused of 'disorganisation' (failing to properly discipline students) and of irregularities such as selling produce from his own farm to the College. The reasons for Hirds' suspension are

---

1   Colin Waugh, 'The "Plebs" Go On Strike', http://www.workersliberty.org/story/2010/09/23/plebs-go-strike, Harold Pollins, *The History of Ruskin College*, Oxford: Ruskin College Library, 1984 and Colin Waugh, '"Plebs": The lost legacy of independent working class education', *Post-16 Educator,* Sheffield, January, 2009.

suggestive of both the alternative culture at Ruskin and the hand to mouth position of teachers at the time. Certainly at other Oxford colleges similar informal arrangements and dependencies could be found, but in the early days of Ruskin – in the embattled context of a 'college of the people' attempting to remain politically neutral and maintain its autonomy – exposure of irregularities was controversial.

During the strike the students demanded their fees and boarding costs back, which they obtained. Many immediately left the college and spread their agitation to the regions. Factions formed and some students grouped together to defend the college. A year prior to the 1909 strike a student group called The Plebs League had formed to press for changes at the College. A war of pamphlets broke out; a publication called 'The burning question of education' published by The Plebs League put forward the students' case. The Plebs League took their name from a lecture by Daniel De Leon, 'Two Pages from Roman History', which made a parallel between the Tribunes and Gracchi and the trade union leaders of the time. This was published as a pamphlet by the Scottish Labour Party. Advocating handing over control of Ruskin College to the workers' movement, the Plebs' worry, according to Plebs League member and Ruskin striker Stan Rees, 'was that the orthodox educationalists were wooing the college away from the labour movement'.[2] In 1906 the Liberal government had appointed union officials to administer welfare measures on behalf of the state. Many socialists shifted left towards syndicalism – a movement that distrusted the relationship of union leadership to the state, and sought to move toward working class autonomy

---

2   'Plebs...', op. cit., p.20.

ORGAN OF THE NATIONAL COUNCIL OF
LABOUR COLLEGES

THE PLEBS

Monthly, 4d.   NOVEMBER, 1929

J.F.H.

This **Class** is great stuff!

JOIN THE N.C.L.C.
AND GET THAT
GINGERED-UP FEELING

N.C.L.C., 15 SOUTH HILL PARK GARDENS, LONDON, N.W.3

Cover of The Pleb: Organ of the National Council of Labour Colleges,
November 1929.

and direct democracy through a rank and file take over of the unions and a collective reorganisation of society. This rejection of (union) leadership was echoed by the Ruskin strikers, some of whom were sponsored by the South Wales Miners Federation. Also influential on the Plebs group and this general shift towards syndicalism were renegades from a Glasgow working class faction of the Social Democratic Federation.

The background to the Ruskin strike was also caught up in the attitudes at Ruskin towards the notionally 'non-political' status of education there. There is some indication that the content of lessons was at stake. Students had reacted to lectures given on the subject of political economy, claiming that teaching was biased against socialist interpretations.

> The majority of students had not heard of – never mind, read – Marx when Mr Furniss began to lecture at Ruskin [...] The students then began reading Marx themselves because of Mr Furniss' distortions.[3]

In 1908 a rule was introduced at Ruskin forbidding students from speaking at political meetings. The founders of Ruskin had hoped that the school would retain some independence, but this turned out not to be the case.

> [Walter] Vrooman had hoped, early on, that the co-operatives would take responsibility for the college, but nothing had come of that. Instead, efforts were made to raise money from two sources: sympathetic, rich benefactors, and the labour

---

3   Stan Rees quoted in 'Plebs...', op. cit., p.9.

movement, especially the trade unions.[4]

By 1908 not only were wealthy benefactors underwriting the school, but Oxford dons were teaching there too. In many ways these developments and the struggle for control over Ruskin were part of increasing efforts by the middle and upper classes to stem a flood of educational initiatives from below. In 1902 the Liberal government had passed an Education Act expanding secondary education, but the act was perceived by some of its critics as highly paternalistic. Two advisers to the Liberal Party shaping the Act were the Fabian Society 'socialist' Sidney Webb and former Toynbee Hall administrator R.L. Morant. Quoting Morant, Colin Waugh makes clear the attitudes of these nominally left educationalists of the time:

> Unless 'the impulses of the many ignorant' were put under the control of the few wise, democracy would be overcome 'by the centrifugal forces of her own people's unrestrained individualism and disintegrated utterly by the blind impulses of mere numerical majorities'.[5]

Sidney Webb contributed to the establishment, early in the 20th century, of the the dual system by which the ivory towers of Bloomsbury and beyond would later flourish.

> We must abandon the simple ideal of equality, identity or uniformity among professors, whether of tenure, salary, attainments or duties, time-table or holidays. The principal

---

4   Ibid., p.16.
5   Ibid., p.7.

professors, on whom mainly we must depend for research, should, of course, have life tenure, high salaries and abundant leisure, whilst the bulk of the university teachers required by so extensive an undergraduate population as that of London will necessarily be engaged for short terms, earn only modest salaries, and work at times and seasons convenient to those whom they serve.[6]

In 1908 a conference and joint report had been co-ordinated by the Workers' Educational Association (WEA) and Ruskin College: 'Oxford and working-class education'. Colin Waugh is dismissive:

In the end it was an attempt by one section of the ruling class to convince other sections, including within Oxford University itself, that the growth of working class power could not be ignored or simply repressed, and that tutorial classes leading to university entrance via Ruskin were the best weapon for combating it.[7]

Following the strike, a conference was held at Ruskin entitled, 'The Democratic control of Ruskin College'. Ruskin made some reforms and concessions to student control. A new governing council was introduced consisting of representatives from the TUC, General Federation of Trade Unions, the Co-operative Union, and the Working Men's Club and Institute Union. A new principal, Gilbert Slater, had firm credentials with a background in organising dockers in Plymouth in 1889; he

---

6   Sidney Webb quoted in Angela Withers, 'A Capitalist History of Bloomsbury', *Rage*, Issue 1, September 2011, http://rageofmaidens. wordpress.com/

7   'Plebs', op. cit., p.13.

was also author of the book *The English Peasantry and the Enclosure of the Common Fields* (1907). Furthermore any working-class body which maintained a student at the college was entitled to a representative on the council. Each year three academics would assume an advisory role only. This advisory position was often held by historians, with Christopher Hill, Asa Briggs and R.H. Tawney all occupying places on it in the post-WWII years. Nonetheless, the general principle that students would be exempt from examinations was not upheld. In 1910 Ruskin students began to sit the Oxford University Diploma in Economics and Political Science, and the college year was adjusted to run from September to July instead of January to December to mirror that of the standard academic year.

Some members of the Plebs League found the concessions obtained were not enough. Instead they founded the Central Labour College in Bradmore Road, Oxford, which later became part of the National Council of Labour Colleges (NCLC) 1923-1964. The NCLC was established in strong opposition to the Workers Educational Association, of which Ruskin was a part, whilst the WEA dismissed teaching at the NCLC as 'mere class-war propaganda and not education at all'.[8]

A perennial discussion at Ruskin concerned whether the college was educating students for the labour movement or for the students' own social mobility. Examinations paved the way for many to use Ruskin as a stepping stone to Higher Education.

It is certainly true that most students do not return to their original occupation. The founders hoped that they would and the claim was often made before 1914 that they did go back.

---

8   Ibid., p.19.

It was a bold claim then; it has been inapplicable for recent decades. Often it is said that Ruskin has become a prep school for university.[9]

Also, given that placements continued to be funded by trade unions, many returned from Ruskin to step into positions within the union bureaucracy or Labour Party. A 1929 Annual Report stated, 'We learn with much interest that four ex-members of staff and fourteen ex-students have been elected to the new parliament'.[10]

Ruskin College in the 1960s and The History Workshop

In English History Proper the people of this island (see under Poor Law, Sanitary Reform, Wages Policy) appear to be one of the problems Government has had to handle [...] Until recently, 'Labour History' has been defined by its antagonism to this orthodoxy. And several of those who gave, in recent years, the greatest impetus to Labour History were teachers who [...] had an unusually wide, participatory relationship with an audience far outside the groves of academe. They addressed themselves to Ruskin College, Left Book Club and Communist Party, the Workers Educational Association [...].[11]

Both Thompson and Samuel identified an undue emphasis in labour history on the discussion of the institutional infrastructure of the labour movement. They felt that this sidelined the labour struggles which didn't fit the pattern

---

9   *History of Ruskin College*, op. cit., p.60.

10   Ruskin College Annual Report 1929, quoted in ibid., p.3.

11   E.P. Thompson, 'History from Below', *The Times Literary Supplement*, April 7, 1966.

of unionisation – social struggles that took place on a wider terrain than the workplace: around informal and irregular work, around crime and the definition of criminality, over consumption and prices, in the domestic setting, etc. This 'institutional bias' could be deflected by attention to these hidden areas of labour history, but could the institutional structure that underpinned and shaped the study of history be altered along the same lines?

A letter of 1968 to fellow Ruskin tutors from Raphael Samuel outlines some of the historian's criticisms of the college. The process of selecting students was a mystery to Samuel, his fellow tutors and students. Further, Samuel argued that Ruskin students were 'shackled' to the exam system, which was based on the attainment of Oxford University Special Diplomas and which restricted the college to a traditional syllabus. The college, he argued, was not independent, moreover it was 'servile' to the administrative apparatus of both the college and the trade unions, producing a highly uncritical environment.

> [Ruskin] plays no part in the *formation* of radical thought in Britain. No-one in British society expects *ideas* to emanate from Ruskin; only a dutiful fulfilment of narrowly restricting obligations to a sector of the local union movement. [...] [Ruskin is] nothing but a poor man's finishing school, smoothing out the rough edges and preparing students for a respectable but subordinate place working for the capitalist class.[12]

These criticisms, and those of Ruskin students, were met

---

12   Memo on Student Democracy at Ruskin College, Raphael Samuel 1968. Available in Raphael Samuel's archive, Bishopsgate Institute, London.

with a bureaucratic response by the college executive, as Bob Purdie points out:

> A joint consultative committee was set up to consider student participation. By the end of the year the pragmatic Victor Treadwell had produced proposals for student representation which channelled 'student power' into a set of committee structures which kept student activists tied up in meetings. The creation of new, internally examined, diplomas ended reliance on the University Special Diplomas. The college had contained the rebellion by routinising it.[13]

The following year, the growth of anti-racist actions by Ruskin students persuaded the Executive to start offering scholarships to immigrant workers.

Samuel's development of the History Workshops – a 'rebellion against the examinations system' – were conceived at least in part as a response to the idea of Ruskin as a finishing school or assembly line for careers in the Labour Party and trade unions. However, Bob Purdie states that:

> students at Ruskin reflected essentially liberal ideas about racism and democracy [...] their radicalism was limited. Many left-wing students [at Ruskin] were hostile to the History Workshop movement and to its conference on women's history which helped to launch the 'women's movement'.[14]

---

13   Bob Purdie, 'Long-haired intellectuals and busybodies: Ruskin, student radicalism, and civil rights in Northern Ireland', in Geoff Andrews, Hilda Kean, Jane Thompson (Eds.), *Ruskin College: Contesting Knowledge, Dissenting Politics*, London: Lawrence and Wishart, 1999, p.59.

14   Ibid. p.78.

Discussing the History Workshop along with organisations like the Federation of Worker Writers and Community Publishers, Ken Worpole suggests there was a turn in the 1970s toward workers' education that sought less to inculcate knowledges as to draw upon and bring into play the existing knowledge of students.

> Whereas earlier working-class adult educational movements in Britain in [the 20th century], such as the National Council of Labour Colleges and the Workers' Educational Association, were strongly predicated on (and organised around) what it was assumed people didn't know, on their 'ignorance', these new forms of cultural struggle are based much more productively and radically on what people do know, and on the value and political significance of their experience and knowledge.[15]

While the quote below takes issue with the lack of 'quantitative' research work carried out by the members of the History Workshops, it throws up the question of value judgements with regards to the self-production of more 'personal' histories. There was a productive antagonism toward methodologies such as the use of statistical analysis in the History Workshops. But their critics' dismissal of the Workshops' 'collection of ephemera' does point to an increasing move toward research based in working class cultural identity, but sidelining its relationship to social power.

> In practice, however, the political purpose of History Workshop and its members has taken second place in its published works

---

15   Ken Warpole, *Dockers and Detectives,* op. cit., p.23.

to the recreation of experience; and there has been little sense, at least in the journal, of wider political objectives. At times, indeed, the style of History Workshop has verged on the antiquarianism of the left, the collection and publication of ephemera of working class life [...].[16]

Warwick: The Business University

Whilst the transformation of labour history into 'people's history' or 'history from below' was taking place in the 1960s and 1970s, there was a wider transformation of higher education. This developed from a broad demand for access to education whilst at the same time leading to the proliferation and reform of educational institutions, as well as an increase in the scope of subject areas offered. However, by the early 1970s, this relative democratisation was on the turn as universities opened themselves up to the funding agendas of private companies.

> There does, however, exist, in the Mid-Atlantic of the Motor Industry, the new University of Warwick. Whatever other instruments the architects may have used on their drawing-boards, they certainly made lavish use of a divider and a ruler.[17]

Warwick University was one of the first UK universities to adopt a business approach to higher education, developing

---

16 Roderick Floud, 'Quantitative History in International Perspective', *Social Science History*, Vol. 8, No. 2 Spring, 1984, p.156.

17 E.P. Thompson, 'The Business University', 1970, http://senatehouseoccupation.wordpress.com/documents/the-business-university-new-statesman-article-by-ep-thompson/

close links with business and exploiting the commercial value of its research. In February 1970, students staged a sit-in of the University Registry, gaining access to confidential files that revealed the University administration had been spying on students and keeping records of their political involvements. In *The Business University* (1970) Thompson, who taught at Warwick, weighed in on the side of the occupations, writing a defence of the 'intellectual autonomy' of the university from the encroachment of corporate interests.

> This is, of course, the corporate society, with all its ways of adapting and tailoring men to industry's needs, the corporate managerial society, with its direct access to the legal process to prevent the truth from being published, making the very air of Warwick this week crackle with tension, as we have been waiting for that alignment of forces to move in on us. It might be thought that we have here already, very nearly, the 'private university', in symbolic relationship with the aims and ethos of industrial capitalism, but built with a shell of public money and public legitimation.

> It might be thought that we have here already, very nearly, the 'private university', in symbiotic relationship with the aims and ethos of industrial capitalism, but built within a shell of public money and legitimation. (The university's published accounts for the year ending July 1969 show that it has already expended from HM Treasury £8,620,519 in non-recurrent grants alone, as against £1,307,856 in private gifts). There are big issues enough to be pondered here. The integrity of a university as a self-governing institution, which now seems like a fading episode of liberalism. Personal rights of privacy and academic liberties. The question of due representation on the lay bodies of institutions

primarily dependent upon public money, as well as the powers of such bodies – and of administrative officers – in relation to the academic staff. And other issues. The attitude of the labour movement towards this kind of spying.[18]

Thompson went on to ask:

Is it inevitable that the university will be reduced to the function of providing, with increasingly authoritarian efficiency, pre-packed intellectual commodities which meet the requirements of management? Or can we by our efforts transform it into a centre of free discussion and action, tolerating and even encouraging 'subversive' thought and activity, for a dynamic renewal of the whole society within which it operates?[19]

One problem with this intervention, which appears only a distant memory as access is even further curtailed by raised fees, is the age-old issue of institutionalised intellectual autonomy as a relatively privileged (let alone impossible) position. In protecting the university from business interests, such a position also risks the protection of established interests within the university – those who can afford to be there – while keeping those producing knowledge outside the university from having a stake in changing academic culture and debate. It is a contradictory and seemingly intractable problem, but we have to start on it somewhere.

---

18   Ibid.
19   Ibid.

Research Agendas in the Big Society

In March 2011, the intellectual autonomy of higher education was again thrown into question when a controversy erupted over the Arts and Humanities Research Council's (AHRC) announcement that the study of the 'Big Society' would be made a research priority in its Delivery Plan, thus securing a favourable funding settlement.

> One of the tasks of research, according to the AHRC's delivery plan, will be to define 'difficult to pin down' values in 'recent speeches on the big society', such as 'fairness, engagement, responsibility, mutuality, individualism [and] selfishness'.[20]

While AHRC declared the decision was not compulsory, 42 academics resigned in disgust. Labour MP and historian Tristan Hunt called the prioritisation of Big Society studies 'grotesque', adding that 'it is disgraceful that taxpayers' money is being spent on this bogus idea.'[21] But sociologist Les Back usefully demystified the announcement, pointing out that government has long tried to shape the research agenda.

> Of course, the 'Big Society' is – sociologically speaking – a nonsense. But is it really any more half-baked than the last government's obsession with 'community cohesion'? It is no secret in the social sciences that research agenda priorities are set politically, but it has come as something of a shock to

---

20 Daniel Boffey, 'Academic fury over order to study the big society', *The Guardian*, Sunday 27th March 2011, http://www.guardian.co.uk/education/2011/mar/27/academic-study-big-society

21 Ibid.

classicists and medieval historians.[22]

Indeed the AHRC's inclusion of Big Society studies appears to be a rebranding of existing research priorities under the banner of 'Connecting Communities' developed under the former Labour government since 2008: 'Enhancing the role that communities play in underpinning economic regeneration and improving quality of life'.[23] It has been argued that the council itself has been more or less influenced by government policy priorities since its inception under New Labour in 2005.

In other areas, Thompson was productively inquiring into the social codes and intellectual values of academic and non-academic work through polemics like *The Poverty of Theory*, from which the following quotation is extracted. Key to the debate here is the notion that historical research could not simply be made 'progressive' or socially aware through limiting its development to interactions between academics, but that the knowledge and analyses produced 'from below' should be brought to bear on established intellectual culture. He also points out that critical thought is for life.

outside the university precincts another kind of knowledge production is going on all the time. I will agree that it is not always vigorous. I am not careless of intellectual values nor unaware of the difficulty of their attainment. But I must

---

22 Les Back, 'Small World, Big Society: Haldane, Willetts and the AHRC', http://sociologyandthecuts.wordpress.com/2011/04/14/small-world-big-society-haldane-willetts-and-the-ahrc-by-les-back/

23 David Haden, 'AHRC rebrands a research priority', http://www.d-log.info/?p=13582

remind a Marxist philosopher that knowledges have been and still are formed outside the academic procedures. Nor have these been, in the test of practice, negligible. They have assisted men and women to till the fields, to construct houses, to support elaborate social organisations, and even, on occasion, to challenge effectively the conclusions of academic thought.[24]

Writing in 2012 when the student fees bill had already been passed, Danny Hayward points out that the defence of intellectual autonomy can serve to wittingly or unwittingly enclose critical thought within the university system and outside the broader field of struggles.

The point [...] is to carry us back to what I called above the liberal 'anti-market' ideology. I have argued that that ideology appears by virtue of its enlightened sneering to oppose 'markets' and to resist their undesirable 'social outcomes'; but that in fact the ideology does not oppose markets but instead contents itself with a polite request that the university be cordoned off from their operations. This doesn't work. The ideology does not deserve to be repudiated because it is 'reformist' but because it has a class basis. That is to say, it assumes that the 'values' which it wishes to protect ought to be protected only within the university and therefore (if implicitly) only on behalf of those who have access to it. [...]

And yet the riposte swells up: doesn't 'higher' education (as in education finer and more spiritual) require independence from the 'social'? Doesn't it require autonomy? But this doesn't mean very much. There must be better forms of autonomy than the type required for the production of 'basic' research which – we

---

24   E.P. Thompson, *The Poverty of Theory*, London: The Merlin Press, 1996.

learn from a University lobby group – contributes vastly more to the haemorrhaging value of HE licensing and spin-outs (the sector specific jargon for commercial enterprise) than so-called 'applied' research. These forms would be better worked out spontaneously in the process of collective action than 'in principle' at the end of an article.[25]

Free Schools, Really?

During recent struggles over education, some have argued that the increasing availability of research, both through official channels and academic piracy, have created the conditions for a 'university without walls', providing you have access to the technologies of dissemination.

Though academia has become obsessed with firewalling and commercializing the products of research, the info-revolution has massively expanded the primary sources of knowledge [...] the open-access revolution is corroding commerce [...] it's now possible to conceive of a situation where the great bulk of academic research will be free, open to all, and transparently cross-referenced. This will destroy the business models of media empires like Reed Elsevier but, arguably, they have already been destroyed.[26]

---

25   Danny Hayward, 'Adventures in the Sausage Factory', http://www.metamute.org/editorial/articles/adventures-sausage-factory-cursory-overview-uk-university-struggles-november-2010---july-2011

26   Paul Mason, *Why it's Kicking off Everywhere: The New Global Revolutions*, London: Verso 2012, p. 46.

Flyer for Open Birkbeck workshop, June 15th 2011

In late-2010 a text authored by Luther Blissett, entitled 'Education's Napster Moment', was distributed at anti-fee increase demonstrations.

> Universities are collapsing. Not as a result of dramatic cuts but because they represent an outmoded model for their primary function, the exchange of knowledge and research. Like the music industry, the education industry is about to experience the same death blow to its infrastructure and profit model that Napster issued to the music industry back in 1999. [...]
>
> Abandon the institution and declare its death, the point at which our apathy for the current state of play is declared, the better. With this change we will be able to destabilise the mediated control of our social trajectory, causing a genuine crisis for those that stand to profit both politically and financially from our existing system. It is the institutions and those that control them that need us.
>
> Create a real crisis, torrent your syllabus, duplicate your id cards and give them to strangers, scan your entire library and post it on AAARG, distribute maps of your university online, relocate your seminars to a space outside of the institution. Invalidate the universities existence, so that together we can begin to build fresh foundations on its grave.[27]

Luther Blissett is a well-known multiple author pseudonym, therefore quite appropriate to a text claiming to herald an era of distributed free universal education. However, when

---

27   Luther Blissett, 'Education's Napster Moment', November 2010, http:// deterritorialsupportgroup.wordpress.com/2011/01/19/educations-napster-moment/

the text was re-posted on the site of The Really Free School, a nomadic squatted social centre in central London established to support the education protests, it elicited vitriolic response.

> I think it's safe to say that they're missing an *absolutely enormous, gaping difference* between the napster-fucking of the music industry and doing the same thing to what is left of publicly funded university education. In short, most of us don't care in the least about the survival of, say, Sony. [...] On the other hand, I'd like to think that we do care about the continued existence and viability of not-for-profit and (let's hope) state funded educational centres.[28]

Whilst none of the organisers of the Really Free School claimed to have authored the text or to necessarily endorse the views expressed therein, it seemed their model of provision of a space for radical self-education, with no fees nor payment for teachers, was sufficient to suggest they were advocating something similar to the dissolution of really existing unfree education. One teacher took exception to this projected model:

> Destroy the university and no one pays me anymore. I spend an awful lot of time and energy on teaching – most months, almost all of my time and energy. The students seem to want me to do it. Maybe it's their interpellation by their ISA [Intellectual State Apparatus] of choice, but they'd be pretty upset to run the seminars on their own or if I just put my syllabi and lectures on-line. [...] Call it me defending my financial interests, but

---

28 'Against the Really Free School', http://adswithoutproducts. com/2011/02/16/against-the-really-free-school/

even given the rough job market I'm pretty sure I could find something amazingly more lucrative to do for a living than this.[29]

Clearly, the author was precisely defending their own 'financial interests' and this revealed a slide into division within the movement against higher education fee increases. On the one side, lecturers and other staff weren't necessarily always fully behind each other when it came to a defence against departmental cuts or fighting for better conditions.[30] On the other, student groups refusing fee hikes took different positions on whether they 1) agreed with fees but just wanted lower fees, 2) wanted to 'save universities' as they were – i.e. institutions which reproduce workers with skills appropriate to the existing division of labour and class society, 3) push for universal free education for all, 4) abolish the universities as they exist and turn them over to student control. The more radical of these positions was rarely expressed and certainly not hegemonic. Amidst a wave of 50 or more occupations in universities around the UK, a number of self-organised groups – the Really Free School, The University for Strategic Optimism, The Bloom Social Centre, London Free School, Glasgow Open School, amongst others – placed themselves on different positions of this political spectrum, but mostly

---

29 Ibid.

30 In this case, the SOAS cleaners struggle to obtain the London Living Wage is an exemplary example of how student activism has connected to labour movements recently. However, the fact that cleaners at SOAS and at other colleges have still not achieved this meagre wage security attests to the lack of solidarity between teaching, administrative and other workers in the sector. See: http://soasunion.org/campaigns/justice-for-cleaners-and-london-living-wage-campaign/

agreed that educational protest went in parallel with showing that they could self-educate and do it themselves. By doing so they were following a rich history of 'self-institutions' which have questioned the 'value', commodification, or ownership of knowledge in a so-called 'knowledge economy'.[31] However, the full ramifications of what that would mean whilst preserving the institutions which administered higher education, let alone primary and secondary education, was explored with less enthusiasm.[32]

In many respects, the tensions over 'really free' versus free-at-the-point-of-use official education reflect the central problematic of self-organisation in a time of austerity. Taking over the functions once provided or paid for (via general taxation) by the state (and its private partnerships) could be seen to play into the hands of the 'Big Society' ethos, care-taking for neglect. But rather than de-stressing the importance of and efforts toward the free university and against the role of education in reproducing capital relations, this dynamic remains a contentious area of debate.

A further division within the education protests became clear as younger students began to join the demonstrations to protest the cancellation of the Education Maintenance Allowance, a payment made by government to teenagers from low income families to pursue Further Education.

---

31   See: http://www.copenhagenfreeuniversity.dk/library.html

32   For attempts to connect up austerity and anti-privatisation struggles in primary, secondary and further education see: *Don't Panic, Organise! A Mute Magazine Pamphlet on Recent Struggles in Education,* http://www.metamute.org/editorial/books/don't-panic-organise-mute-magazine-pamphlet-recent-struggles-education

We're from the slums of London, yeah? How do they expect us to pay £9,000 for uni fees? And EMA, the only thing that's keeping us in college – what's stopping us from doing drug deals on the street anymore? Nothing.[33]

The sequence of demonstrations, particularly those of November and December 2010, offered a brief combination of energies between students in higher education and those in Secondary and Further education and numerous others to letting off steam on the streets of London. Attacking the Conservative party headquarters, the police, and other symbols of a government hell-bent on hastening delivery of the ever-narrowing non-future of overpriced education and shit-jobs. However, this combination had little to do with the nominal 'defend education' agenda, as Danny Hayward concludes:

Middle class students might piously hope that working class teenagers will be allowed to 'access' universities and become more like them; but in fact the similarity is more likely to become visible not at the 'point of access' to universities but, instead, at their exits. And it's the view from the exit, from which can be seen the greatest expanse of nothing at all, which will perhaps give the clearest indication of how UK education struggle ought to proceed.[34]

---

33   Anonymous video, 'We're from the Slums of London' 9th December, 2010, http://youtu.be/k1BsTl4QRjl

34   'The Sausage Factory', op. cit.

Friends I Am Creating a Way of Life in Which Your Ingredients Will Be Returned to You

In 2010-2011 a classroom of 9-10 year olds were shown various outpourings and manifestos from the occupations and produced their own manifesto.

Friends I am creating a way of life in which your ingredients will be returned to you / Our lives are controlled by rules, restrictions, limitations, hatred and big concrete things./ So, as of this Tuesday I am removing power from our government and parliament an other rulers. This city shall be run by the elder generations like grandparents and generally old people. / The old leaders will go to the naughty step where they will destroy all presentations and fax machines and become natural beings. / I am confiscating all mansions and making them flats for the homeless. / All property developers will report to the roof for training in building in the clouds. / Nothing will be barricaded it is free country no limits. / Small family businesses are the only ones aloud and no money either everything is free or you trade products. / Everyone shall be taught the art of sewing to make ones clothing. / There will be no big stores or mass produced products every thing must have a history no smoking alcohol on unessential drugs. / We all shall learn how to milk a goat./ There shall be compulsory napping from one till two for over worked adults and smallish children. Therefore they must not walk but ride around on beds with wheels. / People must share what they don't need. / We will tear down all offices and work places and replace them with more farmland. / Each of us will learn how to Lindy hop / We can travel if we want to but not all year round. / The air of the city will smell of freshly baked bread. / There will be free bikes and tricycles for all / The city will be filled with the sounds of running water, and bird song. / Cheese will be small and humans will be cheerful. / Adults will make giant teacup can sleep in it. / We will grow all our own fruit and vegetables / Cornflakes and potatoes will be plentiful / Visitors need not bring anything but Joy. / This is My Homage to you.

BIG SOCIETY

In the 'Big Society' rhetoric of the UK coalition government (2010-present), we discern the recuperation of much recent discussion on the left over matters of self-organisation and working class autonomy. This has involved the fabrication of a contradictory and *weak* anti-capitalist discourse which has been mobilised under a pro-austerity agenda. 'History from below' is in large part a history of (often socially and politically antagonistic) self-organisation in the face of oppression, dispossession and poverty. Today we reach a point where those complex acts and principles are actively invoked – in politically sanitised form – by the ConDem government and its official opposition as a means of 'plugging holes in the gaps' left by the dismantling and privatisation of welfare. Here we will identify the instrumentalisation of aspects of history from below by two key thinkers and party ideologists, Maurice Glasman and Phillip Blond, who are respectively associated with the 'Blue Labour' and 'Red Tory' tendencies and whose thinking was, at least initially, seen as central to the renewal of their political parties.

Rebranding, 'renewal' and ideological manoeuvrings by both major parties has always been in operation. The particular and highly provisional mode of ideology we address in this chapter is a response to a particular economic moment. In the wake of the financial crisis, and the transformation of the state required to make UK PLC a viable going concern in its aftermath. Labour and the Conservatives have sought to define themselves in distinction from the legacies of Thatcherism and the Blair years. For both parties this process is incomplete, partial and ongoing, and none of the doctrines discussed in this chapter have really achieved full formation. We see these political formations, and their use of aspects of radical history, as reactionary means of both acknowledging and glossing over the financial crisis; in doing so, they lend 'authenticity' to subsequent transformations of the state as directions out of the crisis, however implausible they remain. The debates fill a vacuum and constitute a struggle over ideological territory in which each attempts to re-connect with notional 'traditions' whilst escaping traumas (the neoliberal 'shock doctrine', the Gulf Wars, economic meltdown) which are the products of their parties' recent policies while in government.If, as Jacques Rancière puts it, 'the power of a mode of thinking lies in its capacity to be displaced'[1], then we should expect the analysis of the struggles of the past to be mobilised, not just on the part of those who are struggling globally in the present, but also by the state and capital. In this respect the use of history from below by Glasman and Blond also *reflects back* on the problems and limitations of works like E.P. Thompson's *Making of the English Working Class*; specifically, the narrow focus of the book in terms of race, gender and nation. But there are also some surprising acknowledgements of the long history of class struggle in Britain, though one suspects that they are only called upon in order to better see them as safely contained in idealised history, and to better claim their heritage for an extension of the neoliberal project – a reordering of class society from above.

---

1   Jacques Rancière, *The Philosopher and His Poor*, Durham: Duke University Press, 2004, p.xxviii.

Red Tory

Phillip Blond is an Anglican theologian associated with the 'Radical Orthodoxy' tendency, author of the book, *Red Tory: How Left and Right Have Broken Britain and How We Can Fix It*, and director of think tank ResPublica. Blond, who was recognised as one of the key ideologists of the renewal of the Tory Party, draws directly upon a (unqualified) reading which credits E.P. Thompson's narrative of working class agency in *The Making of the English Working Class* and uses it to justify the dismantling of public services.

> The welfare state, I believe, began the destruction of the independent life of the British working class [...] making the populace a supplicant citizenry dependent on the state rather than themselves.[2]

Blond invokes an illusory past prior to both the monolithic state and the market economy. The subtitle of *Red Tory* inadvertently mirrors a statement made by Thompson in 1980: 'The state, whether the Conservative or Labour administrations, has been taking liberties, and these liberties were once ours.'[3] Blond cites Thompson to celebrate the London Corresponding Society, a body organised by London artisans in 1792 and networked across the country to agitate for the extension of the vote to working class men, which

---

2   Phillip Blond, *Red Tory: How the Left and Right Have Broken Britain and How We Can Fix It*, London: Faber and Faber, 2010, p.15.

3   E.P. Thompson quoted in Peter Linebaugh, 'The Who and Whom of Liberty Taking', December 2008, http://www.metamute.org/editorial/articles/who-and-whom-liberty-taking .

was finally suppressed by the Pitt government in 1799. He even goes so far as to celebrate working class self-activity:

> There never really was an illiterate working class mob. Always and everywhere one can find examples of cogent, intellectual and practical proletarian resistance. Mobs, such as they were, rarely acted spontaneously. Often they were products of political organisation and design operating at the behest of radical factions to secure political advantage [...].[4]

Yet, this rosy view of a righteous battle, without any clarity over which forces it opposed, is mainly used to establish and admonish the present working class and its perceived decline:

> A history that reveals the present state of working-class diffidence and powerlessness as a historical aberration.[5]

It is a persuasive and deft argument which chimes with some historians' (e.g. Eric Hobsbawm's) views that the post-war social contract had manufactured an overly docile working class. But Blond's history restores 'working class' agency with little struggle or humour. Whilst it's worth considering his attempt to absorb a radical history of working class self-organisation as a measure of how influential the work of history from below has become, we cannot but read the invocation of this history as a way to evade taking a racially mixed and gendered class seriously in the present. In a review of *Red Tory*, Jonathan Raban ruthlessly satirises Blond's

---

4   Ibid, pp.12–13.
5   Ibid, pp.12–13.

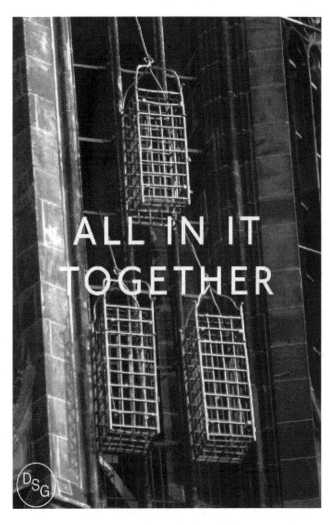

All in It Together poster by Deterritorial Support Group, c.2010

Edenic vision.

> Once upon a time, long before the Industrial Revolution spoiled everything, it was different: Britain had an 'organic culture', a 'vibrant agrarian culture' with a 'prosperous and relatively secure British peasantry'. In the good old days, everyone went to church, of course, and religion supplied the 'transcendent idea of the good', whose absence in our sorry, secular society is the root cause of our national misery. What we must now do, the parson says, is somehow resurrect the 'British culture of virtue'; we need 'a civil society built around the practice of virtue and exploration of the good'. For a start, schools must provide 'education into the good', but we 'cannot have a moral society without a moral economy', and it's on the matter of the moral economy and the 'moral market', and how they might be achieved, that Blond's sermon builds to its utopian climax.[6]

Blond complains that between market fundamentalism and the state the 'civic middle' is squeezed. The 'civic middle' is supposed to represent the working class, though a very sanitised view of them characterised by 'virtue', thrift, friendly societies, churches, trade unions, independent insurance associations. These, according to Blond, are the institutions the working class set up to reproduce itself and which the welfare state destroyed or undermined. For example, the 1911 National Insurance Act met opposition from both right and left:

---

6   Jonathan Raban, 'Cameron's Crank', *London Review of Books* Vol. 32 No. 8 · 22 April 2010, pp.22-23. http://www.lrb.co.uk/v32/n08/jonathan-raban/camerons-crank

'Sections of the Conservative party opposed the Act considering that it was not for taxpayers to pay for such benefits. Some trade unions who operated their own insurance schemes and friendly societies were also opposed'.[7]

Blond disingenuously characterises welfare as the invention of a 'middle-class elite' intended to 'deprive the poor of their irritating habit of autonomous organisation'.[8] Yet, this celebration of the 'autonomous organisation' of the poor is stripped of antagonism. It is based on an extremely selective reading of Thompson, but interestingly one that has been repeated as Labour-aligned thinkers have attempted to respond to Red Toryism.

Blue Labour

Maurice Glasman, an academic and Labour life peer, coined the term 'Blue Labour' drawing on the history of the Labour Party to disinter 'a deeply conservative socialism that places family, faith and work at the heart of a new politics of reciprocity, mutuality and solidarity'.[9] Glasman, like Blond, draws upon E.P. Thompson's idea of radical continuities and traditions as the means the working class used to resist the development of industrial capitalism. Howerver, Glasman, like Blond, erases working class history of its antagonisms,

7   'National Insurance Act 1911', http://en.wikipedia.org/wiki/National_Insurance_Act_1911

8   *Red Tory*, op. cit., p.15.

9   Allegra Stratton, 'Labour: Now it's Kind of Blue', *The Guardian*, 24 April 2009, http://www.guardian.co.uk/politics/blog/2009/apr/24/blue-labour-conservative-socialism

effectively emphasising and affirming the actively conservative and managerial aspects of Labour's position on the left:

> The founders of the labour movement understood the logic of capitalism as based upon the maximisation of returns on investment, and the threat this posed to their lives, livelihoods and environment, but they did not embrace class war, and clung stubbornly to an idea of a common life with their rulers and exploiters.[10]

Glasman is explicit about the way that 21st century Conservatives have successfully annexed Labour values of mutualism and that this requires a response, albeit one which affirms the conservatism of Labour rather than opposing the conservative framing and appropriation of progressive aspects of labour movement history.

> The Labour tradition has never been straightforwardly progressive, and that is not a defect which we are on the verge of overcoming, but a tremendous strength that will offer the basis of renewal [...] Labour is robustly national and international, conservative and reforming, christian and secular, republican and monarchical, democratic and elitist, radical and traditional; and it is most transformative and effective when it defies the status quo in the name of ancient as well as modern values.[11]

John Cruddas, Labour MP for Dagenham and Rainham,

---

10 Maurice Glasman, 'Labour as a radical tradition', *Soundings*, No.46., pp.31-41, p.33.

11 'Labour as a radical tradition', op.cit, p.31.

reproduces many of Glasman's arguments and also invokes E.P. Thompson within a highly conservative framework of nationalism and tradition: 'Thompson articulated the conservative nature of English socialism – how it is a love of home, of place and of the local.'[12] As Stuart Hall points out, Cruddas' use of such identifications is based in the context of campaigning against the far right in his constituency. But Hall goes on to note that the elevation of these particularities assumes that they can easily be politically willed into doing the work of politicians.

> I came to the UK at the age of 19 and I didn't know anything about the working-class tradition, the Labour Party and the unions. I learned it. And in doing so, I came to appreciate that, if you're going to intervene politically, you'd better bloody well know something about the class on whose side you want to align yourself. But I never took the line – which I think was Edward Thompson's – that the heart and soul of the left was out there, and down here was what he called, in a sort of William Cobbett way, the 'Great Wen' [...].

> I think I understand [Cruddas'] preoccupations rather more than Maurice Glasman's. In a constituency like Cruddas's, where you're fighting the far right, you have to think about those things [English identity, immigration]. But you have to be careful about how you recruit them. He came to talk to me about the New Left, which, of course, was interested in the popular language of the nation. But I had the feeling he was raiding the

---

12   John Cruddas, 'A country for old men', *New Statesman*, April 2011,
     http://www.newstatesman.com/uk-politics/2011/04/english-labour-
     tradition

past, out of context, in a way.[13]

Indeed, Glasman's appeal to values of 'Faith, Flag and Family' – a phrase he appears to have borrowed from the Cornerhouse Group in the Conservative party – quickly backfired. In 2011 he called for an end to all immigration to the UK in an interview with the *Fabian Review* which was picked up by the *Daily Telegraph*. He also came under sustained criticisms by feminists for his perceived paternalism, his belief that 'male entitlement' had been eroded; and for blaming women's independence for the breakdown in social order. Blond too, in evoking a nostalgia for a pre-welfare working class 'autonomy', also appears to have harked back to a time when women were expected by many men to be in a subordinate position and women's unpaid work in the home and restrictions within it were taken for granted.

Blond appears to have been left behind by the Tory party. Buffetted by scandals over the Levenson Inquiry, David Cameron and other conservative figures' personal and professional ties to dubious media practices, and the handling of the financial crisis, the coalition government has seemingly dropped any of the experiments proposed by Blond. His ideas have provided a very thin gloss on austerity policies which Labour were in any case introducing during the so-called 'boom' that led up to the financial crisis of 2008.

---

13   Jonathan Derbyshire, 'Stuart Hall: "We need to talk about Englishness"', *The New Statesman*, August 2012, http://www. newstatesman.com/politics/uk-politics/2012/08/stuart-hall-we-need-talk-about-englishness

Tory Marxism

Red Tory and Blue Labour may seem mere anomalies indicative of an era of confused politics which has broken out in the early 21st century. But there are some deeper threads which connect radical social history and the crude ideological posturings adopted by party politicians. Maurice Cowling, a historian at Peterhouse College, Cambridge University, played mentor to a number of Conservative politicians, political advisors and journalists at the *Telegraph*; Michael Portillo being the most famous of these. Effectively a 'talent-spotter' for the Tories, 'Cowling's brand of ultra-Toryism was well to the right of the Conservative Party and of practical politics'.[14] Cowling's contrarian stance led him to invent the term Tory Marxism, which served to bait Liberals, Lefties and Conservatives alike.

> he was a self-confessed proponent of 'Tory Marxism', who endorsed its 'cynical truth' that 'inequalities, sufferings and alienations' were 'vital concomitants of the freedom, discipline and social solidarity of modern societies'. Tory Marxism was an exquisite instrument of provocation. Nothing was more certain to trigger fear and loathing among his real class enemies – the liberal jellies of Hampstead – than the reactionary menace which inhered in the idea of class warfare waged from above.[15]

Whilst Cowling was exceptional, his importance as a recruiter for the Conservative party indicates how modern history as

---

14   Colin Kidd, 'Sabre-Toothed Teacher', *London Review of Books*, vol. 33, no.7, 31 March 2011, http://www.lrb.co.uk/v33/n07/contents

15   Ibid.

an academic subject has remained an important aspect of the education of the UK's politicians and a key foundation for the development of political arguments, which sometimes, and unevenly, inform policy. Cowling's student Michael Portillo had been a strong candidate for Tory leadership in the 1990s but after losing his seat in the 1997 general election he has pursued a career as a broadcaster, specialising in history documentaries for radio and television. In one of these he interviewed Peter Linebaugh on the liberties enshrined within the Magna Carta and the Charter of the Forest.[16]

Before the UK general election in 2009, Douglas Carswell MP – an advocate for 'radical localism' – played up to the Tory self-image of 'progressive' conservatives and antagonists to the centralised state by suggesting that David Cameron was the 'heir to the diggers and levellers'.

> It must be right that those who exercise the coercive power of the state should be held to account by those whom they serve. That is a progressive cause. It is the cause for centuries of the parish constable against the remote magistracy. It is the cause of London Labour councils and the South Yorkshire police authority through the 1980s. It is the cause of the Levellers and, indeed, the Diggers, to which my hon. Friend the Member for Esher and Walton referred earlier. However, it is a cause today that is represented not by the Opposition, but by the Prime Minister, my right hon. Friend Mr Cameron, who represents not just Burford, but democratic ideals of the Levellers who lost

---

16 'Was Magna Carta really the document that defined our freedoms?', The Open University, http://www.open.edu/openlearn/history-the-arts/history/social-economic-history/was-magna-carta-really-the-document-which-defined-our-freedoms

their lives there.[17]

Participating in Blue Labour's undue elevation of national and local particularities to first political principles, popular historian Dominic Sandbrook picks up on the apparent parochialism of some of England's radical history, but suggests this is what Blue Labour needs.[18] Sandbrook says the peasants revolt was led by 'a local landowner, Thomas Baker, while another leading agitator, Geoffrey Litster, held the title of bailiff and was a literate local official'; the participants attacked immigrants and foreigners, beheading 35 Flemish weavers in one street. Robert Kett's attack on the enclosures was, according to Sandbrook, motivated by a rival landowner bribing peasants to smash up his enclosures. Sandbrook also describes Thomas Spence as an avowed localist who took parochialism to an extreme (although both Spence and his followers, including Robert Wedderburn, developed an international vision of freedom from slavery, freedom of movement and the redistribution of land and property).

Ideological Inversions

The recent ideological inversions carried out by Labour and the Conservatives are less unusual than at first they may seem. In the *Revoltes Logiques* essay 'From Pelloutier to Hitler', for which the shorter essay 'Links in the Chain' provides a

---

17 Daniel Hannan, 'A Model Maiden Speech', *The Telegraph* 28 June 2010, http://blogs.telegraph.co.uk/news/danielhannan/100042748/a-model-maiden-speech/

18 Dominic Sandbrook, 'Family, faith and flag', The New Statesman, http://www.newstatesman.com/society/2011/04/labour-party-english-england

theoretical prelude and ally,[19] Jacques Rancière examines the
way in which certain forms of workerism and productivism
were absorbed by Petain's collaborationist Vichy state
leading to collusion between pro-Nazis and trade unionist
elements in France between 1940 and 1944. It is a powerful
reminder to social historians that the Nazi movement drew
its origins from the left and closer examination might find
painful proximities in the history of any territory. Even more
controversially, it is a powerful rebuke to those in France
who would like to imagine, without complication, a glorious
continuum of socialist history cemented by the victory over
Nazism. Rancière misses few opportunities to hammer
home the reactionary consequences of idealist forms of anti-
capitalism: alternative currencies, democratic negotiation
between bosses and workers, workplace hygiene and even
workers' autonomy are all exposed as platitudes through
which to transform genuine grievances into management
schemes. During this brief period all these measures were
recommended by trade unions or militants in favour of
collaboration and found some approval from the Vichy
powers. These workers' advocates greatest treason lay in
the way they sought to organise workers' needs in order to
better direct them via the state. Rancière conveys well the
complex context through which such arguments unfolded,
found material motivation, were contorted and contested.
Moreover, the attempt to mobilise heroic socialist traditions
of hard work, loyalty and dignity in the service of collaboration
lends great weight to his thorough questioning of whether
these ideals were native to the working class at all. In the

---

19   Jacques Rancière, *Staging the People: The Proletarian and His
      Double*, London: Verso, 2011, pp.122–174.

context of the Parti Communiste Française's debates over the relationship between workers and intellectuals, this research had the function of authorising Gauche Prolétarienne's ultra-leftism and discrediting the more distanced and economistic approach of the party. Though arguments against workers' control have typically been mobilised to authoritarian ends, syndicalist-style self-management can also become coercive under certain pressures. Michael Seidman's study *Workers Against Work* explores the conflicting problems of self-management and workers' resistance to work in Paris and Barcelona in the 1930s in a period in which anarchosyndicalists and socialists took power in these cities.

When revolution erupted in Barcelona in 1936, union militants of the anarchosyndicalist CNT (Confederación nacional de trabajo) and the Marxist UGT (Unión general de trabajadores) inherited a backward industrial structure that they were compelled to modernize under difficult conditions of civil war in Spain. These militants – whether anarchosyndicalist, Communist, or Socialist – copied elements from the Western and Soviet models of economic development and accumulation. While attempting to build the productive forces, they quickly encountered what I shall call workers' resistance to work. The anarchosyndicalists of the CNT, the most important working-class organization in Barcelona, were forced to jettison their theories of workers' democracy and participation to make the rank and file work harder and produce more. The anarchosyndicalists and Communists in the newly collectivized firms reestablished piecework, initiated severe controls on the shop floor, and embarked on an intensive campaign that included both odes to

Stakhanovism and socialist realist art.[20]

From this perspective it is possible to see that self-management could also preserve capital and labour as antagonistic, but functioning, poles of a relation which ensure ongoing exploitation. For Seidman, however, the celebration of 'workers against work' could equally tend towards supporting the opposite pole of the political spectrum by affirming such tendencies as a form of nihilism excluding any revolutionary perspective.[21]

Autonomy and the Big Society

As the UK state continues to enact enormous social spending cuts carried out under the rubric of the 2008 financial crisis, a degree of self-organisation was, and is, to be expected. What Westminster's two main parties have done is anticipate, promote and brand this as policy. Across the political spectrum politicians have affirmed the socially beneficial effects of co-operation and volunteering. Since the early 1990s, self-organisation and 'self-activity' have been circulating as key terms in debates between anti-globalisation activists and

---

20 Michael Seidman, *Workers Against Work: Labor in Paris and Barcelona during the Popular Fronts,* Berkeley: California University Press, 1991, p.11.

21 Ibid. Seidman's analysis is interesting, but risks lapsing from critical pessimism into simplistic nihilism as he emphasises worker's dislike for work and desire for travel and cars. Similarities with Rancière are evident in Seidman's problematic arguments for re-introducing 'individuality' back into historical research. See also: Michael Seidman, *Republic of Egos: A Social History of the Spanish Civil War,* Winsconsin: University of Winsconsin Press, 2002.

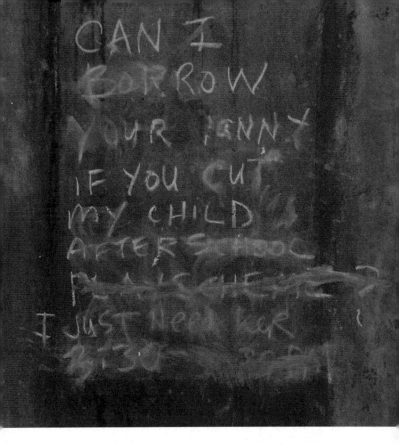

Anon. Graffitti near Coram's Fields Nursery, London c.2010

post-autonomist political theorists. A report by *The Commune* on a community-run library on Woodberry Down Estate in Hackney neatly summarises this bind.

> The Tories are talking about the Big Society; anti-capitalists are talking about self-organisation and the commons; and the anti-cuts campaigns are demanding the preservation or re-

instatement of state run and controlled services. Amongst this finding a radical critique of the state whilst defending those state services; finding a critique of self-exploitation whilst acknowledging the great things communities and small groups are doing to change lives and empower people – is not always easy.[22]

As Mark Fisher notes below, there is a profound irony in the co-option of ideas of autonomy in 'Big Society' rhetoric, but for him this does not invalidate Marxist autonomist ideas.

The much derided idea of the Big Society is, in effect, a right wing version of autonomism. The work of Phillip Blond, one of the architects of the 'Big Society' concept, is saturated with the rhetoric of self-organisation. In the report 'The Ownership State' which he wrote for the ResPublica think-tank, Blond writes of 'open systems' which 'recognise that uncertainty and change render traditional command-and-control ineffective'. While Blond's ideas have been seen by many as obfuscatory justifications for the neoliberal privatisation agenda, Blond himself positions them as critical of neoliberalism. Blond notes a paradox that I also discuss in *Capitalist Realism*: rather than eliminating bureaucracy, as it promised to, neoliberalism has led to its proliferation [...] far from indicating any deficiency in autonomist ideas, the co-option of these ideas by the right

---

22   Lady Stardust, 'An Image of the 'Big Society'? a report from woodberry down community library', *The Commune*, November 2010, http://thecommune.co.uk/2010/11/29/an-image-of-the-big-society-a-report-from-woodberry-down-community-library/

shows that they have continuing potency.[23]

It is easy to ridicule the rhetorical appropriations of radical histories by politicians, but equally they force us to critically re-examine the sources they borrow from, and consider what is living and what is dead in the radical history they wilfully plunder.

---

23   Mark Fisher, 'The Future is Still Ours: Autonomy and Post-Capitalism', Mark Fisher, in *We Have Our Own Concept of Time and Motion*, AutoItalia South East, http://www.charliewoolley.com/post/19956452384/the-future-is-still-ours

UNHISTORICAL SHIT

Here we wade into some of the disputes and controversies the 'historians from below' initiated, or were the focus of. It's important to recognise that not only did the techniques, approaches and subject matter developed by communist historians meet resistance from within the historiographical establishment of their times, but also, politically they met challenges from Marxists and other critics too. Positions on historical events which we now group together began from different starting points and indulged in polemics over what might seem now only minor differences. In the post-WWII period history was a powerful tool in the projects of both decolonisation and national reconstruction taking place across the world. The alignment of Marxist groups and national communist parties with historical research in certain key periods was one way in which crucial political differences were articulated and played out.

The English Revolution

In the years immediately following WWII, growing energy was thrown at the study of the complex dynamics behind the English Revolution of the 1640s. The Marxist reading of the English Civil War was of a bourgeois revolution which set the conditions for the development of agrarian, and later industrial capitalism. In the midst of this dynamic, the Communist Party Historians Group unearthed the contrary radical tendencies that emerged during the conflict, most famously the Diggers and Levellers. The English Revolution became a mainstay for the proponents of 'history from below', and effectively popularised their work, as it became a significant influence on social movements following the New Left. E.P. Thompson attributes this significance as a factor in him pursuing history politically.

> A certain breakthrough in British radical history, associated particularly at that point with the Marxist tradition, took place some forty-five years ago. (I'm sorry to use military imagery.) We are still exploiting the terrain that was opened up with that breakthrough. For me as a school student in 1940 it came through the work of Christopher Hill: his first brief study of 1640. I sat down at the age of sixteen to write for the sixth form history society a paper on the Marxist interpretation of history and the English civil war, leafing through Christopher's work, and Bernstein, and Petagorsky, and Winstanley's pamphlets and such Leveller tracts as I could get, and some Marx, Engels, and Plekhanov. And there followed upon this other breakthroughs: one thinks of Eric [Hobsbawm]'s magnificent essay on 'The Tramping Artisan'. The rest of us followed through that gap.[1]

Writing in 1949 on the Tercentenary of the English Revolution, C.L.R. James took stock of the then recent interest in the great period of social unrest from which secular democracy in Britain sprang forth.

> The contemporary interest in the Puritan revolution of the 17th Century is an outgrowth of the crisis of bourgeois democracy and dates from the 1929 depression. Two groups have concerned

---

1   E. P. Thompson, 'Agenda for Radical History', *Critical Inquiry*, Vol. 21, No. 2. (Winter, 1995), pp. 299–304.

themselves with it – the liberal intellectuals who preoccupy themselves with the Levellers and the Stalinists who give their main attention to Winstanley and the Diggers. In this they have recently been joined by the Catholics. The Stalinists made no contributions of their own to the understanding of the Levellers and ignore the work which has been done during the recent past. A gulf separates them from Marx who called the Levellers 'a functioning communist party.' It is the gulf between the revolutionary-class struggle and a bureaucratic, authoritarian conception of society and politics.[2]

The work of Christopher Hill, possibly at the time one of the 'Stalinists' James denigrates above, is often more explicit than most about the historical parallels between the period of tumult which is his specialism and those he was living through.

The new economic developments of the sixteenth and seventeenth centuries made the old economic and social and political system hopelessly out of date. Those of its defenders [look] regretfully back to the stability and relative [sic] the peasantry in the Middle Ages were quite unrealistic and in effect reactionary. Their role was the same as that of many liberals at the present day who think how nice it would be if capitalism could still work in the, 'liberal', nineteenth-century way, without having to resort quite so frequently to fascism and war. But fine words alter no historic processes. History has passed on and left these apologists of an imaginary system

---

2   C.L.R. James, 'Ancestors of the Proletariat', *Fourth International*, Vol.10 No.8, September 1949, pp.252-255.

standing, just as it left Charles I's defenders.[3]

However, it is a common misconception that members of the Communist Party Historians group were the first to seriously revive radical groups and figures of this period from 'historical oblivion'.

I am afraid that it is not true to claim that there was a dearth of works on the Levellers before Christopher Hill and other members of the Communist Party's Historians' Group began work to rescue them from historical oblivion or that this was the responsibility of Whig historians. S.R. Gardiner considered the Levellers' influence in the period from 1647-1649 in some detail in Volume IV of his history of the English Civil War and in his biography of Oliver Cromwell: the first Agreement of the People, now known to be the product not of Leveller thinking but of a group of radicals around Henry Marten, appeared in 1889 in his Constitutional Documents of the Puritan Revolution. It was C.H. Firth who edited and published The Clarke Papers, which throw such light on relations between the leaders of the New Model Army, the Agitators and Levellers, between 1891 and 1901. Eduard Bernstein's book, *Cromwell and Communism; socialism and democracy in the great English Civil War* was published in German in 1895 and in an English translation in 1930. [...] The truth is that there had been a significant amount of work done on the Levellers long before they attracted the attention of Christopher Hill or of the Communist Party's Historians' Group.[4]

---

3   Christopher Hill, *The English Revolution*, http://www.marxists.org/
     archive/hill-christopher/english-revolution/

4   From, http://keith-perspective.blogspot.co.uk/2011/06/historians-on-
     levellers-and-english.html

Eduard Bernstein was a German socialist and member of the German Social Democratic Party (SPD). His opposition to Bismark forced him into exile in Zurich in the 1880s, and he moved to London in 1888. Bernstein had close contact with Freidrich Engels and Karl Kautsky as well as Henry Hyndman and circles around the first socialist party in Britain, the Social Democratic Federation. Bernstein published his book *Sozialismus und Demokratie in der grossen englischen Revolution* in Germany in 1895 and it was translated into English the same year. The significances of Bernstein's book are several. Bernstein sidelined the romanticism with which the period had been treated in English historiography, he elevated the significance of the English revolution and compared the radical changes it wrought to those of the French revolution of 1789.

> The English Revolution as it advanced, resembled the great French Revolution in outstripping the aims that were proclaimed at its commencement. During its course the various parties, and the different classes behind them, came to the front, one after another, and played a leading part in the direction of events [...][5]

Within communist, socialist and Marxist circles Bernstein was a proponent of revisionism and reformism. He believed socialism would come about through the perfection of capitalism and not through its destruction. His position was explicitly critiqued by Rosa Luxemburg in her essay 'Reform

---

5   Eduard Bernstein, *Cromwell & Communism: Socialism and Democracy in the Great English Revolution*, H.J. Stenning (trans.), New York: Schocken Books, 1963, p.10.

or Revolution', published in 1900. Bernstein proposed significant revisions of Marx's ideas, particularly his 'law of value'.

Despite this he was an unorthodox socialist, one of the first to publish progressive views on homosexuality (with regards to Oscar Wilde's trial), and provided a significant connection between the English socialism of Hyndman, William Morris and the German Marxist left. Bernstein's book on the English Revolution approached the social movements behind it in economic and class terms. He framed the Diggers and the 'true' Levellers as communist currents within a broader social revolution.

> It was only at the height of its power that the Leveller movement produced a genuinely communistic offshoot in the sect or group of 'true Levellers'. This sect not only made an experiment in communistic self-help of remarkable originality, but left behind it a noteworthy sketch of communistic reconstruction which seems to have escaped the notice of historians of the English Revolution.[6]

Progressivism and Modernity

One of the general critiques of Marxist concepts of history is that of a perceived 'progressivism' or teleology: the set narrative of the development of modern industry, together with the increasing power of the industrial proletariat, into the ultimate victory over capitalism. (In this respect the Marxist idea of progressivism should be distinguished from the use of 'progressivism' in mainstream politics, which finds

---

6   *Cromwell & Communism*, op. cit., p.10.

increasingly vague usage by most UK mainstream parties including the Conservatives. But it is or should be inclusive of the common notion of achieving progress against all forms of discrimination, which is a feature of left politics generally.)

The critique of progressivism has come from both left and right. Here, a correspondence between bloggers Dave Renton and 'Reading the Maps', suggests that the work of British Marxist Historians was the product of the Popular Front ideology of the Communist Party of the 1930s.

I think the defining characteristics of the 'HFB' [history from below] school derive not from a new interest in the experience of ordinary people – I think Marxists were always interested in that – but from an agenda set by the turn towards Popular Frontism in the mid-[19]30s. In Britain as elsewhere, the construction of a Popular Front required the rehabilitation of progressive or allegedly progressive aspects of national history and national cultural traditions. The British communists thus began discovering Coleridge as the English dialectician, the English Civil war as the English version of the French revolution, ye olde traditions like the Norman Yoke, and so on, and drawing deeply on a radical liberal intellectual tradition documented in Raymond Williams' 'Culture and Society'. This trend was reinforced by the adoption of the British Road to Socialism programme after the war. I think that [E.P.] Thompson's idealised working class tradition is thus ultimately the expression of a peculiarly British political and intellectual conjuncture, not some simple interest in a hitherto-neglected subject.[7]

---

7   'On History from Below': http://histomatist.blogspot.co.uk/2006/02/on-history-from-below_08.html

Raphael Samuel draws attention to how the focus of Marxist historians on the English Revolution localised or nationalised communism for an English context.

> Homage was paid to the Bible as the 'revolutionists' handbook' of the sixteenth and seventeenth centuries, and revolutionary Puritanism was called upon to give Communism an English lineage: 'Is it not of some value to English Socialists', wrote Joseph Needham, 'tired of hearing Communism identified with foreign-sounding names and doctrines, to know that the Communists of the seventeenth century had names that run like English villages – John Lilburne, William Walwyn, Gerard Winstanley, Robert Lockyer, Giles Calvert, Anthony Sedley? So it will be again, and not for failure'.[8]

The histories being uncovered within the communist movements fed into practical politics and (party organised) popular festivals – although Dave Renton points to the potential problems of a progressive national history bound too tightly to the idea of a nation, noting the grim ironies of the Communist Party's use of the image of Oliver Cromwell in the 1930s, given his participation in the oppression of Ireland.

> In Britain, the cultural politics of the Popular Front was expressed in the form of historical pageants. May Day parades were lead off by men and women carrying the symbols of Britain's folk-history – a story which might have had less 'progressive' meaning in other countries such as Ireland. Raphael Samuel

---

8   Raphael Samuel, 'British Marxist Historians 1880–1980', *New Left Review*, I/120, March–April 1980.

reports that Communists 'set about deliberately fostering a sense of democratic heritage, and in these 'March of History' pageants which the Party organised in 1936, Cromwell's portrait was borne proudly aloft along with those of John Ball and Wat Tyler.' Such politics continued, with further twists and turns, reaching its high-point in the wartime anti-fascist alliance of 1941-5.[9]

While there is good reason to reactivate popular memories of a radical heritage, the particularities of English radicalism, as we explored in our chapter on the Big Society, are easily elevated at the expense of both the global reality of capitalist exploitation, and the global interconnectedness of the struggles against it.

An example of how Popular Frontism and the reanimation of the English Revolution were impacting mainstream parliamentary politics is given in Peter Linebaugh's discussion of Aneurin Bevan, who was later Deputy Leader of the Labour Party and architect of the National Health Service in 1945:

In an hour of looming military defeat, on May Day 1942, Aneurin Bevan [...] published an article under the name 'Thomas Rainsborough'[10] which helped to initiate the wartime political

---

9   Dave Renton, 'English Experiences: was there a Problem of Nationalism in the Work of the British Marxist Historians' Group?', http://www.dkrenton.co.uk/research/cphg.html

10   Rainsborough was the leading spokesman for the Levellers in the Putney Debates (a series of discussions between members of the New Model Army concerning the makeup of a new constitution for England) and famously declared that 'even the poorest he [..] hath a life to live'.

discussion that culminated in the Labour Party's victory in 1945. Bevan summarised the [Putney] debates in a single brilliant chiasmus of two breaths: 'Either poverty must use democracy to destroy the power of property, or property in fear of poverty will destroy democracy.' Bevan's project was the industrial welfare state; its subject was the industrial worker.[11]

An example of the kind of 'conjuncture' Dave Renton mentions above can be seen in a struggle over the term 'modernity'. Former comrades in the Communist Historians Group, particularly on the question of the Civil War and its modernity, were keen to stress 'not their debt to the past, but the extent of their departure from it'. Take, for example, Leveller Richard Overton's 'A Remonstrance' quoted by former CHG member A.L. Morton in his *The World of the Ranters: Religious Radicalism in the English Revolution* (1970):

> Whatever our forefathers were, or whatever they did or suffered, or were enforced to yield unto; we are the men of the present age, and ought to be absolutely free from all kinds of exorbitances, molestations, or *Arbitrary Power*.[12]

We can say that politically this is a significant point for Morton and his peers, and the reason for its significance is that it says several things at once. Firstly, there is the question of modernity. If the Levellers were to be understood

---

11   Peter Linebaugh and Marcus Rediker, *The Many Headed Hydra*, London: Beacon, 2001, p.108.

12   Richard Overton, 'A Remonstrance' quoted in AL Morton, *The World of the Ranters: Religious Radicalism in the English Revolution*, London: Lawrence & Wishart, 1970, p.15.

as precursors or 'ancestors to the proletariat', as C.L.R. James put it, then they need to be understood as both *of* their times and *ahead of* their times; their authority in being able to tell us about their contemporary situation, and their ability to speak to our present, rest on this.

To a certain extent this mixes two forms of modernity in order to strengthen the argument that they were modern. The Levellers were politically modern because they had conceptually grasped the division of state, religion and citizenry. The formulation of 'arbitrary' power suggests that Overton stands not just in opposition to tradition, but in opposition to anything which justifies itself on the grounds that it simply *is*. This formulation has a close relation to reason and Enlightenment thought in general, but even more significantly it expressly addresses a political relation of domination.

Overton's statement recognises no authority, be it religious, hereditary or royal, but only rational, intentional or 'constituent' power. The Levellers were also modern in the 20th century sense because their conceptions express their own times ('the present age') and indicate a futurity of what 'ought to be'. The modern, especially in art, is the uncanny mixture of the present and the future. It is prescient. For A.L. Morton and others, this is not only an old question, but still very much a current one. Whilst some left historians, particularly crude Marxists, would like to present these histories as neat precursors to a gradual historical process leading up to the revolutions of the 20th century, we believe this is not what Morton was doing – in fact it is something more complicated than simply constructing a coherent narrative.

For Morton, Hill and others, it is not that Overton and the Levellers were a stage through which we have passed or a marginal presentiment of what is now commonly believed. Instead, it is in some part all of these things, and the contingent site of a blockage – what Overton expressed then could still be said today. We are still confronted by 'arbitrary power'. And 'we' means in Morton's time and our own!

Therefore, there is a question of where we locate the Levellers and their statements. They may have materially lived in the past, but they didn't see themselves as being consigned to tradition, nor reliant upon it. This is radical, in the sense that it stages a rupture with the past rather than a reliance on stable continuity, and this is something the best accounts by the historians cited above emphasise. The Levellers and other oppositional groups often formulated their demands in terms of birthright, but as the quote indicates, and Morton's book goes on to argue powerfully, theirs was an offensive struggle rather than a defensive one.

As we discussed in our introduction, by the 1970s C.L.R. James had shifted his political position away from Trotskyist micro-parties, and the core group who'd participated in the Communist Historians Group had left behind their Communist Party loyalties. Essentially by then, most of these figures can be seen to be largely in agreement, emphasising the qualities of class antagonism, leaderless resistance, plurality and radical egalitarianism at work in the period leading up to and after the English Revolution. This fed into the values of the New Left in Britain, and to a certain extent also influenced, met or cross-pollinated with movements in the U.S. such as the Students for a Democratic Society (SDS) and the San Francisco Diggers, who were just one of the many splinter groups which developed out of SDS.

Structure and Agency

The tradition of writing history from below, with its emphasis on the capacities of working class and/or subaltern as well as other subjects to resist and effect historical change, served to reignite controversies over the question of structure and agency: to what extent were historical actors shaped and determined by external forces, and to what extent could they think and act for themselves? The development of the historians we have focused on tends towards a complex view of the question of structure and agency, taking into account the specific social and economic contexts, limits and possibilities according to which the subjects they examined acted and organised themselves into social movements. By the 1970s, historians broke out in a series of polemical interventions around the absolutism of either category of 'structure' or 'agency' which centred on reactions to the work of the French philosopher Louis Althusser, and his growing influence on historical studies and political activism. In France, Jacques Rancière characterised the overbearing dynamic of Althusser's thinking thus:

> The idea that the dominated are dominated because they are ignorant of the laws of domination. Eventually [for intellectuals] this exalted task dissolves into a pure thought of resentment which declares the inability of the ignorant to be cured of their illusions, and hence the inability of the masses to take charge of their own destiny.[13]

---

13   Jacques Rancière, *Althusser's Lesson*, London: Continuum, 2011, p.xvi.

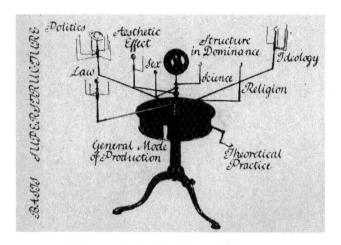

'Althusser's Marxist Orrery'. From E.P. Thompson,
The Poverty of Theory, London: Merlin Press, 1995, p.134.

Rancière went on to elaborate and resist the implications of his former master's work throughout the course of his career, to the point that Althusser remains a ghostly negative presence in introductions to his work.

Mirroring the switch after 1968/1969 within Althusser's circle, events took their revenge upon *Annales* in the years following the revolt of 1968. According to Peter Burke, 'A major change – not to say "purge" – was carried out in 1969.'[14] The school responded immediately by hiring younger historians. In this turn, or schism, initiatives on the political and academic left reoriented themselves away from the doctrine of structure towards the particularity of events or (in Alain Badiou's terms) *the event* – in its singularity and

---

14   *The French Historical Revolution*, op. cit., p.43.

departure from given and established models. The rejection of the history of events (*l'histoire événementielle*) had been a constant theme of *Annales*; Fernand Braudel, for instance, had compared the study of events as to 'prick holes of the night without illuminating it'.[15] Pierre Nora's essay 'The Return of the Event' was symbolic of a major shift and it carried out foundational work in foregrounding the ramifications of the newly recognised influence of events in the light of industrial society and the intensification of new technologies. Rancière poetically illuminates the promise of events for Marxists as the unveiling of 'appearance' in *Proletarian Nights*.

> it is in the moments when the real world wavers and seems to reel into mere appearance, more than in the slow accumulation of day-to-day experiences, that it becomes possible to form a judgement about the world.[16]

For E.P. Thompson, people's thoughts and actions are determined socially and economically in the first instance. But our capacity to reflect and make conscious choices with and against such determination, and to act upon them, is what gives us a measure of agency.[17] Thompson's idea of agency is always subject to the thoughts, actions and mediating behaviours of those around us as well as to broader

---

15   See the introduction to Pierre Nora's essay, 'The Return of the Event', 1974 in Lynn Hunt and Jacques Revel (eds), *Histories: French Constructions of the Past*, The New Press, 1994. pp.427–436.

16   Jacques Rancière, *Proletarian Nights: The Worker's Dream in Nineteenth-century France*, London: Verso, 2012, p.19.

17   E.P. Thompson, 'Socialist Humanism: An Epistle to the Philistines', from *The New Reasoner*, No.1, Summer 1957, pp.105–143, http://www.marxists.org/archive/thompson-ep/1957/sochum.htm

political and economic forces. This conviction was the central plank in Thompson's critique of Althusser in the 1970s. In a protracted essay entitled *The Poverty of Theory* (1978), he attempted to 'storm the citadels' of Structuralist theoretical practice. There are two main threads to Thompson's critique of Althusserian Marxism. First, he identified it as a denial of human agency in historical processes, which ultimately served to confirm the idea that nothing could be changed while preserving the arbitrary power of the institutionalised intellectual. Second, and related to the first point, he was stung by what he saw as the Althusserians' total rejection of historical method, in particular the following assertion from British philosophers Barry Hindness and Paul Hirst.

From the quarter of Louis Althusser and his numerous followers there has been launched an unmeasured assault upon 'historicism' [...]. Not only does it turn out that men have never 'made their own history' at all (being only träger [carriers] or vectors of ulterior structural determinations) but it is also revealed that the enterprise of historical materialism – the attainment of historical knowledge – has been misbegotten from the start, since 'real' history is unknowable and cannot be said to exist. In the words of two post-Althusserians, whose merit is to have carried Althusserian knowledge to its own *reductio ad absurdum*:

> Marxism, as a theoretical and a political practice, gains
> nothing from its association with historical writing
> and historical research. The study of history is not only
> scientifically but also politically valueless.[18]

---

18   E.P. Thompson, *The Poverty of Theory*, London: Merlin, 1996, p.194.

Thompson related the world view of the Althusserian Marxists to the particular dynamics of the academic world they worked in.

> [...] experience, then, does not arrive obediently in the way that Althusser proposes. One suspects that some very aetiolated notion of knowledge is here. He has offered us less an epistemology which takes into account the actual formative motions of consciousness than a description of certain procedures of academic life. He has abandoned the lamp-lit study and broken off the dialogue with an exhausted table: he is now within the emplacements of the Ecole Normale Superieur. The data has arrived, obediently processed by graduates and research assistants at a rather low level of conceptual development (G I), they have been interrogated and sorted into categories by a rigorous seminar of aspirant professors (G II), and the G III is about to ascend the rostrum and propound the conclusions of concrete knowledge.[19]

In this respect, Althusser's disciples are described by Thompson as pursuing 'diversionist' politics; a means of 'acting out revolutionary psycho-dramas' in academia on the way to becoming 'internal émigrés'.[20] Having made a series of *ad hominem* attacks, he goes on to defend the political importance of addressing lived experience, which he conceptualises as a 'junction concept between social being and social consciousness'. Here, we find the productive conflict between structure and agency, objectivity and attention to the subjective world view,

---

19   *The Poverty of Theory* op. cit., p.11.

20   Ibid, p.4.

which marks out the work of the 'historians from below' as a powerful contribution to the understanding of the social world. For Thompson, not only are historical conditions to some extent 'lived' – not merely internalised – but in their practice, through acting on the disjunctions between expectations and realities, people can sometimes effect change on those conditions and contribute to an alteration of the world.

> For we cannot conceive of any form of social being independently of its organising concepts and expectations, nor could social being reproduce itself for a day without thought. What we mean is that changes take place within social being, which give rise to changed experience; and this experience is determining, in the sense that it exerts pressures upon existent social consciousness, and affords much of the material which the more elaborated intellectual exercises are about.[21]

Thompson's polemic met productive challenges from his contemporaries. *The Poverty of Theory* was the centrepiece of a History Workshop debate on 'Peoples' History and Socialist Theory' in 1979. The debate, between Thompson, Stuart Hall and director of the Centre for Cultural Studies Richard Johnson, was dramatically staged in a floodlit, ruined church in Cambridge. Stuart Hall warned against an anti-intellectual disregard of theory *per se* in the development of left politics, and argued that Thompson had elided the complex interplay between ideology and consciousness.

---

21   Ibid, p.377.

All experience is penetrated by cultural and ideological categories. This does not render it 'false consciousness'. But it must undermine the notion that 'experience' can simply be read for its meaning, rather than being interrogated for its complex interweaving of real and ideological elements.[22]

For Hall, Thompson's insistence on the importance of lived experience, and downplaying of the role of ideology, risks leading the historian to produce an image of the working class as,

always really in its place, at the ready [to be] summed up for socialism [...] what I think of as a sometimes too-easy invocation of an existing and unsullied radical 'populism', which can be a heartening thought in dark times but may not prove to be as willing a force [...] as is sometimes supposed.[23]

The Poverty of Theory was also widely perceived as an attack on Perry Anderson. His book *Arguments Within English Marxism*, in which he attempted to pin down the concept of agency, responded to Thompson's criticisms. Arguing that 'if agency is construed as conscious, goal-directed activity, everything turns on the nature of the "goals"', Anderson goes on to unpick what political 'agency' might mean. He determines three main types of agency. The first, that of 'the overwhelming majority of people for the overwhelmingly major part of their lives', is the pursuit of:

---

22   Stuart Hall, 'In Defence of Theory', in, *Peoples History and Socialist Theory*, London: Taylor and Francis, p.382.

23   Ibid, p.385.

'Private' goals: cultivation of a plot, choice of a marriage, exercise of a skill, maintenance of a home, bestowal of a name. These personal projects are inscribed within existing social relations, and typically reproduce them. Yet they remain profoundly intentional enterprises, which have consumed the greater part of human energy and persistence throughout recorded time.

There have also, of course, been collective or individual projects whose goals were 'public' in character: quantitatively far fewer, involving lesser numbers in more fitful endeavours, but normally more interesting and important for the historian [...] However, these too in their overwhelming majority have not aimed to transform social relations as such-to create new societies or master old ones: for the most part they were much more limited in their (voluntary) scope [...].

Finally, there are those collective projects which have sought to render their initiators authors of their collective mode of existence as a whole, in a conscious programme aimed at creating or remodelling whole social structures. On a major scale, the very notion of it scarcely pre-dates the Enlightenment. The American and French Revolutions are the first historical figurations of collective agency in this, decisive sense. Originating as largely spontaneous explosions and ending with politico-juridical reconstructions, however, they still remain at a great distance from the manifestation of a full popular agency desiring and creating new social conditions of life for itself. It is the modern labour movement that has really given birth to this quite new conception of historical change; and it is with the advent of what its founders called scientific socialism that, in effect, for the first time collective projects of social transformation were married to systematic efforts to understand the processes of past and present, to produce a premeditated future.[24]

For Anderson, these definitions of agency depend upon the development of knowledge. But the knowledge Anderson addresses is ultimately to be exercised within a predetermined teleological framework, with the implied guidance of a 'scientific' party elite.

If anything, with the knowledge of the global interconnectivity of struggles as well as the global reach of capital, today the conditions are ripe for decisive forms of agency as never before, perhaps not in the ways Anderson might recognise. There are, nonetheless, considerable obstacles. Peter Hallward, recently discussing what might make up 'The Will of the People' in context of the Arab Spring and parallel global revolts, assumes a distributed ability to overcome obstacles that are personal, cultural, geographical, ideological, material. Hallward's is a self-consciously voluntarist conception of popular will – a kind of Jacobinism from below:

> Unlike Rousseau or Hegel, however, my concern here is not with a people conceived as a socially or ethically integrated unit, one that finds its natural horizon in the nation-state, so much as with the people who participate in the active willing of a general will as such [...]. 'The people' at issue here are simply those who, in any given situation, formulate, assert and sustain a fully common (and thus fully inclusive and egalitarian) interest, over

---

24   Perry Anderson, *Arguments Within English Marxism*, London: Verso, 1980, pp.19-21.

and above any divisive or exclusive interest.[25]

Hallward points to a tricky problem. If participation is key to mobilising popular will, who gets left out of the will of the people? Who structures and informs it? Is the voluntarist assumption that the participants act truly inclusively enough? Hallward also prompts us to ask what are the obstacles that need to be overcome. They are not simply composed of the structures and oppressions enacted by individual states, but also their relationship to global capital. Is it possible to depose capital as a social relation by mere acts of 'will'?

Dead Man Working?

In the opening pages of Peter Linebaugh's *London Hanged* the author points out several problems of structuralist influenced history; its tendency to reify ideology as dominant over action or practice and the overwhelming habituation to defeat such a perspective produces.

> I wish to draw attention to the activity of freedom in contrast to its ideological or theoretical expressions. I see that activity as a counter-tendency to a recent historiographical trend exemplified by Michel Foucault, who stresses incarceration in 'the great confinement' and who makes the rulers of government seem all-powerful.[26]

---

25   Peter Hallward, 'The Will of the People', available at, http://abahlali. org/files/hallward_will_of_the_people.pdf
26   *The London Hanged*, op. cit., p.3.

By contrast, Linebaugh's book develops a counter-action of 'ex-carceration', calling upon the folk legend of Jack Sheppard and his legendary escapes.

> Freedom is treated literally to mean escape from confinement; it is as much a matter of action as it is of words.[27]

Carl Cederström and Peter Fleming's recent Zero Books publication *Dead Man Working* offers a different kind of escape – a prescription for political agency that, at least objectively speaking, is not really agency at all. All domains, they argue, in a slickly satirical book, are saturated with the logic of work.

> What makes capitalism different today is that its influence reaches far beyond the office. Under Fordism, weekends and leisure time were still relatively untouched. Their aim was to indirectly support the world of work. Today, however, capital seeks to exploit our very sociality in all spheres of life. When we all become 'human capital' we not only have a job, or perform a job. We are the job. Even when the work-day appears to be over. This is what some have called the rise of bio-power, where life itself is put to work: our sociality, imagination, resourcefulness, and our desire to learn and share ideas.[28]

Many of Fleming and Cederström's insights may be true, but these authors take their argument to an absurd conclusion. Instead of actively confronting the problem (as there is 'no outside' to the logic of capital), the modern worker should

---

27 *The London Hanged*, op. cit., p.xxvi.

28 Carl Cederstrom and David Fleming, *Dead Man Working*, London: Zero Books, 2012, p.7.

instead 'become invisible'. There are echoes here of the idea of the human strike – involuntary and impersonal forms of resistance to capitalist exploitation – but as David Winters points out,

> The argument here is sophisticated, recalling Foucault's approach to the introjection of power. But this comparison could be instructive for less appealing reasons: as with Foucault, there's little scope for resistance in the foreclosed culture of *Dead Man Working*. Instead of examining insurrectionary tactics, Cederström and Fleming praise 'symbolic' acts of suicide, and, perhaps even more problematically, the 'unfathomable' aura of female children. In the book as a whole the word 'strike' is only cursorily mentioned; blink and you'll miss it.[29]

The problem underpinning their argument is clear: the authors produce a world in which any critical thought, choice or action is simply folded back into the logic of capital – with a deft wave of the philosopher's hand. In Cederström and Fleming's world, knowledge of the forms of domination enacted and reproduced in the world can only produce immobility or an apparently self-interested internal flight. All the better, then, to abdicate from any active and deliberative attempt to confront capital, or to voice or listen to, however partially, the true complexity of its effects, if every attempt to do so simply reproduces it or is recuperated in turn.

---

29   David Winters, 'Mordant Modernity', *Mute,* 5th June 2012, http://www.metamute.org/community/reviews/mordant-modernity

A History of Defeat?

> Marxist historians who have seen all history as class struggle
> culminating in a preordained end – 'the proletariat', in
> Linebaugh's words, 'would bring to birth a new society from
> the ashes of the old' – can't plausibly go on writing as if
> nothing much has happened, even though the inevitable end
> has turned out to be a dead one, and a phenomenally false
> start.[30]

So says the late Sir Ian Gilmour, former Lord Privy Seal to
Margaret Thatcher's Prime Ministership, reviewing *The
London Hanged* in 1991. It is a decidedly topsy-turvy view of
history which Sir Ian spouts: no one could accuse Linebaugh,
least of all the 'historians from below', of presuming history
to have a preordained end. It is apposite that a Conservative
critic invokes a 'preordained end' at the very same moment
Francis Fukuyama was triumphantly declaring the end of
history. Well, if arguments raised against this idiocy at the
time weren't strong enough, it certainly seems no longer
tenable for Fukuyama. Since 2008, history has begun again.

Raphael Samuel suggests that a limited form of
'progressivism' can be drawn from the study of the historical
defeats that are often used to undermine Marxist history. In
re-invigorating the lost battles of the past through renewed
attention to both conflict and possibility, we derive resources
for use in future struggles.

> Optimism, though a main ingredient of the 1930s progressivism,
> is in principle quite separable from it. It may operate within

---

30   Sir Ian Gilmour, *The London Review of Books*, 5th December, 1991.

a quite limited compass and even on the terrain of historical defeats. As the women's movement has shown, one does not need to be a triumphalist in order to keep faith with the past, or to use it as a revolutionary and critical vantage point with which to view the present.[31]

E.P. Thompson ironically grasps a contracted idea of progress and historical legacies:

> London and its environs would have no parks today if commoners had not asserted their rights, and as the nineteenth century drew on rights of recreation were more important than rights of pasture, and were defended vigilantly by the Commons Preservation Society. We owe to these premature 'Greens' such urban lungs as we have. More than that, if it had not been for the stubborn defence by Newbury commoners of their rights to the Greenham Common, where on earth could NATO have parked its Nukes.[32]

The greening of London could also be understood as a history of defeat, or at least a register of conflict and class struggle from above. In his pamphlet on the history of Kennington Park, Stefan Szczelkun connects the embodiment of amnesia in the production of space to several hundred years of social struggles, the construction of history and historiographical objectivity.

History is not objective truth. It is a selection of some facts

---

31   Raphael Samuel, 'British Marxist Historians', 1880–1980, Part 1, *New Left Review*, 1/120, March – April 1980, pp. 21–96.

32   E.P. Thompson, *Customs in Common*, London: Merlin Press, 1991, p.126.

from a mass of evidences to construct a particular view, which inevitably, reflects the ideas of the historian and their social milieu. The history most of us learnt in school left out the stories of most of the people who lived and made that history. If the design of the Victorian park means anything it is a negation of such a people's history: an enforced amnesia of what the real importance of this space is about. A history of life, popular discourse and collective struggle for justice is replaced with a few antique objects and some noble trees.[33]

Re-Animating the Dead

I wanted to say: this is what we do, or what we believe we do; we make the dead speak, we rescue the myriads of the unconsidered from the enormous indifference of the present.[34]

Carolyn Steedman's comment in an obituary of Raphael Samuel expresses the sense of responsibility a historian may feel for the voices of the long dead. And Benedict Anderson, in his examination of the 'Imagined Communities' of nationality, wittily locates Jules Michelet, 'self-appointed historian of the French Revolution', as progenitor of this trend of exhumation and ventriloquism.

Michelet [...] was the first self-consciously to write on behalf

---

33   Stefan Szczelkun, *Kennington Park: The Birthplace of People's Democracy*, London: Past Tense, (undated), p.1-2.

34   Carolyn Steedman, 'Obituary Raphael Samuel, 1934-1996' *Radical Philosophy*, March/April, 1997, http://www.radicalphilosophy.com/obituary/raphael-samuel-1934%E2%80%931996

of the dead. [He] made it clear that those whom he was exhuming were by no means a random assemblage of forgotten, anonymous dead. They were those whose sacrifices, throughout History, made possible the rupture of 1789 and the self-conscious appearance of the French nation, even when these sacrifices were not understood as such by the victims. The formulation is probably unprecedented. Michelet not only claimed to speak on behalf of large numbers of anonymous dead people, but insisted, with poignant authority, that he could say what they 'really' meant and 'really' wanted, since they themselves did not understand. From then on, the silence of the dead was no obstacle to the exhumation of their deepest desires.[35]

Michelet (1798-1874), whose twenty-three volume history of France included a two volume set on the French Revolution written shortly before the final establishment of Napoleon III, was said to have taken history very personally. Describing the writing of history as an act of resurrection, he went so far as to describe himself inhaling the dust of the dead in the archive, and asked whether this was indeed the dust of death, or exhumed life. Attentive to the problematics inherent in recovering hidden voices, Steedman affectionately points to Michelet's tendency to think of himself as tending and caring – becoming responsible – for the voices of the dead, despite the complex problems of doing so in projects for national construction. John Burrow identifies the influence on Michelet of Giambattista Vico, a Neapolitan philosopher of the early 18th century, for whom,

---

35   Benedict Anderson, *Imagined Communities*, London: Verso, 1983, p.189.

culture was the collective product of whole peoples. Mythology, in particular, gave a key to the mentalities of the 'first peoples, who were everywhere naturally poets.' Through it we can 'trace a history of the ideas, deeds and customs of mankind', because they were the 'manner of thinking of entire peoples'. These, lacking the ability to form abstract concepts, expressed their ideas through personifications [...] In this way Vico establishes what were later to become almost a set of commonplaces, which were certainly subscribed to by Michelet, namely a set of antitheses not only between earlier and later times but between the popular and the educated mentality, in which the former is poetic and sensuous, the latter metaphysical and abstract.[36]

Vico understood myth as sedimented human history and his thinking was to have a huge influence on Karl Marx and historians working in a Marxist vein. We return again to the question of the relationship between a historian and their sources, and this matter of how personally the historian guides or shapes the exhumed voices of the dead is an eternal problem in history from below.

History and Contingency

To submerge oneself in historical material is to raise the prospect of one's own confrontation with the forces of the present, and work through its contradictions beyond the limited scope of a book. History from below cannot rest peacefully on its achievements, but must be disinterred,

---

36   John Burrow, *A History of Histories*, London: Penguin, 2007, p.391. The quoted passages are from Giambattista Vico, *New Science*, London: Penguin, p.352.

exposed to new perspectives and pored over again and again, finding new readers and new forms of activation according to the demands of the present and future. Re-reading the past opens previous struggles to contingency, and this in turn animates the forms of contingency and possibility available to the present. We hope to have made a contribution to this process, and introduced new readers to a rich historiography whose legacy can be maintained only through contestation.

Max Ernst, engraving from *Une Semaine de Bonte*, 1933.

BIBLIOGRAPHY

An extended bibliography for this book can be accessed at
http://strickdistro.org/all_knees

Books and Articles

A Trumpet of Sedition, 'Historians on the Levellers and the English Revolution 1642-1652', http://keith-perspective.blogspot.co.uk/2011/06/historians-on-levellers-and-english.html

Henry Abelove et al (Eds.), *Visions of History*, Manchester: MARHO: The Radical Historians Organisation & Manchester University Press, 1983.

Ads Without Products, 'Against the Really Free School', http://adswithoutproducts.com/2011/02/16/against-the-really-free-school/

Amro Ali, 'Saeeds of Revolution: De-Mythologizing Khaled Saeed', http://www.jadaliyya.com/pages/index/5845/saeeds-of-revolution_de-mythologizing-khaled-saeed

Benedict Anderson, *Imagined Communities*, London: Verso, 1983.

Perry Anderson, *Arguments Within English Marxism*, London: Verso, 1980.

Geoff Andrews, Hilda Kean, Jane Thompson (Eds.), *Ruskin College: Contesting Knowledge, Dissenting Politics*, London: Lawrence and Wishart, 1999.

Anonymous, *The History of the Blacks of Waltham in Hampshire*, 1723.

Anon, 'General Ludd's Triumph', c.1811, http://campus.murraystate.edu/academic/faculty/kevin.binfield/songs.htm

Anon., *The Republic of Letters*, London: Comedia/Minority Press Group, undated c.1983.

Anon., 'The London Riot Re-enactment Society', http://anathematician.c8.com/lrrs.htm

Anon., 'Strike, Riot and Fire amongst the Garment Workers: a working class revolt in Bangladesh', London: 56a Infoshop, 2006, http://zinelibrary.info/strike-riot-and-fire-among-garment-workers-working-class-revolt-bangladesh-0

Bibliography

Anon., 'Report and reflections on the UK Ford-Visteon dispute 2009 - a post-Fordist struggle', http://libcom.org/history/report-reflections-uk-ford-visteon-dispute-2009-post-fordist-struggle

Les Back, 'Small World, Big Society: Haldane, Willetts and the AHRC', 2011, http://sociologyandthecuts.wordpress.com/2011/04/14/small-world-big-society-haldane-willetts-and-the-ahrc-by-les-back/

John Barrell, 'Radicalism, Visual Culture, and Spectacle in the 1790s', http://www.erudit.org/revue/ron/2007/v/n46/016131ar.html

Walter Benjamin, 'The Storyteller: Reflections on the Works of Nikolai Leskov', *Walter Benjamin: 1935–1938 v. 3: Selected Writings*, Boston: Harvard University Press, 2006.

Eduard Bernstein, *Cromwell and Communism*, George London: Allen & Unwin, 1963.

Kevin Binfield, *Writings of the Luddites*, Baltimore: John Hopkins University Press, 2004.

Luther Blissett, 'Education's Napster Moment', November 2010, http://deterritorialsupportgroup.wordpress.com/2011/01/19/educations-napster-moment/

Phillip Blond, *Red Tory: How the Left and Right Have Broken Britain and How We Can Fix It*, London: Faber and Faber, 2010.

Daniel Boffey, 'Academic fury over order to study the big society', *The Guardian*, 27 March 2011, http://www.guardian.co.uk/education/2011/mar/27/academic-study-big-society

Pierre Bourdieu, 'Education and the Autodidact', http://www.autodidactproject.org/other/bourd1.html

Peter Burke, *The French Historical Revolution: The Annales School, 1929–89*, Cambridge: Polity Press, 1990.

Trevor Burnard, 'Goodbye, Equiano, the African', *Historically Speaking: The Bulletin of the Historical Society*, Volume VII, Number 3, January 2006, http://www.bu.edu/historic/hs/janfeb06.html#burnard

John Burrow, *A History of Histories*, London: Penguin, 2007.

Elias Canetti, *Crowds and Power*, Harmondsworth: Penguin, 1973.

The Cable Street Group, *The Battle of Cable Street*, Nottingham: Five Leaves, 2011 (first published 1995).

George Caffentzis, 'Summer 2012, A Report from Greece', http://uninomade.org/report-from-greece/

Craig Calhoun, 'E.P. Thompson and the Discipline of Historical Context', *Making Histories: Studies in history-writing and Politics, Volume 1*, Taylor and Francis, 2006.

John Carey, *The Intellectuals and the Masses: Pride and Prejudice Among the Literary Intelligentsia, 1880-1939,* London: Faber, 1992.

Carl Cederstrom and David Fleming, *Dead Man Working*, London: Zero Books, 2012.

Théorie Communiste, 'The anti-CPE struggle report', January 2007, http://libcom.org/library/the-anti-cpe-struggle-report-theorie-communiste

Melinda Cooper and Angela Mitropoulos, 'In Praise of Usura', http://www.metamute.org/editorial/articles/praise-usura

Alain Corbin, *The Life of an Unknown: The Rediscovered World of a Clog-Maker in Nineteenth Century France,* New York: Columbia University Press, 2001.

Emilia Viotta da Costa, *Crowns of Glory, Tears of Blood: The Demerara Slave Rebellion of 1823*, New York: Oxford University Press, 1994.

W.W. Craik, *The Central Labour College 1909-29. A Chapter in the History of Adult Working-Class Education*, London: Lawrence & Wishart, 1964.

John Cruddas, 'A country for old men', *New Statesman*, April 2011, http://www.newstatesman.com/uk-politics/2011/04/english-labour-tradition

D'Log, 'AHRC Rebrands a Research Priority', http://www.d-log.info/?p=13582

Muriam Haleh Davis, 'From Cairo to Madison: The New Internationalism and the re-mystification of the Middle East', Jadaliyya, http://www.jadaliyya.com/pages/index/678/from-cairo-to-madison_the-new-internationalism-and

Oliver Davis, *Jacques Rancière*, Cambridge: Polity, 2010.

Marc Demarest, 'Controlling Dissemination Mechanisms: The Unstamped Press and the "Net"', http://www.noumenal.com/marc/unstamped.html

Jonathan Derbyshire, 'Stuart Hall: "We need to talk about Englishness"', *New Statesman*, August 2012, http://www.newstatesman.com/politics/uk-politics/2012/08/stuart-hall-we-need-talk-about-englishness

Bibliography

Olaudah Equiano, *The Interesting Narrative of the Life of Olaudah Equiano, or Gustavas Vassa, The African, Written by Himself,* (with an introduction by Vincent Carretta), London: Penguin, (originally published 1789) 1995.

Lucien Febvre and Henri Jean Martin, *The Coming of the Book,* London and New York: Verso, 1976.

Silvia Federici, *Caliban and The Witch: Women, The Body And Primitive Accumulation,* New York: Autonomedia, 2004.

Mark Fisher, 'The Future is Still Ours: Autonomy and Post-Capitalism', in *We Have Our Own Concept of Time and Motion,* AutoItalia South East: http://www.charliewoolley.com/post/19956452384/the-future-is-still-ours

Roderick Floud, 'Quantitative History and People's History: Two Methods in Conflict?', *Social Science History,* Vol.8, No.2 Spring, 1984.

Roderick Floud, 'Quantitative History in International Perspective', *Social Science History,* Vol. 8, No. 2 Spring, 1984.

Elizabeth Gurley Flynn, *Sabotage: the conscious withdrawal of the workers' industrial efficiency,* 1917, http://archive.org/details/SabotageTheConsciousWithdrawalOfTheWorkersIndustrialEfficiency

Pier Paolo Frassinelli, 'Cyril Lionel Robert James', http://www.generation-online.org/p/pclrjames.htm

Peter Fryer, *Staying Power: The History of Black People in Britain,* London: Pluto Press, 1984.

Eduardo Galeano, *The Open Veins of Latin America: five centuries of the pillage of a continent,* (Trans. Cedric Belfrage), London: Serpent's Tail, (originally published 1973) 2009.

Paul Gilroy, *The Black Atlantic: Modernity and Double Consciousness,* Massachusetts: Harvard University Press, 1993.

Sir Ian Gilmour, *The London Review of Books,* December 1991.

Maurice Glasman, 'Labour as a radical tradition', *Soundings,* Number 46, pp.31-41, Winter 2010.

Maurice Glasman, 'The Left's Favourite Tories: Edmund Burke', *New Statesman,* October 2011, http://www.newstatesman.com/uk-politics/2011/10/institutions-burke-labour

James Albert Ukwasaw Gronniosaw, *A Narrative of the Most Remarkable Particulars in the Life of James Albert Ukwasaw Gronniosaw, an African*

Prince, As Related by Himself, Bath, 1772.

Nicholas Guyatt, 'Our Slaves Are Black', *London Review of Books*, Vol. 29 No. 19, 4 October 2007, pp.19-22.

Stuart Hall, 'In Defence of Theory' in Raphael Samuel (Ed.), *People's History and Socialist Theory*, London: Routledge, 1981.

Peter Hallward, 'The Will of the People: Notes toward a Dialectical Voluntarism', *Radical Philosophy* 155, 2010, pp. 17-29, http://fass.kingston.ac.uk/faculty/staff/cv.php?staffnum=734

Peter Hallward, 'Staging Equality: On Rancière's Theatocracy', http://www.scribd.com/doc/65081668/Hallward-Staging-Equality

Daniel Hannan, 'A Model Maiden Speech', *The Telegraph*, 28 June, 2010 http://blogs.telegraph.co.uk/news/danielhannan/100042748/a-model-maiden-speech/

Douglas Hay, Peter Linebaugh, John G. Rule, E. P. Thompson and Cal Winslow, *Albion's Fatal Tree*, London: Penguin, 1977.

Douglas Hay, 'Property Authority and the Criminal Law' in Douglas Hay, Peter Linebaugh, John G. Rule, E. P. Thompson and Cal Winslow, *Albion's Fatal Tree*, London: Penguin, 1977.

Danny Hayward, 'Adventures in the Sausage Factory', http://www.metamute.org/editorial/articles/adventures-sausage-factory-cursory-overview-uk-university-struggles-november-2010---july-2011

James Heartfield, 'Eric Hobsbawm and the tragedy of the left', October 2012, http://www.spiked-online.com/site/article/12936/

Jack Heyman, 'A Class Struggle Critique: The ILWU Longshore Struggle in Longview and Beyond', http://www.transportworkers.org/node/90

History is Made at Night, 'Jubilee – the trumpet shall sound', http://history-is-made-at-night.blogspot.co.uk/2010/10/jubilee-trumpet-shall-sound.htm

Christopher Hill, *The English Revolution 1640*, London: Lawrence & Wishart, 1940, http://www.marxists.org/archive/hill-christopher/english-revolution/

Christopher Hill, *World Turned Upside Down: Radical Ideas During the English Revolution*, London: Penguin, (first published 1972) 1991.

Christopher Hill, *The Experience of Defeat: Milton and Some Contemporaries*, London, Chicago, Melbourne: Bookmarks, 1984.

Bibliography

Eric Hobsbawm, 'The Machine Breakers', http://libcom.org/history/machine-breakers-eric-hobsbawm originally published in *Past & Present*, No. 1. February 1952, pp. 57-70.

Eric Hobsbawm, *Labouring Men: Studies in the History of Labour*, London: Weidenfield & Nicolson, 1964.

Eric Hobsbawm, *Primitive Rebels*, New York: Norton, 1965.

Eric Hobsbawm, *Bandits*, London: Weidenfield & Nicolson, 2000.

Martin Hoyles, *The Axe Laid to the Root: The Story of Robert Wedderburn*, London: Hansib, 2004.

Lynn Hunt and Jacques Revel (Eds.). *Histories: French Constructions of the Past*, New York: The New Press, 1994.

C.L.R. James, *The Black Jacobins: Toussaint L'Ouverture and the San Domingo Revolution*, London: Penguin, 2001.

C.L.R. James, 'The Philosophy of History and Necessity: A Few Words with Professor Hook', *The New International*, Volume IX, Number 7, July 1943, pp. 210-213, http://www.marxists.org/archive/james-clr/works/1943/07/hook.htm

C.L.R. James, 'Cromwell and the Levellers', *Fourth International*, Vol.10 No.5, May 1949, pp.143-148.

CLR James, 'Ancestors of the Proletariat', *Fourth International*, Vol.10 No.8, September 1949, pp.252-255. http://www.marxists.org/archive/james-clr/works/1949/09/english-revolution.htm

C.L.R. James, 'Free For All: the Nine Year Old Leader', *Race Today*, 14, 3, May-June, 1982.

Harvey J. Kaye and Keith McClelland (Eds.), *E.P. Thompson: Critical Perspectives*, Cambridge: Polity Press, 1980.

Colin Kidd, 'Sabre-Toothed Tory', *London Review of Books*, 31 March 2011, http://www.lrb.co.uk/v33/n07/colin-kidd/sabre-toothed-teacher

Anja Kirschner & David Panos, 'The Last Days of Jack Sheppard', http://kirschner-panos.info/index.php?/projects/the-last-days-of-jack-sheppard-2009/

Anja Kirschner & David Panos, 'A Response to Peter Linebaugh', January

2010, January 2010, http://www.metamute.org/community/your-posts/response-to-peter-linebaugh

Lawrence Liang, 'Interview with Jacques Ranciére', Lodi Gardens, Delhi, February 2009, http://kafila.org/2009/02/12/interview-with-jacques-ranciere/

Marcel Van der Linden, *Workers of the World: Essays toward a Global Labor History*, Leiden: Brill, 2007.

Peter Linebaugh, 'The Tyburn Riot Against the Surgeons', in Douglas Hay, Peter Linebaugh, John G. Rule, E.P. Thompson and Cal Winslow, *Albion's Fatal Tree*, London: Penguin, 1977.

Peter Linebaugh, *The London Hanged: Crime and Civil Society in the Eighteenth Century*, London: Penguin, 1991.

Peter Linebaugh, 'Days of villainy: a reply to two critics', *International Socialism Journal*, Issue 63, Summer 1994, http://pubs.socialistreviewindex.org.uk/isj63/linebaugh.htm

Peter Linebaugh, 'A Letter to Boston's "Radical Americans" from a "loose and disorderly" New Yorker', in Midnight Notes, IV No.1, (undated).

Peter Linebaugh and Marcus Rediker, *The Many Headed Hydra: Sailors, Slaves, Commoners and the Hidden History of the Revolutionary Atlantic*, Boston: Beacon Press, 2000.

Peter Linebaugh, 'An American Tribute to Christopher Hill', *Counterpunch*, May, 2003, http://www.unz.org/Pub/CounterpunchWeb-2003may-00129

Peter Linebaugh, 'Charters of Liberty in White Face and Black Face: Race, Slavery and the Commons', Mute Vol.2 Issue 2, 2006.

Peter Linebaugh, 'Jubilating: or, How the Atlantic working class used Biblical Jubilee against Capitalism, with Some Success', undated, http://www.midnightnotes.org/pdfnewenc12.pdf

Peter Linebaugh, 'Jack's Back! In the Movies at last!', January 2010, http://www.metamute.org/editorial/articles/jacks-back-movies-last

Peter Linebaugh, 'Introduction to the works of Thomas Paine, *Rights of Man* and *The Commonwealth*', http://libcom.org/history/peter-linebaughs-new-introduction-works-thomas-paine

Peter Linebaugh, *Ned Ludd & Queen Mab: Machine-Breaking, Romanticism, and the Several Commons of 1811-12*, Oakland: PM Press, 2012.

Ian McCalman (Ed.), *The Horrors of Slavery and Other Writings by Robert Wedderburn*, Princeton: Markus Weiner Publishers, 1997.

Bibliography

Saree Makdisi, *William Blake and the Impossible History of the 1790s*, Chicago: University of Chicago Press, 2003.

Karl Marx, *Preface to A Contribution to the Critique of Political Economy*, 1859, http://www.marxists.org/archive/marx/works/1859/critique-pol-economy/preface.htm

Karl Marx, *Capital* Vol.I, London: Penguin, 1990.

Karl Marx, *Grundrisse: Foundations of the Critique of Political Economy*, London: Penguin, 1993.

Paul Mason, *Why it's Kicking off Everywhere*, London: Verso, 2012.

Jules Michelet, *La Sorcière*, 1863. Translated as: *Satanism and Witchcraft: A Study in Medieval Superstition*, (Trans. A.R. Allinson) Lyle Stuart/Citadel Press, 1939.

Roger Mills, *Everything Happens on Cable Street*, Nottingham: Five Leaves, 2011.

Nicholas Mirzoeff, 'Back to organising', http://www.nicholasmirzoeff.com/02012/category/strike-debt/

A.L. Morton, *The World of the Ranters: Religious Radicalism in the English Revolution*, London: Lawrence & Wishart, 1979.

A.L. Morton, *A People's History of England*, London: Lawrence & Wishart, (first edition published 1938) 1999.

Jeanne Neton & Peter Åström, 'How One Can Still Put Forward Demands When No Demands Can Be Satisfied', *Sic* #1, http://communisation.net/How-one-can-still-put-forward?lang=fr

David Parker (Ed.), *Ideology, Absolutism and the English Revolution: Debates of the British Communist Historians, 1940-1945*, London: Lawrence & Wishart, 2008.

Michelle Perrot, 'Workers on Strike: France, 1871-1890 in Lynn Hunt and Jacques Revel (Eds.). *Histories: French Constructions of the Past*, New York: The New Press, 1994.

Karl Polanyi, *The Great Transformation*, Boston: Beacon Press, 2001.

Harold Pollins, *The History of Ruskin College*, Oxford: Ruskin College Library, 1984.

Jonathan Raban, 'Cameron's Crank', *London Review of Books*, Vol. 32 No. 8 April 2010, pp.22-23. http://www.lrb.co.uk/v32/n08/jonathan-raban/camerons-crank

Jacques Rancière, 'The Myth of the Artisan', *International Labor and Working Class History*, Number 24, Autumn 1983.

Jacques Rancière, '"Le Social": The Lost Tradition in French Labour History', in Raphael Samuel (Ed.), *People's History and Socialist Theory*, London: Routledge, 1981.

Jacques Rancière, *The Names of History*, Minneapolis: University of Minnesota, 1994.

Jacques Rancière, *On the Shores of Politics*, (Trans. Liz Heron), London and New York: Verso, 1995.

Jacques Rancière, *Althusser's Lesson*, London: Continuum, 2011.

Jacques Rancière, *Staging the People: The Proletarian and His Double* (*Staging the People*, Vol.I), London: Verso, 2011.

Jacques Rancière, *Proletarian Nights: The Worker's Dream in Nineteenth Century France*, London: Verso, 2012.

Jacques Rancière, *The Intellectual and His People: Staging the People* (*Staging the People*, Vol.II), London: Verso, 2012.

Daniel Rasmussen, *American Uprising: The Untold Story of America's Largest Slave Revolt*, New York: Harper Collins, 2011.

Dave Renton, 'English Experiences: Was there a Problem of Nationalism in the Work of the British Marxist Historians' Group?', http://www.dkrenton.co.uk/research/cphg.html

Dave Renton, 'The History Woman', *Socialist Review*, Issue 224, November 1998, http://pubs.socialistreviewindex.org.uk/sr224/renton.htm

Marcus Rediker, 'The Poetics of History from Below', in *Perspectives on History*, September 2010, American Historical Association, http://www.historians.org/perspectives/issues/2010/1009/1009art1.cfm

Stan Rees, 'The Ruskin strike in 1909' in *Plebs*, Vol. XLIV, No. 7, July 1952, pp.152–155.

Adrian Rifkin and Roger Thomas (Eds.), *Voices of the People*, New York: Routledge, 1988.

Jonathan Rose, *The Intellectual Life of the British Working Classes*, New Haven, CT: Yale University Press, 2000.

Sheila Rowbotham, *Women, Resistance and Revolution*, London: Pelican, 1972.

Bibliography

Sheila Rowbotham, Woman's Consciousness, Man's World, London: Pelican, 1973.

Sheila Rowbotham, *Hidden from History: 300 Years of Women's Oppression and the Fight Against It*, London: Pluto Press, 1975.

George Rudé, *The Crowd in History*, London: Serif, 1999.

Olive D. Rudkin, *Thomas Spence and His Connections*, New York: Augustus M. Kelley, 1966.

Raphael Samuel, 'British Marxist Historians 1880-1980', *New Left Review*, I/120, March-April, 1980.

Raphael Samuel (Ed.), *People's History and Socialist Theory*, London: Routledge, 1981.

Sukhdev Sandhu, 'At the Hop', *London Review of Books,* Vol. 19 No. 4, 20 February 1997, pp.23-24.

Sukhdev Sandhu, *London Calling: How Black and Asian Writers Imagined a City*, London: Harper Perennial, 2003.

John Saville (Ed.), *Democracy and the Labour Movement: Essays in Honour of Dona Torr*, London: Lawrence & Wishart, 1954.

Michael Seidman, *Workers Against Work: Labor in Paris and Barcelona during the Popular Fronts,* Berkeley: California University Press, 1991.

Michael Seidman, *Republic of Egos: A Social History of the Spanish Civil War*, Winsconsin: University of Winsconsin Press, 2002.

Beverly J. Silver, *Forces of Labor: Workers' Movements and Globalization since 1870*, Cambridge: Cambridge University Press, 2003.

Josephine Berry Slater (Ed.), *Don't Panic, Organise! A Mute Magazine Pamphlet on Recent Struggles in Education,* December 2010, http://www.metamute.org/editorial/books/don%E2%80%99t-panic-organise-mute-magazine-pamphlet-recent-struggles-education

Thomas Spence, *The End of Oppression*, 1795, http://thomas-spence-society.co.uk/7.htm

Lady Stardust, 'An Image of the "Big Society"? a report from Woodberry Down community library', *The Commune,* http://thecommune.co.uk/2010/11/29/an-image-of-the-big-society-a-report-from-woodberry-down-community-library/

Carolyn Steedman, 'Raphael Samuel, 1934-1996', *Radical Philosophy*, No.82, 1997.

Carolyn Steedman, 'Something She Called a Fever: Michelet, Derrida, and Dust', *American Historical Review*, Vol.106, Issue 4, October 2001, http://www.historycooperative.org/journals/ahr/106.4/ah0401001159.html

Carolyn Steedman, *Dust*, Manchester: Manchester University Press, 2001.

Carolyn Steedman, *Labour's Lost: Domestic Service and the Making of Modern England*, Cambridge: Cambridge University Press, 2009.

Allegra Stratton, 'Labour: Now it's Kind of Blue', The Guardian, 24 April 2009, http://www.guardian.co.uk/politics/blog/2009/apr/24/blue-labour-conservative-socialism

Stefan Szczelkun, *Kennington Park: The Birthplace of People's Democracy*, London: Past Tense, (undated).

Barbara Taylor, *Eve and the New Jerusalem: Socialism and Feminism in the Nineteenth Century*, New York: Pantheon Books, Keith Thomas, *Religion and The Decline of Magic*, London: Penguin, (first published 1971) 1991.

Dorothy Thompson, *Outsiders: Class, Gender and Nation*, London and New York: Verso, 1993.

E.P. Thompson, 'Socialist Humanism: An Epistle to the Philistines', *New Reasoner*, No.1, Summer 1957, pp.105-143, http://www.marxists.org/archive/thompson-ep/1957/sochum.htm

E.P. Thompson, *The Making of the English Working Class*, London: Gollancz, 1963.

E.P. Thompson, 'History from Below', *The Times Literary Supplement*, 7 April 1966.

E.P. Thompson, 'Time, Work-Discipline, and Industrial Capitalism', *Past and Present*, 38(1), 1967.

E.P. Thompson, 'The Business University', *Writing by Candlelight*, London: Merlin Press, 1970, http://senatehouseoccupation.wordpress.com/documents/the-business-university-new-statesman-article-by-ep-thompson/

E.P. Thompson, 'An Open Letter to Leszek Kolakowski', *Socialist Register*, 1973, p.91.

E.P. Thompson, *Customs in Common*, London: Merlin Press, 1991.

E. P. Thompson, 'Agenda for Radical History', *Critical Inquiry*, Vol. 21, No.

Bibliography

2.,Winter, 1995, pp. 299-304.

E.P. Thompson, *The Poverty of Theory*, London: The Merlin Press, 1996.

E.P. Thompson, *The Essential E.P. Thompson*, (Ed. Dorothy Thompson), New York: New Press, 2000.

E.P. Thompson, *Witness Against the Beast*, New York: Norton and Co., 1995.

Dona Torr, *Tom Mann and his Times*, Vol.1, 1956 (prepared for publication after her illness by Christopher Hill and A.L. Morton).

The Open University, 'Was Magna Carta Really the Document that Defined Our Freedoms?', The Open University, http://www.open.edu/openlearn/history-the-arts/history/social-economic-history/was-magna-carta-really-the-document-which-defined-our-freedoms

T.W., 'Biblioclasm and the Book Bloc', *Rage*, Issue 1, September 2011, http://rageofmaidens.wordpress.com/

Colin Waugh, '"Plebs": The lost legacy of independent working class education', *Post-16 Educator*, Sheffield, January 2009.

Robert Wedderburn, *The Forlorn Hope or a Call to the Supine*, 4 and 11 October 1817.

Cal Winslow, 'The ILWU Longshore Struggle in Longview and Beyond', http://www.counterpunch.org/2012/08/10/the-ilwu-longshore-struggle-in-longview-and-beyond/

Angela Withers, 'A Capitalist History of Bloomsbury', *Rage*, Issue 1, September 2011, http://rageofmaidens.wordpress.com/

David Winters, 'Mordant Modernity', http://www.metamute.org/community/reviews/mordant-modernity

Alan Woodward, 'Ford Visteon Enfield Workers Occupation', 2009, http://libcom.org/history/ford-visteon-enfield-workers-occupation-alan-woodward

Ken Worpole, *Dockers and Detectives*, London: Verso, 1983.

Michael Zimmer, 'Facebook's Zuckerberg: Having Two Identities for Yourself is an Example of a Lack of Integrity', http://michaelzimmer.org/2010/05/14/facebooks-zuckerberg-having-two-identities-for-yourself-is-an-example-of-a-lack-of-integrity/

Resources

Brycchan Carey's online resources on Slavery, Emancipation, and Abolition, http://www.brycchancarey.com/

Copenhagen Free University online library, http://www.copenhagenfreeuniversity.dk/library.html

The History Cooperative is a pioneering non-profit humanities resource offering top-level online history scholarship, http://www.historycooperative.org/

Hossam el-Hamalawy's collection of links on bossknappings in Egypt, http://www.diigo.com/user/elhamalawy/bossnapping

Hydrarchy: Power and Resistance at Sea conference organised by Gasworks Gallery at UCL, 18 September 2010, http://www.gasworks.org.uk/exhibitions/detail.php?id=564

Mary Kemp-Ashraf, 'An Annotated Bibliography of the Works of Thomas Spence', http://thomas-spence-society.co.uk/5.html

Luddites Bicentenary, http://ludditebicentenary.blogspot.co.uk/

The Luddites Without Condescension, documentation of a conference held 6 May 2011 at Birkbeck University of London, The Luddites Without Condescension, http://backdoorbroadcasting.net/2011/05/the-luddites-without-condescension/

The *Oral History Journal*, run by the Oral History Society, online resources, http://www.oralhistory.org.uk/resources.php

Raphael Samuel archive, Bishopsgate Institute, London. Contains extensive materials on Ruskin College and the History Workshop.

Shahadat special on 'The Popular Writing of Tahrir', http://issuu.com/arteeast/docs/shahadat_january25_final?mode=embed&layout=http%3A%2F%2Fskin.issuu.com%2Fv%2Flight%2Flayout.xml&showFlipBtn=true

Bibliography

Films

Anonymous video, 'We're from the Slums of London', 9 December 2010, http://youtu.be/k1BsTl4QRjl

BBC, 'The Luddites', from the CBB 'Horrible Histories' series based on the books of Terry Deary, http://youtu.be/IgBiGrpWNQU

Luke Fowler, *The Poor Stockinger, the Luddite Cropper and the Deluded Followers of Joanna Southcott*, 2012. Film exhibition, http://www.fvu.co.uk/projects/details/the-poor-stockinger-the-luddite-cropper-and-the-deluded-followers-of-joanna/

Richard Broad, *Luddites*, Thames Television, 1988.

Kevin Brownlow & Andrew Mollo, *Winstanley*, 1976.

Mark Carlin, *For Memory*, 1983.

Bill Douglas, *Comrades*, 1986.

Patrick Keiller, *Robinson in Ruins*, 2011.

Anja Kirschner, *Supernumeraries*, 2003.

Anja Kirschner & David Panos, *Polly II: Plan for a Revolution in Docklands*, 2006.

Anja Kirschner and David Panos, *Trail of the Spider*, 2008.

Anja Kirschner & David Panos, *The Last Days of Jack Sheppard*, 2009.

Penumbra Productions, 'Talking History: C.L.R. James & E.P. Thompson in conversation', 1983, http://youtu.be/Ml7n7M6nAOA

Peter Watkins, *La Commune (Paris, 1871)*, 2000.